FROM MOAB TO BETHLEHEM... journey to the King

a devotional study on the book of Ruth

by

Cynthia Shomaker

FROM MOAB TO BETHLEHEM...journey to the King
a devotional study on the book of Ruth
by Cynthia Shomaker

Printed in the United States of America

ISBN 978-1-60791-163-0

www.xulonpress.com

Dedication…

To Mark and Debbie Meadows, for patiently pursuing the vision

To Terry Beh, for editing, advice, and encouragement

To the precious ladies who took this journey with me…

And to Eric, Karaline, and Harrison, my husband and children who have prayed faithfully for this work, I love you.

TABLE OF CONTENTS

Chapter 1- Root of a Famine 13
Chapter 2- Seeking the Enemy's Bread 19
Chapter 3- An Unexpected End 25
Chapter 4- All Things Work Together 31
Chapter 5- The Checed of God 35
Chapter 6- Leaving Moab 41
Chapter 7- Orpah, Fearful and Unbelieving 53
Chapter 8- Crossroads 59
Chapter 9- But Ruth... 67
Chapter 10- Don't Look Back 75
Chapter 11- While You're Walking, He's Working 87
Chapter 12- Our Kinsman Redeemer 99
Chapter 13- Where the Harvest Begins 111
Chapter 14- Barley, the Bread of Life 121
Chapter 15- Watching and Working 131
Chapter 16- Listen to Me, Child 141
Chapter 17- Don't Go 151
Chapter 18- Watch the Fields 161
Chapter 19- Favor for Foreigners 171
Chapter 20- Stepping Out and Stepping Under 181
Chapter 21- Soaring Under the Wings of the King 191
Chapter 22- The Bread and the Wine 201
Chapter 23- Gleaning Where You Are 211
Chapter 24- More Than Enough 219

Chapter 25- Enough To Share 229
Chapter 26- What's In a Name? 239
Chapter 27- The In-Between Time 249
Chapter 28- Lessons From the Threshing Floor 257
Chapter 29- Changing Clothes 265
Chapter 30- Watching and Praying 275
Chapter 31- Knowing Who and Whose You Are 287
Chapter 32- Young Things and Impossibilites 297
Chapter 33- Pondering and Prospering 305
Chapter 34- The Life-Changing Power of Hope 313
Chapter 35- Doing Business in the Meantime 325
Chapter 36- Seeking and Keeping Covenant 335
Chapter 37- The Obligation of Confirmation 345
Chapter 38- Mere Business or Beloved Bride? 353
Chapter 39- Blessing or Cursing? 363
Chapter 40- Ruth Became 373
Chapter 41- New Birth 383
Chapter 42- Suffering's End 391
Chapter 43- Generational Blessings 399
Chapter 44- Conclusion 411

Introduction

The Word of God is mighty, powerful, fresh, living and active. I have found that as you sit with that Word open and cry out for the Holy Spirit to illumine its pages to your tender heart, to pour it in like new wine and feed it to your hungry soul like the finest of bread, you will discover it coming to life in you. The Lord tells us in Psalm 81:10, "Open your mouth wide, and I will fill it." Not with religion, but with Truth itself.

As I have done this morning after morning, year after year, I've been utterly overwhelmed at the Lord's faithfulness to answer that cry. He has caused my heart to tremble before His Word, to love and crave it and to seek it as the finest treasure. It has pricked my flesh and deeply offended me, then led me to repentance and wholeness. It has blown me away, leaving me in a puddle of grateful tears at my dining room table. God's holy Scriptures have become a consuming fire in my soul, burning away its chaff and setting it ablaze for Christ alone. He has let me see myself and my great need and then allowed me to glimpse His amazing fullness. *My heart is captured.* I want Him like nothing else.

I am compelled to write down what the Lord teaches my heart. My purpose in writing is not to put pen to paper with some sort of profound eloquence to impress anyone. I simply sit with the Word of God open and my heart surrendered in prayer and try to process in ink what the Holy Spirit reveals, convicts and teaches. I write of necessity—it's become as critical to my soul as breathing is to my body. I have notebooks full and daily add freshly scribbled pages, and as I've asked the Lord what to do with them, slowly He's called me to start sharing what they contain. My flesh has shrunk back from this, as it opens doors for criticism. I am not a writer or scholar. Yet, God has finally brought me to a place where I see that His glory is far more important than my fear of what anyone may think of me. He has absolutely laid me low with the conviction that it's not prideful to pour out what He pours in, but rather sinful to hold it back. With that in mind, I share with you these pages from my heart.

This book is simply a recorded exchange of my personal journey through *Ruth*, forged in the early morning hours through prayer and listening to the Holy Spirit, with the Word laid open before me. It was not intended to be shared, except with a small group of precious women who asked me to. However, because the Lord has made it possible for this to be in your hands, I know He has a direct word to plant in your heart through it. I am praying that you will hear His voice in these pages, not mine, and that through this devotion He will do for you what He has done for me—peel back heart layers, lead out of anything that is not of Him and, by His presence, release you into sweet, priceless freedom. My hope is that God will lead you from your "Moab," that place far from Him, straight into "Bethlehem," that indescribably intimate place in the chamber of the King of Kings. *The trip is worth it. Freedom like you've never tasted and joy the best of the world can't produce awaits you. The King Himself waits for you.*

I don't know how many times I've read the account of *Ruth*. I've heard some excellent teaching on it from Beth Moore and others, *but nothing compares to walking through the Word yourself, guided and taught by the Holy Spirit*. As

Job said, "Who teaches like the Lord?" I would urge you, then, to go to the text yourself and ask the Lord to speak to your own heart- but in obedience to Him, I share with you what He has laid on mine...

1

Root of a Famine

In the days when the judges ruled, there was famine in the land, and a man from Bethlehem in Judah, together with his wife and two sons, went to live for a while in the country of Moab, **Ruth 1:1.**

"*In the days judges ruled...*" Let's step back and get a picture of what brought Israel to the point of famine. Judges 2:10 says that after (Joshua's) generation had been gathered to their fathers, *"another generation grew up, who neither knew the Lord nor what He had done for Israel."* As a result of this, Judges 3:7 informs us that, *"The Israelites did evil in the eyes of the Lord; they forgot the Lord their God and served the Baals and Asherahs."* By the time we reach Judges 16:5, God's Word tells us that, *"In those days Israel had no king; everyone did as he saw fit."* Why were judges ruling Israel, and what brought the famine?—ignorance about the Most High God, serving idols and everyone doing as they pleased, or, as some translations put it, "what was right in their own eyes."

One generation is to proclaim the wonders and glory of the Lord to the next. The people of Joshua's generation apparently died without burning into the hearts of their children the profound power of the Lord. Their children grew up, and "neither knew the Lord nor what He had done for Israel."

The Israelites had seen the mighty hand of God lead them from captivity, part the massive Red Sea, test and train them in the wilderness and crumble Jericho's fortress walls. They'd settled in the land of promise, established by God Himself. They were blessed beyond blessing. Why didn't they tell—with every waking breath—what the Lord had done? Were they so taken with abundance that they allowed their passion for the King of Kings to subside? Were they so consumed with taking care of their fields that they forgot where the harvest came from? Did they conquer the Promised Land by obeying God's voice, but then hide the light of God under a bushel? Did they raise a selfish, spoiled generation that demanded their every whim be satisfied—one that could care less about the things of God? A generation easily influenced and swayed by the idolatry and evil around them, because they had no passion for the One True God? Did the older not recognize a lack of faith in the younger, and hit their knees on their behalf?

How that pierces my heart with conviction to TELL MY CHILDREN what the Lord has done: to tell of the way He led me out of the wilderness, grabbed my heart and made it His, has answered and moved as I've cried out to Him and has set the Word on fire in my soul. Whether our children want to hear or not, we must TELL IT. If we do, the Holy Spirit will drive it home for them and bring it to remembrance just when they need it.

What have you seen the Lord do *in your life*? Have you seen your soul melt before the Lord and your heart of stone become as tender as flesh? Have you seen the mighty hand of God divinely order your steps? Has He opened doors before you that He alone could open? Has He delivered you from something—an addiction, an unhealthy emotion, a bad relationship, fear, jealousy, persecution...? Has He renewed your mind with His living Word? Has He shown you Truth, and by it set you free? Has He lifted your life from the pit, and established it on the solid Rock of His Risen Son? Have you been led from captivity? Have you seen impossible seas part before you, the Enemy devoured by the deep waters of the Word, the hand of God lead you across the wilderness, hindering walls and fortresses crumble before your cry of faith-filled praise and the land of promise stretch out before you as sacred, blessed ground? THEN TELL IT!!! Don't take the miracle of salvation for granted, and don't forget from where you've come! The next generation desperately needs to know. The well being of some coming behind us will be deeply affected by our testimonies being sown in their hearts—they need to see "up close and personal" a life transformed by Almighty God. Go show them yours.

What was the result of the generation following Joshua "neither knowing the Lord nor what He had done?" They forsook the Living God. It's almost unbelievable to me that the descendants of a mighty man of faith like Joshua could turn from the Lord. That drives the point home to me that *we can't count on our children having a passion for the Lord just because we do. We can't assume they'll make good choices. We can't count on them being immune to the evil in the world. It's CRITICAL that we pour the Word into them.*

The Word of God is where the Lord makes Himself known. It's the Word that gives us Jesus, that arms and equips us, that tells us we overcome by "the power of the blood and the word of testimony." May we be faithful to pour the Word, along with our testimony, into our children's hearts. Not just our physical children—the ones we commit to train up "in the fear and admonition of the Lord" when we dedicate them to Him as babies—but those in the Body of Christ, those who visit in our homes, relatives, those from broken homes, neighbors...*any little soul the Lord puts before us.*

Then, there's our spiritual children—the ones we've led to Christ, or are new in their faith. They need to hear the Word sprinkled through our conversation. They need to hear about what the Lord is doing in our lives and teaching our hearts, and to see the living, active Word of Truth living actively in us. In fact, we are called to affect not just our own families, *but a whole generation.* Not hiding from it, but speaking truth to it.

The people in Judges 16:5 had no king, so they did as they saw fit. They weren't ruled by wisdom, but by whatever looked or felt good to them. Pleasure and self-protection were their gods. They did what evil hearts do and worshiped what wicked minds worship. *And they reaped for themselves the only thing idolatry can produce: distress and famine—* famine that stretched far beyond mere physical hunger; a famine that dried up their souls and left them with a yearning thirst no water could satisfy.

WHAT THEY SAW FIT TO DO LED THEM TO *GREAT* DISTRESS. Idolatry always opens the door for the Enemy to come in and *plunder.* How I pray that won't be our children. May they see us proclaiming the wonders of the Lord in our speech, actions, songs, scrapbooks, journals- every creative way we can- as Psalm 78:4 says, "We will not hide them from their children, telling the generation to come the praises of the Lord, and His strength and His wonderful works that He has done." May they hear us delighting in Almighty God. May they observe His power saturating our hearts. May they know He lives, *because He lives strongly in us.* May they watch us truly worship, and desperately crave what we have. May the world's offerings be rubble in their eyes. May they forever seek true wealth—the kind far too costly for earthly currency.

May we continually pour out what the Lord pours in to our families and beyond. We're to freely pour the oil our Savior gives us into every empty jar He brings our way.

Just as the widow in 2 Kings 4 gathered empty jars from her neighbors and poured miraculous overflow into them in obedience to the Lord, so ought we. There's a limitless supply. We're supplied by God Himself, anointed with holy oil, as Psalm 23:5 says, *"You anoint my head with oil; my cup runs over."* We need to give up our fear of being poured out. Our "jar" won't run dry, no matter how many others need filling. *May we never send a jar away empty.*

I want the Lord Himself and no other. I want to know Him in the most intimate, holiest place, and I want to make Him known. I want my idols destroyed, with the Lord Jesus ruling over all. In Ezekiel 36:25, the Lord says, *"I will cleanse you from all your idols."* Idolatry leaves greasy, messy stains on our hearts the blood of Christ alone can cleanse. Thank God, He's willing. I pray we'll be a generation cleansed, who passionately proclaim Christ to those coming behind. They need to see more than a warm pew—they need to see a fire in our hearts. ASK FOR IT. Then ask the Holy Spirit to fan that flame, so that you take revival everywhere you go—*and affect a whole generation.*

Questions & Applications

1. **If you feel like there's "famine" in your life, have you considered its root?**
2. **With what are you seeking to fill and feed it?**
3. **Ask the Lord Jesus to light a holy fire of passion for Him and His Word within you as you go to His table and allow Him to "give you this day your daily Bread."**
4. **Ask for a contagious, bold, lived-out yearning for no less than the feast of the King of Glory Himself. Fall on your knees and cry out for the generation coming behind. You can't pass on what you don't have yourself.**

2

Seeking the Enemy's Bread

...there was famine in the land, and a man from Bethlehem in Judah, together with his wife and two sons, went to live for a while in the country of Moab. The man's name was Elimelech, his wife's name Naomi, and the names of his two sons were Mahlon and Kilion. They were Ephrathites from Bethlehem, Judah. And they went to Moab and lived there, **Ruth 1:1-2**.

The distress brought on by idolatry sent them packing. Yet, Elimelech was from Israel. His feet had walked on holy ground. Surely he'd heard the name of the Lord *somewhere*. Couldn't he see the root of Bethlehem's famine? Why didn't he dig his heels into that holy soil and repent? Why didn't he cry out to the living God? Where was repentance and trust? Why did he grab his family and run?

Elimelech didn't believe in God for himself. Maybe he had some head knowledge, but his heart was far away. *His heart was in Moab long before his feet got there.* He wasn't willing to fall on his knees and seek the way of the Lord, but trusted in his own wisdom and counseled himself. *NOT A GOOD IDEA.*

Just as the Lord let Elimelech go, He won't strap us to His perfect will. He lets us choose. I cry out for my own unbelief, foolishness and head knowledge that has yet to affect my heart. And I pour out my heart like a river before the Lord for my children. They, like Elimelech, are being raised in Bethlehem—the "House of Bread"—a place where they hear the name of Jesus. How I pray they'll STAY THERE, worshiping with all their heart, mind, soul and strength, regardless of their circumstances. I pray they, and I, will always see Moab for what it is: not a city of refuge, but a deceptively well-laid trap.

On a business trip to Dallas a few years ago my husband and I took a cab to dinner, but when we came out of the restaurant our hotel seemed so close we decided to walk back. After making a wrong turn, we found ourselves in the middle of dozens of homeless people wandering the streets of downtown. We felt very uneasy but kept walking, and men soon began approaching us, asking for money. Unsure of how to handle that, we walked a little faster.

Finally, a man approached us by himself, requesting $5 to stay in a shelter for the night, telling us he was out of work and penniless. We didn't know shelters charged, but something about him made us comply. As Eric handed it to him, I said, "Sir, what you really need is the Lord Jesus." To my shock, he replied, "I know. My Dad's a pastor." We talked with him a little while, and then with a grieving heart we dashed into a convenience store, complete with barred windows, pulled out the business card of a cab driver, made a quick call and soon crawled into a very welcome car. We were never really sure if the fellow was truly out of work, or if homeless shelters actually charge a fee.

When we mentioned the story to the cab driver, he said, "I want to show you something." He drove a few blocks over, and I was horrified to see many, many homeless gathered in an empty lot. Noticing children among them ripped my heart, and I wanted to run out and rescue them all. The driver told us there'd be hundreds huddled out there by morning. It was February, and the temperature hovered around 40 degrees. That encounter touched and challenged my heart, hitting me especially hard as a mother. In fact, that moment, the Lord planted a desire in me to help the homeless, even as we had to fly back to our tiny, mountain resort town where no homeless live. I flew home with the realization that a homeless, orphaned heart doesn't necessarily live on the street. They may live in a lovely home on a mountain—or even a parsonage. I was also left with a renewed desire to cry out for my children and others coming behind.

To think that somewhere, if the homeless man's story was true, there's a pastor whose son made choices that landed him on the streets of Dallas sends chills down my spine. It drives home the point that we can't make our kids' choices for them, or count on them loving the Lord Jesus merely because we do. It was a huge wake-up call for me to hit my knees and pour my heart out for the lives of my children NOW—to ask and keep asking the Holy Spirit to grab their hearts at a young age, to give them a love for the King of Kings that surpasses all others, to bless, prosper, guide and direct them and to mold them early and grant them teachable hearts. To keep them firmly planted in His will, in "Bethlehem," not wandering down the wrong physical or emotional streets.

BACK TO MOAB

Moab was a pagan, Baal-worshiping nation east of Israel. The king of Moab, Balak, denied Israel passage through the country as they traveled out of Egypt, sending for a prophet to curse them instead (Numbers 22-25). Then, the Moabite women attempted to seduce the Israelite men and lead them into the worship of Baal. To put it mildly, *their history with Israel wasn't good.* So much so that in Deuteronomy 23:3-4, the Lord commanded that *"no...Moabite or any of his descendants may enter the assembly of the Lord, even down to the tenth generation. For they did not come to meet you with bread and water on your way when you came out of Egypt, and they hired Balaam to pronounce a curse on you."*

Elimelech was running to Israel's enemy, seeking food from the very ones who had refused bread to his ancestors and blessing from people that attempted to curse his whole nation. *What was he thinking? And why would he drag his family to such a place?* This man willingly led his family away from the Holy Land onto unholy ground. However, instead of finding life, he and his sons found death, leaving his wife Naomi with two daughters-in-law in a desperate place named Moab. We have this choice, too. God gives us the freedom to venture into enemy territory if we wish, but once there we'll either perish or need help getting out.

Serious offenses against the Lord were going on in Moab. It was a pagan culture, where people lived as they pleased apart from the true God. Baal-worship saturated their lives and was blatant, open and "in-your-face." Watching the news today, can we really say we're any better, or do our idols just look different? Packaging is everything. Our enemy brings the same old stuff to market; he just wraps it in snazzy, new, contemporary wrapping. It's the same ol' same ol'. We may think ourselves too "sophisticated" to fall before a statue, but there are certainly many things we *do* fall for: obvious ones like money, power, pleasure, position, "love," false religion, selfishness, relationships, etc. Not idols made of stone or carved from a tree, but involving worship just as deceptive, dangerous and deadly.

Then, there are the not-so-obvious idols: bitterness, anger, pain, unforgiveness, our own opinions, self-righteousness, jealousy, past wounds, sickness...Whatever it is, if you're focusing all your strength, energy, thoughts and conversation on that *thing*, then it's become an object of worship to you—an idol. We can even focus our hearts inappropriately on good things, such as family, career, friends, hobbies or what may come wrapped in a church package, like tradition, a dynamic leader, a personal ministry, a movement or cause. Elevated too highly, even positive things can assume a wrong position in our heart. *But there's no such thing as a "good idol," and they, too, will eventually smother us. When raised where they don't belong, their weight becomes destructively unbearable.* In their proper place, they're weightless, serving the Lord's purposes and blessing your life instead of being a burden. In short, idolatry is the worship of *anything* besides the Most High God

To me, Moab represents those places we often run to apart from Christ, where the idolatries of self-gratification, unbelief, deception and rebellion reign supreme. It's where we walk in flesh and falsehood, instead of spirit and Truth. We can travel there in obvious ways, openly rejecting the King, or inconspicuously. I once heard Billy Graham state that a huge percentage of souls sitting in church pews every week have no relationship with Christ at all. Jesus said in Matthew 15:8, *"These people honor Me with their lips, but their hearts are far from Me."* They come to church and say one thing, BUT THEIR HEARTS ARE IN MOAB.

That should stir us to ask, ask and ask again for true revival, for a fresh wind of the Holy Spirit, for the flame of passion for the King to be fanned by His very breath, for the Word to wash, renew, transform, empower and fall like rain on parched land and for the fires of renewal to be lit in us and spread to all we touch. In Ezekiel 37, the prophet was shown a valley of dry bones. I see it as the valley of Moab, a parched, dusty place of death. In verse 3 the Lord asked, *"Son of man, can these bones live?"* Ezekiel replied, *"O Sovereign Lord, You alone know."* I love what the Lord says next in verse 4, *"Prophesy to these bones and say to them, 'Dry bones, hear the Word of the Lord!'"* That whole army of skeletons came to life as Ezekiel spoke God's Word to it. *LIFE CAME TO THAT DEAD PLACE THROUGH THE WORD OF THE LIVING GOD,* just as life comes to us—even we Moabites.

Questions & Applications

1. **Are there any obvious or not-so-obvious idols you need to lay at the foot of the Cross? Are you tempted look to anything besides our Wonderful Counselor—the Prince of Peace, Almighty God, Jesus Christ Himself—for comfort and fulfillment?**
2. **Have you ever run to something or somewhere that you previously swore you'd never go? If so, what was it and what made you go there?**
3. **Identify the things you think about most, talk about most and spend most of your time on. Then honestly ask yourself if any have assumed too lofty a place in your life.**
4. **Ask the Lord to search your heart for any hidden idols that may exist there, things of which you may not even be consciously aware. He doesn't seek to condemn you, but to release you from their blinding grip.**

3

An Unexpected End

> *Now Elimelech, Naomi's husband, died, and she was left with her two sons. They married Moabite women, one named Orpah and the other Ruth. After they had lived there about ten years, both Mahlon and Kilion also died, and Naomi was left without her two sons and her husband,* **Ruth 1:3-5**.

Elimelech went to Moab searching for a better life, but found death instead. There's no life out there in Moab. THERE IS NO LIFE APART FROM CHRIST. Moab comes with dire consequences: trouble, pain, sorrow, loss of dreams, empty promises and eventually death. Everything it offers inevitably crashes into a million pieces. For Elimelech and his sons, it only took about ten years. *How grateful I am for the Lord's patience and longsuffering,* otherwise I, too, would have died in Moab long ago! (I think it's interesting that Ruth bore no children in Moab. The Lord kept her from conceiving in the dead place, because He had true fruitfulness awaiting her in the Place of Redemption.)

Like Elimelech, you can grow up around Truth. You can live where it's all around you, but still refuse to grab it with your own two hands. If you're not truly grounded in the Word and don't know the Lord for yourself, Moab can start looking pretty attractive. You might say to yourself, "Good things are going on in that far country. The people there seem to have more fun, more money—an easier life. What am I doing here?"

Be assured, however, that the Enemy won't reveal the traps waiting for you there. He'll always make it look better than what you have right now. He'll tell you Bethlehem's road is too hard; that Moab is where you'll find "the good life." He'll whisper softly in your ear that you *deserve more*...he just won't reveal what the more is. The Word tells us the devil will try to deceive even the elect. What could possibly deceive the saved, except something that appears *really good?* Yet, if we run to whatever IT is for security, provision, strength and satisfaction, instead of to Christ, it'll lead us astray. There's only *one* House of Bread—and it isn't in Moab.

Has something that looked deceptively good to you become a dry, dusty, idolatrous wilderness? Has your soul been swallowed up in pain, and sent you running to the wrong place? Have you run to a Moab in search of relief, to soothe yourself or to forget your troubles? Did you go there looking for help, only to find yourself stuck in a place of serious compromise? Has idolatry and the distress it brings forced you into foreign lands where you weren't meant to dwell? Have you departed to the wrong place to find satisfaction? Allow the Lord to search deep in your heart here (as He loves to do with me). Never condemning, He'll expose the hidden places of our souls so that we can be set free. Ask Him to show you if any movement, program, person, possession, feeling, relationship, goal, dream, fear, hurt, desire or anything else has become a Moab in your life.

Ruth 1:1 said that Elimelech went to live in Moab "for a while." Have you ever told yourself something like that? "I'll just go see what ______ has to offer...nothing permanent...just a little temporary relief. I know God will understand." After all, you reason, you have every intention to *eventually* return to Bethlehem—especially when it starts looking more like a House of Bread. I remember hearing someone say in college, "I know what's right. I just want to have fun in college and come back to the Lord later." It's a fool's game to PLAN seasons of rebellion. What if we pack our bags and head out to Moab, but like Elimelech, NEVER MAKE IT OUT? Idolatry tends to blind our hearts to the dangers of stepping off the King's soil, removing us from His protection and exposing us to serious peril.

When is it wise to camp out in sin, even if our intention is only to linger there "for a while"? How can we ever prosper or find satisfaction in a place like that? When will it produce a righteous harvest of joy and blessing? What could it possibly bring, but distress and death—the only things of which it is capable? Sure, the grass "over there" often looks better from a distance, just as Moab looked awfully inviting to Elimelech, but please be warned: YOU CANNOT PROSPER THERE! Oh, that our hearts would long instead to continually abide in the most intimate place of the Lord's presence, resting in Him and feeling our belovedness as the Apostle John did, far, far away from Moab.

Elimelech died in Moab. His "just for a while" turned into forever. His sons married foreign wives, a sin against the Law and a disgrace, and then died there too. *They followed in Daddy's footsteps.* The father's compromise led to the sons', and his wife was suddenly left in a foreign, idolatrous land as a childless widow. What good came to Elimelech and his family in Moab? WHAT GOOD *EVER* COMES FROM UNFAITHFULNESS AND COMPROMISE?

I don't know about you, *but I've been to Moab*. I know what its soil feels like. I know how it smells and tastes. I know how sweet it appears, but how bitter it is going down. I know how pain and desperation can make you grab your running shoes and head there. I know how wide Moab stretches her arms, and how welcoming she can be. *But there's no fine print on her welcome mat—she won't tell you what's waiting for you inside.*

I know the road into Moab very well, but, thank God, I also know the road out. For much of my life I wanted to be a "good Christian," but I also wanted to stand on the outer edge of Truth, just on the borders of Moab, blending in to both sides. That's a lukewarm place, a place of confusion and trouble far from Bethlehem's fiery passion, but not quite frozen by Moab's cold waters. *Worse than that, it's dangerous ground*, because the Lord says in Revelation 3:15-16, *"I know your deeds, that you are neither cold nor hot. I wish you were either one or the other! So, because you are lukewarm—neither cold nor hot—I am about to spit you out of My mouth."* (The very morning I typed these words, my shower water for some reason never got really hot. Maybe the Lord was driving home the point: LUKEWARM IS NOT GOOD!) What results from it? Those with feet in Bethlehem but hearts in Moab, like those who claim to be Christian but live just like the world, do great harm to the kingdom of the Risen Christ. No wonder He wants us to be one or the other.

But what if you were raised in Moab and know nothing else? What if its bitter strongholds ensnared you even as a child? What if you worship the things of this world because you were taught to? What if the roadways of Moab are the only paths your feet have ever walked? What if your only spiritual heritage is idolatry and dysfunction?

Have you jumped from one thing to another in Moab—relationship after relationship, job after job, friend after friend, drink after drink, possibly even perversion after perversion—searching for what you've yet to find? IN YOUR HEART, you KNOW there's so much more. You have a deep yearning and a restless longing for true satisfaction. But everything you try merely leaves you with a deeper void, and greater emptiness or feelings of despair. Are you desperate to still your soul and find rivers of peace? Do you hunger for a life that satisfies? I assure you these things exist, and invite you to step out and find the high road to Bethlehem. Whether you realize it or not, you have these desires because Almighty God planted them in your heart. The truth is, the Lord made you for Himself and put a hunger for Him within you. As the French philosopher Pascal once said, "Man has a God-shaped void in his heart that nothing else can fill."

It doesn't matter if you were born in Moab or ran there- you don't have to stay. You were meant for Bethlehem, for the fields of the King. One name on your lips will take you to the place you are destined for- Jesus.

Perhaps your feet are firmly planted in the House of God, but you have relatives and friends far away in Moab, as do I. (Having lived there too long myself, I TRY NEVER TO JUDGE ANYONE FOR BEING IN MOAB. God forgive us for our all-too-often condemning, critical spirits!) I pray the Lord will draw my loved ones to Bethlehem by the power of His Word and the breath of His Spirit! I beg Him not to let them die out there like Elimelech! I persevere in asking that their hearts will be opened to Truth and their feet turned to run to the mighty, open arms of Christ. I implore the King to help them desire His abundant fields, where they can drink in His soothing presence and glean from His harvest.

WHAT WOULD HAPPEN IF WE *ALL* COMMITTED TO PERSEVERE IN PRAYER FOR THOSE WE KNOW IN MOAB? While I haven't always persevered in praying for everyone on my list, I make a concerted effort when it comes to my family, some of whom aren't yet saved. I have photos of them sitting on the buffet beside the table where I meet with the Lord. As I look at those pictures, I cry out to Jesus to BRING SALVATION TO MY LINEAGE AND SEED, every last one of them—every soul that still has breath, though some are in their 80's and 90's; not one dying without the Truth prospering in their hearts—even those, or *especially* those, whose darkness and dysfunction have deeply wounded my heart. I ask the Lord for every family link to Moab to be broken, for every stronghold and generational curse to be covered by the blood of Jesus and for redemption and restoration to soak us all. Let it be, my King. Let it be.

Imagine what it would be like if EVERY "MOABITE" IN OUR FAMILIES CAME HOME! What if hearts were healed, and we could all gather with joy around our holiday meals without distress? What if dysfunctional, unhealthy families could establish new patterns of CELEBRATING RESTORATION and walking with redeemed feet? How incredibly could *that* affect future generations? Mighty, holy King Jesus, BRING US OUT OF MOAB! Bring those we love out of Moab. Bring us to Your precious, tender feet, and guide us to Bethlehem's rich fields of grace.

Questions & Applications

1. **Are you crying out for lost and lukewarm hearts—maybe even your own?**
2. **Will you commit to bring before the Lord continually those you know who are in "Moab," or who are lost?**
3. **James 5:16 tells us that "the prayers of a righteous man are powerful and effective." As you abide in the presence of the King and in His Word, you can expect to see the prayers you are lifting answered with power. You will never waste your time when you're on your knees. Those cries are effective.**

4

All Things Work Together...

> *Now Elimelech, Naomi's husband, died, and she was left with her two sons. They married Moabite women, one named Orpah and the other Ruth. After they had lived there about ten years, both Mahlon and Kilion also died...***Ruth 1:3-5a**.

Raised in a culture steeped in idol worship, pressure surrounded Ruth on every side to follow the ways of her deceived people. I believe she fully expected to marry some handsome, young Baal-worshipper and live out her days in Moab. *Yet, there was something about that man from Bethlehem, Naomi's son, that caught her eye*. Kilion was a foreigner in Moab, a man of a different people, a man from Israel—forbidden to marry someone like her. But they were drawn to each other. Perhaps it was her elegance that charmed him, or her passion that captured his heart. Whatever it was, despite the scandal of it, Ruth became his bride. But that was a temporary situation. As verse 5 already informed us, death took the young groom, leaving a grieving widow and a bitter mother.

The Lord God Almighty had a deeper, broader, sweeter plan for Ruth. The sorrow of Moab was going to lead her straight to destiny—and to more than she ever dared imagine. In time, as she stepped into the place of honor prepared for her by God Himself, that sorrow would melt into a distant memory. The words of Psalm 119:67 and 71 come to mind, *"Before I was afflicted I went astray, but now I obey Your Word...It was good for me to be afflicted so that I might learn Your decrees."* THE PAIN OF MOAB WAS GOING TO CATAPULT HER STRAIGHT TO THE FULLNESS OF GOD'S GREAT PLAN.

How often do we despise affliction and pain? Personally, I'd say, *"EVERY TIME."* Yet, it may be the very thing the Lord uses to glorify Himself in our lives and set us in a never-imagined place of honor. When we see the plan of God unfold and understand how that despised experience was used for good, I believe praise will fill our hearts in a place we never thought it could.

We're given breath each day so we can praise the King of Kings—*even when we can't understand our painful circumstances*—not to waste it on complaining. In 2002, my immune system went haywire following a bout with strep throat. The pain was so severe that I had to leave my teaching job. After years of doctors and specialists, I was finally labeled in the "fibromyalgia" category, and my health has been like an unpredictable yo-yo. I didn't experience death like Ruth tasted it in Moab, but I did walk through a dying of sorts. Death to my normal energy level. Death to the independent part of me that liked earning a paycheck. Death to counting on feeling well when you woke up in the morning. Death to the kind of exercise I enjoyed- long walks, aerobics, running after my young children. Death to thinking I could do it all.

One night I couldn't sleep because of terrible pain. I tossed and turned physically and spiritually. I kept crying out to the Lord, "TAKE THIS THING! HEAL ME! I'M

YOURS—SURELY YOU DON'T WANT ME TO HURT LIKE THIS!!!" The Lord spoke loudly but gently in my heart and said, "You need to be thanking Me for this." How strange. Thank Him for pain wracking my body, for swollen joints and weak muscles and for no energy in a household that demands a lot of it? THANK HIM?

Yes. Thank Him. That disability put me on my face before the King. That despised thing stripped me of all confidence in my flesh. The Lord used it to start peeling back my heart and to set me on a path of truly seeking His. I began to ask Him for three things- show me Your glory, illumine Your Word, and let me see the unseen. I begged Him to show me all of Him that flesh could behold on this earth without falling dead before His holiness. AND PRASIE GOD, HE BEGAN TO DO IT. He didn't deliver me in a dramatic healing event, but He began to unfold His heart and His Word before my weak, trembling soul. He gave me a desire for His presence that reached far deeper than my desire for healing. He put a thirst for His Word in me that exceeded my thirst for physical strength. The living Word became living and active in me, and I am forever hooked. *And that's a reason for gratitude. That's an "all things working for good" kind of deal, a momentary affliction working out an eternal weight of glory, a reason to join the Psalmist in saying, "It was good that I was afflicted..."*

Sometimes the hardest things turn out to be the best things. I believe Ruth, not to mention Naomi, eventually came to a point of praising God for all that happened in Moab. May we also *truly* give thanks in all things, even those we may now despise.

Questions & Applications

1. **Has there been a "despised thing" in your life that's brought you to your knees before the**

King? Is there even now an affliction you can't understand?

2. **Are you expecting to see the Lord use it for good, draw you to Himself and show you His mighty strength?**
3. **Will you dare to praise Him, even when you can't make sense of your circumstance? Even when the answer hasn't come in the way you wanted? Will you trust His Word that is forever true and tells us, "And we know that in all things God works for the good of those who love Him..." (Romans 8:28). Will you trust His indescribable love for you, even when you hurt?**

5

The Checed of God

When she heard in Moab that the Lord had come to the aid of His people by providing food for them, Naomi and her daughters- in-law prepared to return home from there. With her two daughters-in-law she left the place where she had been living and set out on the road that would take them back to the land of Judah," **Ruth 1:6-7.**

Powerful testimony hit the ears of Naomi, Orpah and Ruth. SOMETHING HAD HAPPENED IN BETHLEHEM—something huge enough for word of it to spread all the way to Moab! The Lord's provision was being spoken of in an idolatrous, foreign land. In spite of labored communication, with no technology, no Internet and no telephones or modern conveniences, THE WORD got out. The Name of the Lord was falling from even the lips of the lost in Moab.

What had happened in Bethlehem? *"The Lord had come to the aid of His people..."* The King of Kings was standing by His covenant with Israel. Faithfulness was being displayed. Mercy had overtaken wrath. Despite their turning away, He was making Himself known. I wonder: had the people of Bethlehem finally hit their knees and cried out to God? Had repentance soaked their hearts and spilled onto the feet of the King? Or had His great compassion alone caused the Lord to move on behalf of His people?

The Hebrew word for mercy is *checed* (kheh'-sed), meaning strength, steadfastness and love. As one of God's most central characteristics, it's used repeatedly to describe the Lord's heart toward Israel. It represents God's strong faithfulness to His promise, His steadfast commitment to His covenant. Beyond promise-keeping, it moves into the realm of generosity, kindness, goodness, pity, compassion and favor. *Strong's Concordance* says of mercy, "...but since God's *checed* is ultimately beyond the covenant, it will not ultimately be abandoned, even when the human partner is unfaithful and must be disciplined." Now, that's *good news!* Even while unfaithfulness was raging throughout Bethlehem, the Faithful One was planning to act with mercy. *Even when faithlessness and unbelief rage in our own hearts, the Lord, through Christ, is laying up mercy for us.* The Lord is faithful in spite of us.

Did the Lord's great mercy poured out on an unfaithful people spark REVIVAL in Bethlehem? Was the move of God so awesome and overwhelmingly gracious that word of it spread like wildfire? AND DOESN'T THE SAME GOD OF MERCY MOVE IN US? Isn't it the same eternal Hand that works on our behalf? Doesn't the same brand of faithfulness cover our unfaithfulness and call us home? SHOULDN'T WORD OF GOD'S MOVING IN OUR LIVES SPREAD—EVEN TO FAR-REACHING, DISTANT PLACES? Shouldn't we be telling everyone we see about the goodness and undeserved favor of the King, of His provision in our famines and of His steadfast love and strength despite our wavering weakness? ARE WE TELLING IT?

I dare say some of the most powerful testimonies in history were from individuals who desired no such thing. I believe they were souls desperate for a touch of God, through whom the King spread the glory of His Name far and wide, as a result of their cries. What would happen among us if we fell on our knees and cried out for the Lord's great *checed* to fall on our hearts, homes, churches and nation? Could it birth a revival that would burst through our borders and reach even far-off, idolatrous places? Is it possible testimonies of it could prove so powerful and far-reaching that Moabites would come running to Bethlehem—God's House of Bread? *Dream big before the Lord. Ask for mercy's wonders. Ask for the breath of His Spirit, the flame of His heart and the living power of His Word to saturate your heart and burst through every border.*

In her time of despair, in a place far from home and far from her destiny, Naomi heard the name of the Lord—and it stirred her heart. She was drawn to the House of the Lord, to her homeland of Judah, to the place where provision was now pouring forth. Her heart longed for deeper, purer and truer satisfaction, the kind Moab couldn't give. Moab had utterly failed her, or she would have stayed put.

Physical hunger had taken Naomi to Moab, but I believe it was a deep, spiritual hunger that turned her back to Bethlehem. Jesus' words in Matt. 5:6 echo here, *"Blessed are those who hunger and thirst for righteousness, for they shall be filled."* The Psalmist also speaks to this in Ps. 107:9, *"He satisfies the longing soul, and fills the hungry soul with goodness."* We won't be served stones in Bethlehem, but fresh, satisfying, pure bread from the table of the King. No matter how far we are from the place God has prepared for us, how distant destiny seems or how darkly sorrow overshadows, the Name of the Lord raises its strong tower and draws us to its safety. The name of Jesus shouts to our hearts and leads us homeward, saying, *"Come unto Me, all you who are weary and burdened, and I will give you rest,"* (Matthew 11:28).

Christ promises salvation, satisfaction and sweet rest for your soul. What does Moab promise, and how have its promises worked out for you? Have they given you rest, or frenzied panic? Have they left you starving for the very things they promised to feed you? Are the things you expected would bring you an enjoyable, easy life killing you instead? Naomi followed a *relationship* out to Moab. That point hit home with me. Did you grow up among God's people, in the church, but choose to follow a relationship out to Moab? Did it work out like you thought or leave you bitter, like Naomi? Did things seem to grow out of that relationship for a time, but still end in death?

Naomi was led astray by her husband, but there are plenty of other relationships that have the potential to lead us away from God's best. It could be a relationship with a leader, a movement, an idea, a dream—perhaps it's with your own independent spirit or self-righteousness—on and on. Whatever it may be in your life, *is it possible the Lord has allowed it to die, because He wants to lead you to a place of joy with Him you never dreamed possible in that foreign land?* Has God allowed some things you've anchored your heart in, apart from Him, to PERISH, to enable you to see your idols for what they are? Are you experiencing pain because He wants you to turn your feet in a new direction and head straight for Him? HE IS GOOD. HIS MERCY ENDURES FOREVER. *Sometimes His mercy hurts.* What will you do then?

There's only one place to go: Bethlehem. As Naomi packed her physical bags, we need to pack our emotional bags and head out for the highway of the merciful King. I cry out with the Psalmist, *"Show me Your ways, O Lord; teach me Your paths,"* Psalm 25:4.

Naomi grabbed those she loved and CHANGED DIRECTIONS. She left the place where she'd been living, a land of Baal worship and sorrow, and put her feet on the

King's Highway. She had no idea what was ahead of her, but deep in her heart she knew she MUST GO. Flesh had driven her to a foreign land, but brokenness was driving her home. *Don't despise the day of brokenness. It can be a vehicle of glory.* There was a breaking, then a turning; a humbling, then a change of direction; a ripping apart, then a redeeming. Proverbs 3:5 says, *"Trust in the Lord with all your heart, and lean not on your own understanding."* Naomi had no understanding or guarantees to lean on; she just knew she had to return to the land of the Lord.

We can't always make sense of our lives, but we can always run with tear-filled hearts to the feet of the Almighty. We can trust Him there to fill us, to give us fresh glimpses of grace, to cover, shield, protect and plant our feet on holy ground. We can trust Him to show us the path of life, fill us with the joy of His presence and let us enjoy the pleasures of His right hand forevermore (Ps. 16:11). We can trust Him to carefully hold our hearts and divinely guide us with His all-seeing eye (Ps. 32:8). *He sees ahead. He hears your current cries and spills tears for your heart as it mourns before Him, but HE KNOWS WHAT'S COMING. He knows the path that will lead you from glory to glory. He knows how to position you to fully receive His blessing. You just want Him to fill you where you are and make you comfortable—He wants to take you to new, never-tasted heights. He didn't bring you immediate gratification, because that would have locked your feet on barren land. He doesn't answer your way—He answers His way, BECAUSE HE HAS SO MUCH MORE FOR YOU THAN YOU EVEN KNOW HOW TO ASK FOR.* How I thank the Lord for *His sovereignty;* for responding to my foolish requests with His often-quiet wisdom...and for changing my direction with His loving heart- even when His mercy has hurt.

Questions & Applications

1. **Could, "Something has happened!" be said of your life, and could testimony of it reach even far off places? Are you asking for a move of God like that?**
2. **The Lord is rich in mercy, abundant in grace and full of plans for your good. Will you trust His purposes when he allows a change of direction you don't understand? Will you believe that He's working out His glory—and your destiny?**

6

Leaving Moab...

And Naomi said to her two daughters-in-law, "Go, return each to her mother's house. The Lord deal kindly with you, as you have dealt with the dead and with me. The Lord grant that you may find rest, each in the house of her husband." So she kissed them, and they lifted up their voices and wept. And they said to her, "Surely we will return with you to your people." But Naomi said, "Turn back, my daughters; why will you go with me? Are there still sons in my womb, that they may be your husbands?...Then they lifted up their voices and wept again; and Orpah kissed her mother-in-law, but Ruth clung to her...[and] said, "...wherever you go, I will go; and wherever you lodge, I will lodge; your people shall be my people, and your God, my God...," **Ruth 1:8-18**.

A decision had to be made. Three grieving women were in the same situation, facing the same options. Yet their hearts were in very different states, states that would have very serious consequences. Naomi's heart was bitter from despair, and she let that bitter root become so HUGE that it literally changed her identity. "Call me Mara (bitter)," she will soon tell others—"Oh, I know Naomi...she's bitter." Orpah's heart wavered. Lacking faith, she looked at the magnitude of the pain, then turned around and ran backwards: back to the familiar, the comfortable, the same ol' same ol'—self-reliance, idolatry, addiction, a man—whatever she looked to in Moab for satisfaction. But Ruth's heart was determined to venture out and press on, even in pain, even into the unknown. She chose to let go of the past, seek new avenues for her hurting soul and move ahead in faith, hope and love. These women all faced the same root of bitterness, but each responded differently.

NAOMI

Naomi's bitter heart blinded her to what the Lord could do. She spoke to her daughters-in-law as if their future depended on HER, not on the Living God. "Am I going to have any more sons?" she says cynically, repeatedly counseling her daughters-in-law to return to their families in Moab. Have we, like Naomi, ever thought we had to arrange circumstances and fix things in our own strength and ability? Have we ever urged someone to do wrong because bitterness was blinding us, even if it sounded like common sense? WISE COUNSEL CANNOT COME OUT OF BITTERNESS! It can neither guide correctly nor encourage rightly. Why would Naomi, a child of the true God, urge those young women to return to households of *Baal worship*? Bitterness said, "Go back." It urged them to follow the flesh instead of the Spirit, to follow the known instead of the unknown, to stay within the boundaries of what had always been—even if what had always been was an absolute offense to the Most High.

Protect us, Holy Spirit, from the counsel of the bitter! Cement our feet to Yours, and lead us in the way everlasting. Silence our ears to the pleas of those around us, even those we love, to stay in the mire of what we've always known! You are higher, deeper, fuller and wiser than anything we have yet tasted. Anchor our hearts, steady our determination and help us take the path of righteousness. Let the clamorings and scorn of the flesh fall on deaf ears. Let Your counsel alone guide our feet.

Bitterness drives us backwards, far from the blessings of the Lord. Bitterness locks us into the place where it was birthed, refusing to let us move forward. *We must never allow it to take root in our hearts, but forsake and walk away from it. So much more lies ahead.*

Bitterness is rooted in self-centeredness and pride. "Things didn't go *my* way. I wasn't treated the way *I* wanted to be. They hurt *me*. God didn't move the way *I* wanted Him to." I, I, I...me, me, me...an absolute inward focus. Our flesh grabs hold of that offense or wound and nurses it right into bitterness, all the while refusing to take responsibility for the role it may have played in the matter; it just looks at its own hurt.

Bitterness can stem from many sources. There can be huge, deep roots that feed bitterness: childhood abuse, rejection, divorce, sickness, loss, unanswered prayers— any painful, life-altering situation. But there can also be small, everyday doors through which bitterness can subtly slip: disappointment, a friend letting you down, a spouse hurting your feelings, being left out of something, unmet expectations and needs, comparing your life to someone else's, your opinions or gifts being overlooked, valid things, silly things, it goes on and on. *However, whether the root of your bitterness is big or small, IT IS STILL BITTERNESS!* You might rate the degree of offense, but you can't rate bitterness. Bitter is bitter. Poison is poison. No matter what the source, it produces the same deadly effect in your heart.

You can continually feed that bitter root, causing it to grow and grow until it completely consumes your joy. You give it life by focusing your thoughts on it, talking about it and giving it a comfortable place in your heart. It loves to be nurtured, stroked and agreed with, and will thus inevitably make itself known in your conversations. It wants to be a dominating factor in your life, and will strangle the sweet fruit the Holy Spirit wants to bear in you.

We don't only grow bitter from our own wounds, but also from those suffered by ones we love. Have you ever taken on someone else's offense and fueled an angry fire in your own heart—gotten bitter because of what happened to them? Have you picked up something that wasn't yours to pick up? Once when a friend of mine was deeply hurt, it fell so heavily on me I literally lost sleep. I went to my closet, hit my knees and begged the Lord to help me deal with that burden. His response in my spirit was simple, but strong. He said, "I didn't ask you to pick that up. Pray for them, but don't take it upon yourself." I was set free as I repented of the bitterness that burden was causing in me and laid it all in the hands of the King. 1 Peter 5:7 invites us to, *"cast your cares upon Him, for He cares for you."* Holding onto our cares, or the cares of others, instead of casting them upon Him will produce bitterness.

Have you ever prayed from a heart of bitterness instead of love? "Lord, that person is WRONG. They hurt me. They hurt my family, my friends... It's unacceptable. They shouldn't be in the position they hold. Bring on justice, Lord! Set them straight!" I never want to be prayed for that way. (*"Do unto others as you would have them do to you..."* rings loudly here.) I want forgiveness. I want mercy. I want grace that I absolutely don't deserve. I want the faithfulness of the Most High to completely override my unfaithfulness. I want to dwell in the shadow of the Almighty and be covered by His sacrifice. I want to walk on righteousness' path of beauty, no matter how long I avoided it in the past. I want the sweet aroma and radiance of the King to soak my life, scandalous as it may be.

That is what we should pray for others, no matter how much our flesh resists. And believe me, *the flesh will resist.* Jesus says, "Pray for your enemies, bless those who persecute you." Ouch. What if those persecuting you are the very ones who are supposed to love you? What if your enemies are sitting in the next pew? I've seen brothers and sisters in Christ deal brutally with each other. What then? *Pray, bless, do unto others, forgive, walk in love*—by the supernatural power of the Holy Spirit alone. The flesh just isn't capable. We have to leave it behind and walk in Spirit and Truth.

The Enemy is after that heart of yours to steal, kill and destroy all the Lord wants to accomplish in it. Bitterness is one of his clever, utterly destructive tools. It won't allow you to be a Kingdom builder—the high place to which we are called—because it only knows how to tear down. Bitterness is barren. It can't produce godly fruit and can never be a springboard of hope- they aren't in its nature. LAY THAT BITTER HEART DOWN! It's too heavy a load, and will forever hinder your feet. The Lord wants your WHOLE HEART because He wants to pour *GLORY* in it, but *He will not share His glory with your bitterness.* He wants to absolutely *dazzle* you. But bitterness blinds your eyes.

The Hebrew word for bitter or bitterness is "marar" (maw-rar). Its meaning includes being bitter, grieved, vexed or provoked. It may refer to a trickle or a drop, and is sometimes compared to the venom of a serpent. *That bitter thing you're holding in your heart is as deadly as allowing a serpent's venom in your IV drip!* Why would we allow poison to trickle into our hearts? If you've ever walked in bitterness, you know its poisonous power. Hard and destructive, unless you step out of it, it leads you to darker and darker places. I believe its venom can affect your heart, soul, mind and strength—the very things with which we're called to love the Lord our God.

In Exodus 15:22-25, the Israelites came to a place of bitter water. They were thirsty and in need of fresh, cool springs. Yet, this water came with serious consequences if drank. Instead of asking the God who had just parted HUGE waters to provide for them now, they grumbled. They complained. THEIR HEARTS WERE DRINKING BITTER WATER EVEN IF THEIR MOUTHS WEREN'T. The Most High God had been able to handle the Red Sea for them. How could they think this little pool was too much for Him now? Had He lost strength? Were miracles now beyond His abilities? Where was faith in this picture? *We have to look back and remember the wonders the Lord has done in our own life as we trust Him for today's need. Journaling is a good way for forgetful minds to recall (maybe the Israelites needed a pen and paper).*

Moses cried out to God on behalf of those grumbling people (I wonder what that prayer sounded like). And God, in His faithfulness, provided the answer for the bitter waters. He showed Moses a piece of wood, a branch that sweetened the water when thrown into it. And God has given us the solution to our heart's bitter waters, as well. It's Cross-shaped wood thrown into the depths of our heart. It's the blood of the Lamb cleansing that poison deep within. It's Jesus standing in our hearts, and doing what Isaiah 60:13 says, *"making the place of His feet glorious."* From bitter to sweet; from death's poison to life's abundance.

I say, "STAND HERE, MY KING!" Put holy feet on bitter ground and CHANGE ITS VERY NATURE! Renew, transform, establish, bear fruit and let glory shine 'round about. "FOR UNTO US A CHILD IS BORN"*—for our bitterness. He was pierced for that transgression. He was bruised for that iniquity. The punishment that brings you peace is upon Him. BY HIS WOUNDS YOU ARE HEALED! (Isaiah 53:5). His hands are open. Don't keep whatever it is in your heart. Let Him take it.*

If bitterness has found a place in your life as it did in Naomi's, I encourage you to take these steps:

1 Ask the Holy Spirit to examine your heart with you and reveal anything that's not of Him. Believe me, *HE'LL ANSWER THAT ONE!* And He may just bring to mind more than you expected.
2 Lay down whatever He reveals to you in the sweet freedom of repentance. Take responsibility for it before Him, then put it in His lap and let the blood of Christ do its mighty work.
3 Forgive the offense against you and make amends if need be.
4 Renew your mind—refocus it on the Word of the Living God. Replace the spot bitterness held with TRUTH.
5 Bitterness creates a self-centered passion of its own. Ask the Holy Spirit to replace that energy with a passion for the Risen Christ.

What could happen among us if every hint of bitterness was replaced with a fiery passion for the King; if every thought was taken captive to Christ and every word out of our lips was a word of wisdom and praise to the Lord? How different would our lives, our homes, our relationships, our churches, our communities and our nation be? What would that look like? I'm on my knees with conviction: *Oh, mighty Prince of Peace, Lamb of God, cleanse my heart. Wash it with the water of Your Word. Sprinkle your sacrifice over my soul and make it new—fill it with NOTHING BUT YOURSELF—and let bitterness find no room.*

There will be plenty of opportunities for bitter roots to grow, even if you're walking in the perfect will of God. *His ways are usually not ours.* My ways usually focus on my comfort. His focus is on Christ's glory.

Mary could have chosen bitterness at Joseph's initial request for divorce. She could have resented having to ride a smelly donkey all the way to Bethlehem. She could have stomped her feet and pitched a nine-month-pregnant, hormonal fit at having to give birth in a dark stable and lay the newborn King on mere straw. She could have been bitter about the welcoming committee being a bunch of animals and some scraggly shepherds. Or, she could have boasted about being chosen by the Most High God and demanded earthly prosperity and honor. She could have resented Joseph's meager carpenter's salary. How could she educate this holy Child properly on THAT? How do you raise a King when you're living in poverty? Herod's fury could have caused bitterness to rage in her heart with innocent babies killed, wailing mothers grieving, life terribly interrupted and having to flee to Egypt of all places. After all, she had no desire to live among the Pyramids—hadn't planned to vacation there, let alone take up residence. Mary had many opportunities to blame God bitterly, rather than trust in His perfect will and timing.

Noah could have resented being asked to do something so strange and illogical, so counter-cultural and consuming, and quickly grown bitter as he became the brunt of cruel jokes. David could have let bitterness toward Saul overtake his heart. He could have flaunted his own anointing and let bitter feelings flow. Had he let bitterness grip his heart, it would have been simple for him to kill Saul when given the chance. Joseph could have allowed bitter roots toward his brothers to completely consume him, focusing on the hurt, refusing to forgive and missing the incredible plan of the Most High. What if that poison had found a place in his heart as he sat day after day in a dark prison? Would the ending have been the same?

John could have grown bitter in his lonely exile to Patmos, sat there in complete self-focus and self-pity, replayed the horrible things that had happened to him and blamed God. After all, he was the beloved of Christ. What was he doing in that desolate place? Didn't he deserve better that that? What if, on the Lord's Day, he was wallowing in bitterness instead of dwelling in the Spirit, as it says in Revelation 1:10? What great wonders he (and we) would have missed!!!

What are we walking in today? Have we allowed bitterness to cause us to miss anything, to blame God for not appeasing our flesh or keep us in the same place when the Lord wants to move us forward? Deuteronomy 8:2 says, *"You shall remember that the Lord your God led you all the way these forty years in the wilderness, to humble you and to test you, to know what was in your heart..."* Have you ever found yourself LED BY GOD into a wilderness? Taken by the King's hand out to a dry place of uncertainty? Followed the pillar of fire and cloud of glory to a place you absolutely couldn't understand? Did it leave you bitter?

Mark 1:4 tells us, *"Now John (the Baptist) came baptizing in the wilderness..."* I believe the Lord takes us out into the wilderness at times to *baptize* us for something new He's planned—to prepare us for what He has ahead—and that our experience there is not meant to foster bitterness, but humility and a revealing of what's lurking in our hearts that we may not be aware of. Completely different things surface in trials than in prosperity. Impurities rise to the surface during hard times. Selfishness makes itself known. Unforgiveness displays its brutality. Bitterness raises its ugly head. If those things aren't dealt with through the power of the blood of Christ, paralysis sets in. Your feet will remain in that barren place, while the Promised Land is waiting for you just ahead. For the Israelites an 11-day trip became a 40-year trial—a test they never passed.

That puts me on my face before the King, pleading for mercy and wisdom. I WANT TO MOVE INTO ALL THE LORD HAS PLANNED FOR MY LIFE. I don't want to march in circles around the same bitter root year after year, when the fulfillment of God's promises lies just ahead. I want my trembling feet to *move* and tread on holy ground. We're told in Hebrews 12:15, "*See to it that no one misses the grace of God and that no bitter root grows up to cause trouble and defile many.*" That bitterness you've been nursing does more than poison your own heart, it will eventually cause trouble for those around you. Bitter hearts get critical. They stop believing good about others. They grow cold and cynical. They hold onto past hurts, and bitter builds on bitter. They can't pray effectively, because they secretly want people to get what they deserve. How desperately I desire a heart the Lord can pour Himself through, not one that spews bitterness.

I CAN'T DO IT IN MY OWN STRENGTH. So I ask the Lord Jesus to stand in my heart, raise His hand of power and speak peace over its bitter waves, wash me with the water of His Word and fly His banner over my soul. As Psalm 23 says, I want Him to lead me (out of bitterness, out of Moab), restore my soul (along with my heart, mind and strength) and take me forward without fear by quiet streams of peace. I want my head anointed with so much oil my cup overflows, making it too slippery for bitterness to hold onto. I desire goodness and mercy, the great *checed* of God, to follow me all the days of my life and keep me in the intimate sanctuary of the Most High—in the secret place—where we abide beneath the shadow of His wing and where grace is poured out, not missed. No blinding bitterness. No turning back. Just pressing in to Christ's freedom with feet aimed toward Bethlehem.

What made you bitter, Naomi? Dreams that crashed to the ground...loss...disappointment...death...despair? Your feet have turned the right way now. Don't take bitterness with you. Yes, you've seen trouble. Yes, sorrow has cloaked your heart. But a great outpouring of mercy is just ahead. Rise up out of self-pity, shed bitterness like an old rag and follow the leading of Jehovah. He is faithful. He is Restoration itself. He is your Redeemer. Bitter is not your name or your home. Keep walking, Naomi, one step at a time. Insert your own name here: Keep walking, ______________, one step at a time. Yes, you've been through some things, but your Redeemer is ever ready to restore. His great mercy is for you. Put one shaky foot in front of the other and follow the Faithful One to all He's prepared in advance for you to do.

Questions & Applications

1. **Every one of us can find an excuse to cling to a bitter root. Are you willing to release yours and ask the Lord to remove every trace of it from your heart?**
2. **Have you ever imagined what the Lord could do through your freed heart?**

7

Orpah, Fearful and Unbelieving

Then Orpah kissed her mother-in-law good-bye... **Ruth 1:14.**

Orpah feared the path ahead and kissed it good-bye. She just couldn't envision what stretched out before her—*"Without vision, the people perish."* She listened to bitter counsel instead of pressing on with a faith of her own, and I believe she paid dearly. We never hear of her in Scripture again. She went back to all she'd known in Moab, walking away from all she could have had in Bethlehem. Surely she, too, heard the report that good things were occurring in Bethlehem—that the Most High had come to the aid of His people; that He was keeping holy covenant with them and mercy was pouring forth. She heard it and believed it for others, *but couldn't believe it for herself.*

Ever been there? You hear of a great move of God. He's doing mighty things in other lives with His Word prospering in hearts and utterly transforming souls, but you can't see yourself in that picture. Or you read and hear the promises of God, but, somehow, can't make the application to your own life—you can't imagine divine power blasting through your own soul.

It's easy to believe the amazing promises of God for that super, in-the-spotlight Christian: Billy Graham, Beth Moore or any famous church leader. They're obviously walking in Truth and blessing. *But what about your own two feet?* Do you believe with all your heart that you'll see the goodness of the Lord in the land of the living? That you'll walk in His wonders? That the power of the Word will actively soak and cover your soul and burn like fire in your heart? That you'll see miraculous answers to prayer as you pray the Word over yourself and others? That the path God has set you on will bring Him much glory? That you'll know the fullness of the Most High through Christ and experience as much of Him as earthly hands can hold? That you'll dwell in His intimate sanctuary *all* the days of your life—not just on one or two super-special ones?

For so long I didn't. I had accepted Christ and believed the Word in a general sort of way, but my feet still pointed toward Moab. I couldn't seem to get a vision of its living, active power in my everyday life. I believed it was there and that plenty of other people had it, but I didn't know how to grab hold of its fullness. I didn't have enough sense to ASK the King for faith and all it brings. I thought I had to muster it up myself. The Lord says, *"ASK, that you may receive."* My life changed DRASTICALLY the moment I began to ask for the glory and wonder of the Risen Christ, for Spirit-produced, not flesh-produced, love and faith, for the living Word of the Holy One to be illumined in my heart and for the ability to absolutely, without a doubt, believe it for MYSELF and tremble with passion and awe before it. I asked that Isaiah 66:2 would begin to describe my heart, *"This is the one I esteem: he who is humble and contrite in spirit and trembles at My Word."* How desperately I want that to be me.

A lack of faith that fails to grab the Word with both hands and take it as our own is crippling. In Matthew 13:58, we're told that Jesus *"did not do many miracles there* [in His hometown] *because of their lack of faith."* What did Orpah miss by not believing the Most High could redeem all she'd walked through? There was risk involved in stepping out with Mrs. Bitter and heading to a new place that required faith to overcome. Who knew what awaited in Bethlehem, and how would they be provided for on the trip? Where would they live once they got there? How would they eat and pay their bills? Would they be homeless beggars? Would they find any available men, and, if they did, would they be cute? Sadly for her, Orpah turned around. Doubt screamed louder. Fear won out.

Have you missed anything by hiding in your past instead of hiding yourself in Christ, wrapped in the shield of faith? Is the Lord calling you to step out in faith, but a million doubt-filled questions fill your mind and hinder your feet? Is risk involved? Does the ground He's calling you to shakily step onto look way too uncertain? Does fear instead of faith fill your heart? And, if so, what then? Here's what: DEAL WITH THE FEAR.

Fear freezes your feet, trapping you where you are in merciless captivity. It's an "equal opportunity" stronghold—anyone can be snared by it. Many times the Lord has opened a door in my path that left me trembling in fear: *leave your job...homeschool your kids...write down what I teach you... share what you've written down...*For a great while, every time He provided an opportunity to publicly share my heart, I'd almost get physically ill. My stomach would hurt, and afterwards the Enemy would drape my mind in such fear of what people might think I'd wish the floor would open up and swallow me whole—or that Jesus would come back just as I finished speaking so I wouldn't have to deal with the response. I listened to fear's whispers, and they totally blocked my vision of what the Lord could do through any weak but willing heart.

Fear would tell me that nobody cared what I had to say, or that I wasn't needed, or that there were enough Bible teachers out there, or that people could always get some great video and there wasn't a place for my voice. Fear would tell me that without my income we'd be strapped financially, that it would just be too tough and I better stick to a 9 to 5. I'd hear it whispered that my kids would need therapy after I home-schooled them, resent me, miss some critical part of their education and be *ruined* for life and that the college they dreamed of wouldn't accept them—that they'd be *ignorant!*

Fear likes to gather reinforcers around itself to help torment us. Have you ever had other people echo your fears right back to you? As she urged her to go back to Moab, Naomi did it to Orpah. I've had many people do it to me, too. "Surely you're not going to teach your kids a subject you never learned yourself." "How long are you going to homeschool? Surely not in high school." "I don't know how educated her kids are, but they're great kids." Or here's a good one—spoken by someone I expected support from that drove a stake through my heart—"Teachers aren't accepted in their hometown." So, are you saying I have to pack up and leave, or what? Nobody in this town cares that the Lord is burning like fire in my heart? Not one soul here will receive what the Lord calls me to share? Is that what you mean? That *really* fed the deep root of insecurity already embedded in my heart. Fear would tell me I could never be more than I already was: no more than my past, no more than the chains that bound me.

Fear is not your friend. It won't help you press on toward Bethlehem. Fear is a liar. It originates in the pit and spews forth from the father of lies. DON'T LISTEN TO IT OR GIVE IT THE SLIGHTEST BIT OF CREDIBILITY. Fear places great value on what others think and say about you, instead of what the Most High God does. It gives the opinions of men a position far above the Word of God. That's treacherous ground. Don't keep standing on it. Ask for the power of the Risen Christ to rise up in you and lead you out—to get you away from there.

The Lord led me to pray with someone about my crippling fear. As I did, I began to see its unbelief and self-focus as sin. I repented, and asked the Lord Jesus to cast it far from my life and never let me give it ground again. That was a POWERFUL moment in my heart, and I truly felt release from fear's deadly grip. The Lord provided evidence for that the next opportunity I had to speak. That time, instead of wanting to throw up, I was filled with nothing but a great desire to PROCLAIM THE WORD OF THE LIVING GOD. Fear was replaced with fresh passion for Him. THAT WAS HUGE! (I still may feel nervous, but not scared to death. It's a different, blessed feeling.) Oh, the Lord is good! *He has so much more for us than fear.*

Questions & Applications

1. **Is the Lord leading you to a place that fear absolutely resists? What is it?**
2. **Have you ever considered fear to be connected to unbelief—why or why not?**
3. **Lay your fears down at the feet of Jesus and ask Him for the strength to press on into all He has planned for your precious life.**

8

Crossroads

...but Ruth clung to her. "Look," said Naomi, "your sister-in-law is going back to her people and her gods. Go back with her." But Ruth replied, "Don't urge me to leave you or to turn back from you. Where you go I will go, and where you stay I will stay. Your people will be my people and your God my God. Where you die I will die, and there will be buried. May the Lord deal with me, be it ever so severely if anything but death separates you and me." When Naomi realized that Ruth was determined to go with her, she stopped urging her, **Ruth 1:1-18.**

Naomi, Ruth and Orpah had come to a crossroads. They faced a choice: press on in bitterness, press on in faith or turn around in fear and unbelief and run. Sooner or later, we all arrive at places like that where we also have to make heart decisions, spiritual decisions, that drastically affect our lives.

The first, obviously, is the crossroads called SALVATION. It's the choice between Christ and the flesh; between humbly embracing the living Word of the Most High God, or pridefully disputing and rejecting it. After we've tasted salvation, we'll find ourselves, more than once—perhaps even every day—standing at the crossroads called OBEDIENCE. We'll face the option of pressing on to what the Lord is opening before us, or turning and running back to what was comfortable.

If you're walking with the Lord Jesus and soaking in the water of His Word, *you will encounter crossroads*. He's going to ask you to take that step away from your comfort zone and do something new in Him, something that requires utter dependence and trust, something that may prick your flesh mercilessly, something that might not make sense, something you can't do without walking in faith, something that makes you vulnerable, something you can't see the end of, *something your flesh wasn't counting on—or wanting*.

You know what's behind you. You know what's in your life right now, but THE ADVENTURE LIES AHEAD. Who wants to swim in stagnant pools? Who wants to walk the same road day in and day out, but never go anywhere? Who wants to run on a treadmill when they could run on majestic, mountain paths? The Lord brings your heart to crossroads because He wants you to move into *more than you know.* Into the sheer thrill of obeying, and seeing Him move through that obedience. Into intimacy with Him you couldn't experience running backwards. Into wisdom you can't gain without moving forward in Him. He brings you to those points because of His great, unfathomable love, not because He wants to make you miserable.

Could crossroads indicate that God has brought us to a place where we've been faithful enough in the small that He can offer us a chance to be faithful in "the more"? *To think that the King has found me faithful and is now willing to put my feet on a path of greater faith and blessing stirs my soul with excitement*. The Lord wants your feet on that wild, adventurous Road of Faith. *He's not a quiet, tame God*. He's passionate, full, rich, deep and amazing. His voice rolls like thunder, or a great, rushing waterfall. The earth is a mere footstool for His feet. Righteousness spreads out before Him, and brilliant glory surrounds His throne. Men who saw the glory of even His angels fell to their knees in fear. Men, like Isaiah and John, who glimpsed but a shadow of God's face ***FELL TO THEIR FACES AS DEAD!***

This is no boring, pew-warming God. I heard a little girl sing a Christmas song on the radio the other day. Instead of "Jesus is born," it sounded like she sang, "Jesus is bored." I just had to smile, because HE'S DEFINITELY NOT BORED, MUCH LESS BORING! This is the King of Kings, the Holy One of Israel, Who parts seas, walks on water, sounds trumpets and crumbles walls, carves His Word in stone and now inscribes it on our hearts; Who commands His angels concerning you, and whose Word set the stars in motion and calls you to shine like them. He's the One who hung the sun and the moon to delight His people, placed His holy feet on vile soil, conquered sin and death, leads captives triumphantly in His train and holds the keys to heaven. His Name *alone* sends the Enemy fleeing.

He is beyond our wildest imagination and our deepest understanding. He's the Lord of Lords, the Light of the World, the Morning Star, the First and the Last! And pressing on with Him at that crossroads will be *the greatest adventure imaginable*. I don't want more of the same. *I want more of Him*. I don't want yesterday's comfort. I want today's faith-adventure. I want greater passion, wider eyes and better hearing. I want wonders down tomorrow's road I've yet to even think of today. I want trembling feet to *dance* on His paths, accompanied by heaven's melodies. I don't want to go where men—or women—following only what seems logical, say to go. I WANT TO WALK WITH THE KING OF GLORY, holding tightly to His mighty hand, following His every Word, moving from glory to glory and strength to strength until heaven's gate opens its doors before me and I fall before His presence in utter, complete worship. At that moment every crossroads, every bump in the road, every gut-wrenching decision of the heart will be absolutely worth it, and *nothing* will compare to His glory revealed. When I stand in His presence, I'll be SO GLAD I chose to move forward every time He asked me too. SO WILL YOU. Don't let fear and unbelief tangle your feet and turn you backward. *You will NEVER regret going forward with God.*

I bet Orpah wished she had. We never see her at that crossroads again. She kisses Naomi good-bye and heads back to her past, back to her people and back to her gods, and that's the last we hear of her. *That puts a fire in my heart to do whatever the Lord puts in my hands while I still can—to take up the task before me when the opportunity is fresh, because it may never return.*

Scripture provides numerous examples of souls encountering a crossroads before the Lord. Over and over, they're brought front and center to something requiring great faith, and they have to choose. Stay where it's comfortable, or march forward with hearts full of trust. Mary, the mother of Jesus, came to a crossroads. An angel announced the plan of the Most High, leaving her with a difficult choice. It could have been, "No thanks...not interested...sounds a little freaky...might ruin my reputation...may be asked to leave the church (synagogue)..." Instead, Mary replied, *"I am the Lord's servant. May it be to me as you have said,"* (Luke 1:38).

Joseph faced a crossroads when the angel appeared to him in a dream and told him not to be afraid to take Mary as his wife (Matthew 1:20). He could easily have attributed the vision to too much spicy food and dismissed it as nonsense, but he chose to believe the Lord and move forward in trusting uncertainty. The Israelites came to a crossroads at the foot of the Red Sea, as the Lord opened those mighty waters and said, "Move forward..." (Exodus 14:15). Their option: surrender to Pharaoh and return to the relative safety of slavery, or press on into the never-before-seen future with the Lord God Almighty. Abraham stood at that door when the Lord asked him to lay down his most precious gift, his son Isaac. Obey, or clutch onto that boy and run?

Joseph encountered it when his brothers bowed before him in complete vulnerability, begging for bread and mercy: forgive, or make them pay dearly? Before they were Jesus' disciples, Peter, James and John faced a major turning point: leave all they'd ever known, done and been and follow this Man they knew little about, or stay put, never knowing more than the monotony of their nets? Christ, Himself, faced crossroads: give in to the Enemy's taunts and challenges in the desert, or refute those lies and temptations with Truth? Take on every vile, earthly sin and pay for it with His own blood, or let man fend for himself? Over and over, the Lord leads His people to places of decision where either fear or unbelief sends them running backwards, or faith and promises believed propel them forward.

We will all come to crossroads in our walk with the King. When we see one another at those points, I pray we'll be great encouragers, speaking faith-filled words of Truth that will inspire each other to press on. May our responses not come from bitterness like Naomi, nor out of fear and unbelief. Instead, may we trust the heart of the Father and nudge each other deeper in Him, no matter how illogical it seems. Instead of saying (or thinking), "Who does that Moabite think she is? I've seen her sin...," may we say, "Look what the Lord can do. He loves and dares to use even Moabites like me and her."

The world is always ready to dispute the Word of the Lord and plant discouragement in our souls. I pray that we, the very Body of Christ, would always believe God and sow our faith into the hearts of others. One of the greatest blessings we can experience on this journey with the King is to inspire others to take it too, and to PRESS ON TOGETHER. *Let it be, mighty Lord.*

To press on, WE HAVE TO BE WALKING IN SPIRIT AND TRUTH. Our flesh is too feeble, selfish and unreliable. It's immature and greatly limited. It hates discomfort and demands to be petted. It has self in mind, not the things of God. It will turn us around and steer us wrong every time. It'll send us back to Moab with Orpah.

Every morning I have to surrender my flesh to the King of Kings. It seems like even in my sleep it can rise up and resist what the Lord is asking me to do. I can't begin to study the Word and expect the Holy Spirit to teach it to me until I've dealt with my flesh. I can't receive Truth until I've rejected all lies. I don't even crack open the Word before I've soaked my heart in prayer, asking for crucified flesh and a receptive spirit; until I've come face to face with the blood of the Risen Christ and pled for the fullness of its power to saturate every part of me—mind, soul and body—until I've looked at my weakness, then gazed on His strength. *That's when He begins to open the Word to me, to lead me through it and astound me, convict me, challenge me and thrill me. It's then He prompts me to study a certain book or part, and then nails it to my heart. I couldn't begin to learn the Word without the active power of the Holy Spirit.*

Through that living, active Word, and in that deep place of prayer, the Lord begins to show me what doors to walk through, what direction to move in, what to let go of and what to do with every ounce of strength. He uses His Word to reveal His purposes and plans for our lives—*something we absolutely do not want to miss!* The Scriptures fine-tune our hearts and focus our eyes on our calling- something the flesh can never do. *God will do this for you* WITH PLEASURE. He will meet you at every crossroad, and guide you forward.

It fascinates me how the Lord calls His servants, like Ezekiel. Something in Ezekiel 1 and 2 strikes my heart powerfully regarding pressing forward on the King's path. In Ezekiel 1, four living creatures and the glory of the Lord are described in detail. In verse 12 it says of those creatures, "*Each one went straight ahead. Wherever the Spirit would go, they would go, without turning as they went.*" THAT'S WHAT I WANT SAID OF MY HEART: "She went straight ahead. Wherever the Spirit would go, she would go, without turning as she went."

Where will the Holy Spirit of the Living God take us if we live like that? What glory will He reveal? What wonders will our eyes see? In the very next verse, we're told that those living creatures looked like *"burning coals of fire, or like torches...and fire moved back and forth among them..."* I believe this is what we'll become in this dark world as we move straight ahead in the Lord. We'll burn for the King like flaming coals or torches, and the fire of His Word will move back and forth among us GREATLY AFFECTING ALL WHO SEE OUR FLAME. May we never turn in fear or unbelief, and may Orpah never be our role model, but may it be always said of us, "They pressed on with, and burned for, the Living God. They left Moab and went straight to Bethlehem."

In Ezekiel 3:15, after Ezekiel received his call from the Lord, he sat among the Jewish exiles in Babylon for seven days, overwhelmed. May it always be the living, personal Word of the Lord Jesus that overwhelms and amazes us, not fear of the path ahead.

Questions & Applications

1. **Have you ever found yourself at a crossroads—led to a place where you must choose to press on or run backwards?**

2. **If you're at such a place now, will you dare to pursue Jesus Christ, to choose to press on in Spirit and Truth, to move ahead by faith?**

9

But Ruth...

At this they wept again. Then Orpah kissed her mother-in-law good-by, ***but Ruth*** *clung to her. "Look," said Naomi, "your sister-in-law is going back to her people and to her gods. Go back with her."* ***But Ruth*** *replied, "Don't urge me to leave you or to turn back from you. Where you go I will go, and where you stay I will stay. Your people will be my people and your God my God. Where you die I will die, and there I will be buried. May the Lord deal with me, be it ever so severely, if anything but death separates you and me." When Naomi realized that Ruth was determined to go with her, she stopped urging her,* ***Ruth 1:14-18.***

Naomi's heart swelled and trembled with bitterness. Orpah's heart swelled and trembled with fear and doubt. "BUT RUTH..." Ruth's heart swelled and trembled with faithfulness, trust and determined love. Bitter, doubting words could not persuade her to turn around. Orpah's retreat back to her people and her gods didn't discourage her. She stood strong against pressure coming from all sides, even from those dearest in the world to her. She had every reason to be as bitter as Naomi and had family, friends and gods to return to, just like Orpah. BUT RUTH anchored her heart in deeper, richer soil. She pressed on to what was before, even though she couldn't see ahead—even as fear tried to override faith and depression surely attempted to undermine determination. Even while sorrow was soaking up every bit of joy Ruth had ever known, even then she exercised faith.

Can you picture the King of Kings leaning over her and cheering her on, delighting in the trust that belied the hurting condition of her heart and rejoicing and singing as her wobbly feet set out for Bethlehem? Can't you almost hear Him whispering to her spirit...

> Keep pressing on, child. The King Himself goes before you; the light of Truth illumines your path. Your feet have chosen solid ground, and this road is leading to GLORY. Keep moving, My love—one foot, one step at a time. It doesn't matter that you can't yet see the end. You have enough of a glimpse to fuel your heart's fire. You would be blown away if you could see the end now. It's further than your wildest dreams ever took you. It is glorious, full, rich and satisfying. My own hand has prepared it for you, and it will bless you beyond your dearest desire. Keep moving, child of My heart. The road does not go on forever. You are heading to a real place, a place I have perfectly anointed you for, a place I am now training you for. Those hard things you thought were My punishment were My preparation. I am making straight a highway in your desert. I am preparing the way of the Lord. I am putting holy feet on earthly ground and moving on your behalf. Do not fear, precious one. Do not turn back. Do not grow bitter because of the past. *There's a new day ahead.* You're wearing new shoes. Keep pressing on. Keep gaining strength from My heart alone, and you will not grow weary. Rely on Me. Angels hover near

with excitement as I command them concerning you. I cover you today and wait with great anticipation to show you what I have for you tomorrow. It is good. It is a future and a hope. If you could see it now, you wouldn't be able to wrap your mind around it. Your face would hit the floor, and I wouldn't be able to get you up from that place of amazement. So I show you what you need for today's journey. I give you everything you require for the next precious step. *And I dance with joy as you take it.*

Hallelujah! He is with us! He is *absolutely* for us! And He is good! Our path is holy ground because He's on it. We can press on in faith, even alone, because He's directing us. We can step out of fear and bitterness, because He's leading our feet. Our heart can settle in sweet peace, because the King of Kings is our Shepherd. Who is like the Lord? Who teaches like Him? Who else guides with eternity's vision? Who else could weave our days in Moab into a thing of glory and beauty—into a testimony that will exalt the Alpha and Omega? Your Alpha in Moab is redeemed, and a glorious Omega awaits you at the end. Christ is now absolutely and forever your beginning and end. His hands are eternally able to hold and redeem your every breath. He's able to soak your soul in pure passion and purpose, *and He's willing!* Trust His heart toward you, no matter how long you lived in Moab.

Paul prays for us in Ephesians 3:17-19, *"that you, being rooted and grounded in love, may be able to comprehend with all the saints what is the width and length and depth and height—to know the love of Christ which passes knowledge; that you may be filled with all the fullness of God."* RUTH GROUNDED HER HEART IN LOVE AND MOVED FORWARD IN FAITH.

Being rooted and grounded in the love of God opens your heart to the vast, mind-boggling fullness of the living

Lord. As you begin to get an inkling of comprehension of its width, length, depth and height, *you will not care about the direction of your path but about the direction of His heart.* You'll only want to move where He moves and go where He goes. Nothing else matters, and nothing or no one can turn your feet. Many will choose the broad, seemingly easy road, but that won't sway your heart. You'll know that you know the King and will run after Him alone, panting for His presence as the deer pants for water. And on His path you'll taste His fullness, drink deeply and love much.

On His path you'll be shepherded WELL. This Shepherd will never leave or forsake you or lead you astray. He won't grow tired of your immaturity, but will direct you with amazing patience and long-suffering. He remembers your feet are merely clay and will wrap them in His own strength. He knows better than you the weakness of your heart and will saturate it with all-sufficient grace. He knows the things of Moab that plague your soul, but covers it all—everything—with the power of His own blood.

You ask this mighty, awesome Shepherd for so little, when He's ready and able to do *"immeasurably more than all we ask or imagine, according to His power that is at work within us,"* (Ephesians 3:20). Your feet are turned toward Him, ASK HIM TO BLOW YOUR MIND. His power is at work within you, ASK FOR THE IMMEASURABLE "MORE." And keep moving. You're the joy of His heart, and much awaits you, as it says in Isaiah 40:11: *"He will feed His flock like a Shepherd; He will gather the lambs with His arm, and carry them in His bosom, and gently lead those who are with young."* Don't fear the path He has for you. The Shepherd will feed you exactly what you need, and it will be the most satisfying of fare. He urges, *"Open wide your mouth, and I will fill it,"* (Psalm 81:10). He satisfies your hunger with holy bread, sacred oil, new wine and honey from the Rock; He quenches your thirst with living water.

He gathers your lamb-like heart in His strong, mighty arms, and there you rest secure. He draws you to lay your sweet head on His massive, warm bosom, where you sense your belovedness, and, like the Apostle John, know you are "the Beloved of Christ." From there, He'll gently lead you on and divinely direct your steps, as you bring young ones of both flesh and spirit along with you. What a Shepherd!

Could that be why He chose to reveal the wonder of Christ's coming first to simple shepherds in the field? Could the reason He chose to let the glory of heaven shine "'round about them" and to crack open heaven's window for them to hear the praise of the heavenly host be because their task reflects His heart? Their flock represents His? Because their night watch reminds us of His ever-seeing eye that never closes in slumber? THERE IS NO INSIGNIFICANT THING IN THE WORD OF THE LIVING GOD. The fact that He first revealed Christ to shepherds is *significant.* No wonder they ran to Bethlehem to see the thing made known. *May we run there too.*

We need to guard ourselves against looking to mere flesh and blood to shepherd our souls. The Lord certainly appoints and uses people to teach and inspire us, but they're NEVER to take His place or be elevated too high—or their word taken as gospel. THERE'S ONLY ONE GOSPEL. There's only one Wonderful Counselor. Only one Prince of Peace. Only one Holy Spirit. Only one Mighty God. Anything or anyone you place on the throne of your life instead of the King of Kings is a false god. And they'll take you right back to Moab, no matter how "holy" they look.

Christ alone is the Chief Shepherd. From His mighty heart of love He allows us to hear His voice as we seek Him in Spirit and Truth. That tender yet powerful voice leads us perfectly down our appointed path. To His will. To the pleasure of His presence. To the most intimate, holy sanctuary. To hope. To a future. To the passion of His heart. To the destiny laid out for us. To the abundance of His Word. To the fullness of His hand. To the place where heaven bends low, touches earth and utterly transforms us. The Hebrew word for "shepherd" means, "to associate with as a friend—to feed, pastor, keep as a companion." The Greek definition is, "one who tends, pastors, guides as well as feeds; involves tender care and vigilant superintendence." The Almighty One who spread out the heavens and formed the earth with His Word draws near to associate with mere Moabites as a friend and perfect pastor; as One who feeds, cares for, guides, protects and comes along beside as a Beloved Companion—One that will never leave nor forsake.

He is holy, and He leads us to holy ground. He is Living Water, and He invites us to quench our thirst. He is the Bread of Life, and He urges us to come and be filled to overflowing. He's the King of Kings, who dares ask us to His royal banquet table to be seated as honored guests. He opens the gate to Bethlehem's treasures and offers Himself as the way in. He wants us out of Moab's sorrow and sin and dwelling with the Lord of Hosts Himself. What an offer! What a Shepherd! What a priceless gift is Christ! *I ACCEPT!* Why do we ever doubt His guidance, or fear moving forward? This perfect Shepherd has given us His mighty Holy Spirit to lead us on, and great is His work within our hearts. The King has chosen us, despite the scandal of it, and perfectly equipped us in Spirit and Truth.

In John 16:7, Jesus says, *"But I tell you the truth:"* [Truth speaks truth!] *"it is for your good that I am going away. Unless I go away, the Counselor will not come to you; but if I go, I will send Him to you."* Christ went to that rugged Cross and bore the heaviness of our sin, and now gives us the mighty power of His Holy Spirit to equip us for the path that stretches before our feet. Ephesians 1:13-14 tells us that we're "sealed" by that power. THERE'S NO POWER THAT CAN BREAK OPEN WHAT THE LORD HAS SEALED.

In Revelation 5, Christ alone is worthy to open the scroll of the Lord and break its seals. *The same hand that sealed that holy scroll seals us.* No matter how hard the path looks or what may come against us as we travel on it, *we're sealed by Him to bring Him glory.* No power in heaven or earth can overcome His. No scheme of hell can alter His mighty plan. HE IS SOLID GROUND. In Him alone is the Kingdom, the power and the glory forever.

We read in John 16 that the Holy Spirit comes to counsel, convict, guide in Truth, speak what the Father says, prophesy and bring glory to Christ by making Him known. In Romans, we're told that the Spirit causes us to overflow with hope and be sanctified; that He leads us to obedience, fills us with love, intercedes and helps us pray, demonstrates power, imparts wisdom, teaches and expresses Truth, gives discernment, dwells within us, bestows gifts, produces spiritual fruit, gives instruction, covers and baptizes us. The Gospel of John also tells us that we're given the Spirit "without limit" and that "of His fullness we have all received." In 2 Corinthians 3:17, we learn that where the Spirit is, there is liberty—freedom. THAT'S GOOD NEWS! *What else could we possibly need?*

Whatever path the King has set you on, the Holy Spirit is there to walk you through it with perfect counsel and complete truth, and we know "the truth will set you free," (John 8:32). He comes to cut the bonds that held you captive, free your soul from Moab's chains and loose you from all that bound. In His hands you're established in true, perfect liberty. Memories and wounds from Moab no longer have to pierce you, nor labels from the world define you.

When I taught in public school, we handed out labels all day long: Learning Disabled, Mentally Handicapped, Language Impaired, ADHD, etc. The world has plenty of names for you, too, good and bad: Beautiful, Ugly, Successful, Failure, Gifted, Hopeless, Wealthy, Poor, Fruitful, Barren, Esteemed,

Rejected, Winner, Loser, Victim, Married, Divorced...*The world names us by our circumstances.* Too often we do the same. BUT THE HOLY SPIRIT OF THE LIVING GOD BREAKS THROUGH EVERY NAME YOU'VE BEEN GIVEN, AND DEFINES YOU BY THE NAME ABOVE ALL NAMES. He bursts through every circumstance and redefines your heart, turning it from stone to flesh, and calls you His treasure—the very object of His joy.

As Ruth presses on, we'll find she's no longer defined as a Moabitess, but as the passion and bride of a great man from Bethlehem, *just as we'll be known.* Not by the things that were, but by the King's heartbeat for us. He'll escort us out of all that was and straight into the more-than-flesh-can-imagine. Out of the Was, strength for the Is and hope for the Is To Come.

> *"Holy, holy, holy is the Lord God Almighty, Who was, Who is, and Who is to come." (Rev.4:8) Thank You, mighty Lord.*

Questions & Applications

1. **You may be surrounded on every side by those who are bitter or who are choosing the broad, familiar path, but could it be said of you, "___________ chose to press on with Christ..."? Ask the King of Kings for that kind of strength.**
2. **Who are you trusting as your Shepherd? Who do you turn to for guidance in life? If it's not the Great Shepherd, the Lord Jesus Christ, ask Him now to take that role.**

10

Don't Look Back

So the two women went on until they came to Bethlehem, **Ruth 1:19**.

My kids love to read license plates in town to see where the cars are from. Not long ago, I read one that said, "Expect it." Then shortly after I saw a bumper sticker that stated, "Engage your faith." I had to laugh at how the Lord speaks through the most unexpected things, as He used those simple messages to stir my faith. He'd already been whispering in my heart, "If I say it, expect it." I had been asking Him to teach me about the journey with Him as related to this verse, and those three little words, "Engage your faith," spoke volumes to my soul.

IF YOU'RE GOING TO MOVE FROM MOAB TO BETHLEHEM, SOME FAITH IS GOING TO HAVE TO BE ENGAGED. How can you press forward without believing that good awaits you? How can you walk on if you have no vision of where you're going? I wonder what conversation passed between those two empty, broken women as they moved down that road away from Moab toward sweet Bethlehem. Did faith flow out from one heart to the other? Did Naomi tell Ruth all she remembered about growing up in Judah? Did she tell her, despite her bitter spirit, all the wonders the Lord had done in Israel? Did she plant seeds of hope deep in Ruth's spirit? Did her words plow the ground of Ruth's heart, preparing her for all that was to come on Israel's soil? Did they sprinkle faith's waters, no matter how shallow they were at the time, on Ruth's sad, dry heart?

What effect do *our* words have? It's the cry of my heart that the Lord will fill my mouth with words of faith and encouragement for this journey we're on. We're not on an easy road and we desperately need the Body of Christ to do what He's called it to do: speak Truth to ourselves and each other, cheer each other on when progress is made and uphold weary hands and hearts when challenges come. We need to recount the wonders of old and the wonders of now, reminding others—as well as ourselves—that the same power is available in our current need. The same mighty God who set Israel's feet on dry ground in the midst of a raging sea is here to establish our feet, too. We need to pour our hearts out like rivers before the Lord on behalf of His Body, His children. I've lived out Lamentations 2:19 many times, which says, *"Arise, cry out in the night as the watches of the night begin; pour out your heart like water in the presence of the Lord. Lift up your hands to Him for the lives of your children..."* The Lord calls us to pray not just for our children, but for His, too. We need to recall and retell how the kingdom of Christ is expanding, encouraging each other to keep pressing on.

As we travel on life's unpredictable path, we're called to be worshipers, warriors, intercessors and proclaimers of Truth. Even non-believers should be able to look at our lives and say, "There's something unusual about the way they walk through life, something sacred, priceless, beautiful and abundant; something different from everything I've known. Their path isn't any easier than mine, but there's a peace about them. A deep-rooted joy, an abundance of love, a mouth filled with praise and encouragement—a hope, even in this stormy world of terror."

While we don't know what passed between the two widows as they traveled, we are told that *they made it to Bethlehem.* They kept moving, despite the hardship of it, and reached their destination. I believe there must have been some encouraging and faith-building words exchanged—words that stirred their hearts, motivated their feet and focused their eyes on Bethlehem, instead of Moab. (Interesting note: Moabites were descendents of Lot's incestuous relations with his oldest daughter, who got him intoxicated and laid with him to preserve the family line [Genesis 19:37]. Sounds like a major lack of faith to me. And what came from that unbelief?—Moab!)

Lot's wife turned into a salt pillar as she looked back toward Sodom. Israel wandered for years as they gazed back fondly toward Egypt, grumbling about their circumstances. *They let unbelief turn their heads.* What would the story have been if Ruth and Naomi had done that? *If you're going to move forward in life, you have to look ahead with faith.* Sounds simple enough, but there are plenty of things and people eager to drag you backward and cement your feet in what you've always known. Plenty of people will jealously resent your desire for "Bethlehem" and mock you for setting out. Lots of voices will speak unbelief and discouragement—sometimes even your own. Many circumstances will arise to tempt you to think you can't make it, that it's just too tough. We need to ask the Lord to hold our face in His mighty hands and *set our gaze straight ahead,* locked on the narrow road He's chosen for our feet: on the path He's laid before us, the mission His Spirit has birthed in ours, the promises of His Word, the glory and power of the risen Christ, the wonders He's done in our life and the lives of others. We need to maintain our focus on His faithfulness, His strength, the depths of His heart and the fullness of His great, passionate love. We must move forward, pressing faithfully on into the "more" of the Lord, more than Moab, more than past dreams, more than mind can imagine, more than whatever plagued our souls yesterday. *You have to move past yesterday to step into what waits ahead.*

How different the book of Ruth would have been if she'd chosen to live her life centered in past pain, trapped in her yesterday and frozen in what was. Would we even know her name if she hadn't hit the road and moved past Moab into the beautiful, abundant fields of Bethlehem? *You don't have to live in yesterday's stuff from a center of old pain.* I believe that's good news for more than just this girl. New mercy from the heart of the King is offered you again today. Take it! Holy hands envelope every moment gone by, and are waiting to tenderly and faithfully lead you to higher ground. *Yesterday is safe in the hands of King Jesus. Let Him have it.*

The Enemy wants to trip you up with old memories and painful reminders of deep wounds. He doesn't play fair. He's bent on your destruction. He loves to use cheap shots—I daresay he pulled out a few against Ruth and Naomi. Try as he might, that foe can't overcome the Word of God planted and prospering in you. It makes him frantic and sends him scurrying to formulate plans to turn you from it. He wants to turn you in his direction and away from marching on with the King of Glory. *He can't have you.* Keep the Word flowing. Take thoughts and memories captive, negating and replacing them with Truth. Stay in continual, intimate communication with Christ, where you're covered by the shadow of His mighty wings, centered in the palm of His awesome hand and shielded from every weapon formed.

Don't worry about the cheap shots. They're just that—cheap. It's the shot of the King against the Enemy of your soul that's priceless and lethal. The blow that triumphed over the kingdom of darkness, and all that would keep you locked in Moab, was given at Calvary. No low-down punches can ever overcome the blood of the spotless Lamb. Nothing can enslave what the Son sets free. He's the Most High. There's none above or beyond Him. His strength is the utmost, and before His Name everything that's held power over you must bow. That long-ago-thing that has your soul trapped in fear and pain must bow. That sorrow of heart and tossing of mind must bow. All those things you can't control, Jesus Christ can. He can take their deadly sting and use it for good, dig out their bitter roots and make them sweet. *I have a quiet nature, but could do some shouting right here.*

Not too long ago during prayer time in our church service, I felt movement at my feet. I looked down, and there was my young son on his knees right at the edge of the aisle. I was amazed, because no one else in the building was in that position. He looked up at me, and said, "Lay your burdens down, Mom." From the mouth of babes.

I can't imagine that Ruth wished for the pain she endured in Moab, but that she just wanted to sail happily through life, content and completely settled on familiar turf. Trouble was, she was settled in the wrong place, far from her destiny. Yet pain, the thing she despised, was the very thing that drove her to the land of bounty and honor. Suffering moved her feet to her life's purpose, and there she discovered more than her heart had dared dream. As she eventually stood among the fields of Bethlehem's best, I'm sure she counted it all joy—even the rough journey through hurt and loss and the long, tedious path to Judah.

Be certain that whatever the Enemy meant to kill you with, the Lord will use to build you. Don't worry about the past. It's being handled and covered by the Most High God. It's being woven into an instrument of praise to glorify the Lord on the earth. *Walking out and pressing on will be worth it.* So I bless the road, hard as it was, that brought me to the feet of the King. I thank Him for loving me enough to not let me settle in foreign lands. The place I longed to plant my feet was pitifully short of His best—and far, far from destiny.

Pain closed Moab's doors, and pushed Ruth's soul onto a new road. When the Lord is shutting doors behind you and opening new ones ahead, you must determine to go with Him in your heart, trusting His strength, not your own, to see you through to the end. I somehow always envisioned walking through doors the Lord led me to would be easy. No hindrances. No setbacks. Smooth sailing to the end. SO FAR, I HAVEN'T FOUND THAT TO BE THE CASE. Instead, in taking baby step after baby step with the King, I've encountered *great* resistance, spiritual warfare and unexpected battles, seemingly out of the blue. I've met with steep hills requiring faith and perseverance, His ways not looking at all like mine and struggles in flesh and spirit. Yet, I believe those are the very things that throw us at His mighty feet; that reveal things of His heart we'd never learn on a carefree, easy, nonchalant path.

I've had a friend for many years that I've never known to have a really bad day or overwhelming circumstance. *She's not the one I call when I need heaven pounded on my behalf.* It seems to me that walking through trials with the King gives you more credibility to minister to others, in order to, as 2 Corinthians 1:4 says, *"comfort them with the comfort we have received ourselves."* Because of her experience, I'd say Ruth had a fresh heart of compassion and tenderness for others as they journeyed through hard times. *It's all used for good.*

Ruth and Naomi were absolutely in the center of God's will as they journeyed to Judah, but their hearts surely came up against battles of flesh and spirit along the way. Their path was not luxurious, without tears, or fears or spiritual battles. They had some major obstacles to overcome before they reached Bethlehem's gate. If you look at a map of the time, you'll see what a trip they had. No paved roads. No automobiles. No speed jets. No smooth, easy time. There were mountains in the way, a body of water to deal with and countless steps of many miles to take. It was going to be A PROCESS for Ruth and Naomi to get where they were going—as I believe our walk will be also. Proverbs 4:11-12 says, *"I have taught you in the ways of wisdom; I have led you in right paths. When you walk, your steps will* not *be hindered, and when you run, you will not stumble,"* (NKJ). The key words here are *led, walk* and *run*, indicating ongoing motion—steps, a journey, a process—not an overnight thing.

So many times I've asked the Lord to do what I wanted NOW, even though my heart was in no way ready for what I was demanding. Ever been there? Ever grabbed hold of something expecting the Lord to give it to you, and maybe sunk into anger or depression when it didn't come? *His timing is not ours.* Only He knows when we're ready for the next step. As I look back on some of my foolish demands, my heart overflows with gratitude that He answered, "no" or "wait." I would have shamed His name and embarrassed myself had He granted them on *my* schedule. *But His timing is absolutely, always and forever PERFECT.* Beautiful. Marvelous. An ideal fit with our souls' journey, bringing glory to His Name.

"Faithful is He who has called you, and He also will bring it to pass," (1 Thessalonians 5:24). This is one of my favorite verses, because it assures my soul that the Faithful One is in control, guiding, guarding and bringing to pass the call He has on my life. The Hebrew definition of "faithful" deeply stirs my heart. The word is "aman," which means, "to build up or support, to foster as a parent or nurse, to be permanent, to be true or certain, sure, established, steadfast, to bring up, to endure." It's also described as, "a firm place; a place into which a peg will be driven so that it will be immovable. The peg will remain firmly anchored, even

though it is pushed so hard that it breaks off at the point of entry." What an awesome thought. The King of Kings, the Most High God, the Mighty, Holy One of Israel, the Prince of Peace, the Wonderful Counselor, the Everlasting Father, the Lord of Lords—the One whose hand holds the universe yet also holds your heart, the One whose Name alone rocks the very gates of hell yet flings open the doors of heaven, the One who needs *nothing* from mere man yet desires everything from him, the One whose wrath we deserve yet whose grace we receive, the One who orders the heavens and earth yet orders your feeble steps—is the One parenting, nursing, supporting, building up and permanently establishing you. He's the One steadfastly planting you in a sure, true, certain, immovable place. YOU'RE THAT PEG DESCRIBED. Your heart and soul are driven deep into His, and from there you won't be moved. You'll be forever, permanently, anchored on firm soil. And from that firm position, He will lead you on. Step by step. Strength to strength. Glory to glory.

In connection with "aman" *Strong's* also says, "...Abram came to experience a personal relationship to God rather than an impersonal relationship with His promises." You've got to know and walk with the King Himself, not just grab His promises in an attempt to make your life better. *He's after your heart, not your comfort*. When I first began dealing with some of the limitations that a chronic illness brings, several people gave me healing verses to claim. I read them, and asked the Lord to perform them in my life. But as time went on and He drew me into deeper and deeper waters with Him, I began to realize how far my heart had been from Him as I prayed those Scriptures. I was seeking His action on behalf of my flesh, not His heart. I wanted every hard thing made easy. I desired my own comfort. I didn't realize that *discomfort* would be the very thing He'd use to draw me into His purpose.

I still pray every day for healing, but not from a list of healing Scriptures. Instead, I dive into study of the Word for myself (because I'm desperate for it) and ask for all of it, THE WHOLE COUNSEL of God's Word. Not just the parts I find appealing, but also those that challenge my heart, mind, soul and strength; that call me to die to self and live to glorify the King; that tell me to keep pressing on when I really want to lie down. The parts that tell me to forgive when I don't want to; to love when it's hard; to take His peace when my flesh is in turmoil and to believe what I've yet to see. *He's worthy of our trust, whether what we're believing Him for is ever manifested or not.* The God of all faithfulness, Who is passionate for your heart, has your best in mind, regardless of whether you understand it. *Strong's* says of Him, "The 'God of the Amen' is the God who always accomplishes what He says; He is a God who is faithful."

There's rest in that knowledge, even if you're weary of the trip, even if you have no clue what the next step will be and you've yet to see His Word accomplished in your current situation. *"Faithful is He who calls you...."* I cry out for the Lord to plant patience and perseverance deep within my being to trust His timing, to push me along and fiercely guard my steps, to keep me from temptation and to deliver me from evil as I move on with Him. How reassuring is 1 Samuel 2:9, *"He will guard the feet of His saints."* Thank God.

Whether you're faced with high mountains or deep waters, the Lord assures that He'll instruct you over, around or through them. He'll show you through His Word and prayer whether you're to get in the boat and set sail, put faith-filled feet on the water and WALK ON IT, raise your staff and watch those waters part or trust Him to still the waves. He'll show you when to put on hiking boots and march, climb or go around seven times, if you have to, until the walls crumble and the mountain flies into the sea. HE

WANTS YOU TO GET THERE. HE WANTS FORWARD MOTION. HE'S ALL ABOUT VICTORY.

I believe every miracle we'll ever need for this journey through life is already demonstrated in Scripture. *"Not by might nor by power, but by My Spirit, says the Lord,"* (Zechariah 4:6). I've boldly begun to ask the King, "If it's in Your Word, let me see it worked out in my life. Every promise. Every amazing thing. Everything Your mighty Spirit would dare to show and do in this weak, tiny heart." I've often told Him, "If You're looking for the foolish and weak, YOU'VE PICKED THE RIGHT GIRL! SHOW THIS WEAK VESSEL HEAVEN'S BEST!!!" *I'm certain He's just waiting for us to ask.*

ASK, then trust Him for the path ahead. He knows the number of your days and orders them from the deep well-spring of His heart. He rejoices over every step forward your sweet feet take. He spreads His mighty wings over your soul as you go, not to strike you down, but to cover and shield you with His favor and delight. His love is completely irrational. He's smitten by you! His heart pounds for you. You're the joy set before Him, the thrill of His soul. How can one describe the perfect, pure passion of the King? How can earthly minds wrap themselves around the depths of His? How can feeble hearts fully grasp the kind of love that DIES for you? HE DIED FOR YOUR SOUL AND LIVES FOR YOUR STEPS—to make intercession, to guide and direct, to order and ordain, to commission and charge, to establish and equip and to illumine and reveal. *Hallelujah!*

He extends His hand to lead you to Bethlehem and lift you over or around the bumps in the road. Can you picture the King ordering your next step, arranging and ordaining your circumstances to exalt His Name and lead you closer to Him? Can you envision Him celebrating with angelic hosts as you move forward in His call, choosing to press on in faith as Ruth did? As you wrap your feet in peace, patience and perseverance? As you suit up in the King's armor, ready to strike whatever would hinder your steps with the mighty Sword of the Spirit? As you soak your mind in Truth and allow its living, active power to become living and active in you? As your faithfulness in the small steps allows the Lord to open giant ones before you? *Your steps thrill Him. His steps in your heart will thrill you.*

Keep moving. Don't let flesh, fear, unbelief, discouragement, ridicule or bitter counsel turn your feet. The labor of your heart and the steps you take in Christ are not in vain. *They're taking you somewhere.* They're leading you to the Promised Land of His presence and blessing, and to the place He's ordained for you—to destiny. Remember what the Lord said to Joshua in Joshua 1:9, *"Have I not commanded you? Be strong and courageous. Do not be terrified; do not be discouraged, for the Lord your God will be with you wherever you go."*

Remember what was said of Israel in Deuteronomy 32:12, *"As an eagle stirs up its nest, hovers over its young, spreading out its wings, taking them up, carrying them on its wings, so the Lord alone led him."* So He leads you.

Remember Isaiah 46:4, where the Lord promises, *"Even to your old age, I am He, and even to gray hairs I will carry you! I have made, and I will bear; even I will carry, and will deliver you."* So He carries you.

Remember what the King says in Isaiah 58:11, *"The Lord will guide you continually, and satisfy your soul in drought, and strengthen your bones; you shall be like a watered garden, and like a spring of water, whose waters do not fail."* So He provides for you.

Remember what the Lord told Joshua in Joshua 13:1, *"There remains very much land yet to be possessed."* Thank God, there's more ahead.

Trust the Lord's words in Isaiah 33:17, *"Your eyes will see the King in His beauty; they will see the land that is very far off.*" Bethlehem stretches before you. *Lead on, beautiful King!*

Questions & Applications

1. **Are you willing to lay your past, present and future in the hands of the King with a joyful expectation of seeing Him move?**
2. **Have you started out with the King of Glory, but turned around when the road got tough? Go back to Him—He waits for you.**

11

While You're Walking, He's Working

So the two women went on until they came to Bethlehem. When they arrived in Bethlehem, the whole town was stirred because of them, and the women exclaimed, "Can this be Naomi?" "Don't call me Naomi," she told them. "Call me Mara, because the Almighty has made my life very bitter. I went away full, but the Lord has brought me back empty. Why call me Naomi? The Lord has afflicted me; the Almighty has brought misfortune upon me." So Naomi returned from Moab accompanied by Ruth the Moabitess, her daughter-in-law, arriving in Bethlehem as the barley harvest was beginning, **Ruth 1:19-22.**

Imagine with me some of the thoughts Ruth may have journaled as they completed the last leg of their long, tedious journey and finally caught a glimpse of all she had been dreaming of:

It was a day of weariness. The bitterness that soaked Naomi's heart had found a place on her tongue; my feet ached and my belly rumbled. Dust and grime covered my entire body, and the veil protecting my head and hiding my not-so-fresh hairdo was a mess. Weary or not, we kept moving as always. What choice did we have? Moab held nothing for us. We were compelled to press on where hope was leading us. We had come so far, yet as we faced one mountain after another, it seemed we could never go far enough. We saw seasons come and go. We walked through searing heat and bitter cold. We dodged thieves and wild animals. We survived on little nourishment (good for our figures, but not for a strenuous trip). To give up on that path would have meant certain death, yet how long could we continue? Would we ever get to the end of this long road, we wondered? Would we ever know joy again? As we put many weary days to rest, we laid down on the hard ground and together prayed desperately for a better tomorrow. As the sun rose and flung its brilliance across the sky, we arose and started off again. Our mood was often no better than the day before, but at least we knew we were one day closer to Bethlehem. That's when it happened. Our bleary eyes landed on a sight we had only dreamed of—the fields of Bethlehem. The mere glimpse of them sent tears of relief streaming own our dirty cheeks and, for the first time, the long journey felt worth it. The houses seemed to shout out a welcome; the streets to open their arms to embrace us. The town folks stirred as we drew closer, and the whispers began. As we drew near those beautiful barley fields, we saw we were right on time. The harvest was just beginning.

Naomi and Ruth had arrived. Tired, hungry and burdened by a widow's bitter pain, they got there. Not in their way or on their schedule, but right on time. Right in the middle of Kingdom purposes. Right in the palm of the Almighty's hand. Right at the beginning of the perfect time of year, when the fields were ready for gleaning. Soon, one named Boaz would be inspecting those very fields. A season of God's favor was about to begin.

Those ladies had walked through some tough, tough times. Yet, I believe those hard things served them well in the end, preparing their hearts for the fullness of Bethlehem, changing their minds, building in them a yearning for the House of Bread and teaching them to walk by faith not by sight. One day my daughter and I put some old pictures in an album, something I really don't like to do. It always reminds me of how fleeting time is and how fast the kids are growing up. But, what I really dislike is looking back at pictures of myself. Besides wondering who told me a "bob" was the perfect hairstyle for me or that bright, red lipstick was my color, they remind me of where my heart was in the past. I can almost visibly see the chains that bound me. I barely recognize the woman in those snapshots.

Yet, with those pictures spread out before me, the Lord gently spoke this lesson from Ruth deep into my spirit. With a whisper that unleashed grateful tears, He said, *"As you were walking, I was working."* Thank God. He doesn't leave us where we are or were. We've taken some tough steps, but He was orchestrating them. His hand was molding, transforming, planting, watering and gathering, even when our blind eyes didn't know it. He's the One who put my stubborn, scared feet on that tough mountain path. He did it, because He wanted to lead me out, over and beyond where I was, far from all I'd ever known and settled in Him- not in that pitiful place where I'd landed.

Naomi and Ruth *needed* that difficult trip, the process, to fully appreciate where the Lord was leading them. They were different, their hearts were fuller and deeper, because of where they'd been and all they'd walked through. *So am I. So will you be*. Go on over the mountains with Him, whatever they represent. With every step, trust. With every step, let go of flesh. With every step, forgive—including yourself. That's been a tough one for me. I've had to forgive myself for not taking care of myself when I was sick, for thinking I had to do everything myself, for self-sufficiency, on and on...

Trips across steep terrain leave no room for excess baggage or hindering weights. Your trips across the mountains, like mine, will serve to shave off the things that weigh down *your* heart. They'll build strength in you and a yearning for the land of the King. They'll humble you, and change your perspective. My own confrontations with mountainous things in my heart have forced its excesses to the surface, completely humbling me and altering my outlook. When the hills get steep and the going gets tough, the "ugly" in me wants to rise up and be heard. It usually sounds like grumbling, complaining, criticizing, whining, arguing or defensiveness—all reflecting a general hardness of heart. *That stuff has to go!* The Lord doesn't want it merely to return to dormancy until the next time, HE WANTS IT GONE! Exterminated with His Word. Covered by His blood. Repented of and replaced. It's of the flesh, and it will cripple you.

Sometimes you don't even realize ugly is there until a mountain rises before you. Until, perhaps, your timeline doesn't go according to schedule, pain rubs your heart raw, you can't figure things out on your own, all your dreams lie in a million pieces or someone receives the very dream you've been dreaming, while you stand empty.

I confess I've faced a few mountains with some weights on my back. I've met some hard things with a bitter heart. I've shouted out to God, "How do You expect me to do this in the shape I'm in???" His reply has been, "I DON'T. Let's work on the shape you're in. Let's sit down in the examining room and take a deep look at your heart and across your life, and allow some weights to fall. Let's trim off the baggage. *You've got places to go those things will keep you from.* Let's wash them away with Truth, with My perfect, powerful Word. Let the Sword of the Spirit cut the Enemy's fingers from every single spot he's grabbed on to in your life." Can't you picture the Lord's mighty Sword—His powerful Word—cutting loose the Enemy's fingers from your heart? I don't picture our foe just letting go. I picture the Sword CUTTING OFF his fingers, so he can't grab hold again (a graphic, but powerful image). Keep cleansing and pruning, my King.

Sometimes the Lord has brought me face to face, front and center with my weakness and sin, and, instead of repenting and falling at His feet, I've said, "Get behind me, Satan," mistaking God's conviction for a spiritual battle. Often it wasn't spiritual warfare at all, but the Lord urging me to look at the *"stuff"* in my life and lay it at His feet; to take it to the Cross and deal with it; to let His Spirit reveal the stumbling blocks in my way, the irregularities in my heart, the things still dwelling in my soul opposing His holiness. *Denial is not our friend.*

The Almighty, the King of Kings, your Redeemer, wants you free from your stuff, so you can move into His. *His stuff is so much better. It's perfect and produces great fruit and abundant harvests. Acknowledgment and repentance from sin by a heart anchored in Truth = freedom.* You can't be free to get over the mountain or climb out of the Valley of Dry Bones until you listen to the Holy Spirit's conviction and begin to hear, speak and live by the Word of the Living God.

Do as the Lord instructed the prophet in Ezekiel 37 and prophesy the Word over those dead, dry, tough places in your life and heart. Speak it as you cross those mountains, doubting you can make it to the other side. Speak it as you see dry bones in your heart, fully expecting them to come to life by the breath of Jehovah. Believe that what seemed hopeless and too far gone will rise up and become a vast army for the Kingdom that will shake the very gates of hell. The Lord said to Ezekiel in verse 4, *"Prophesy to these bones and say to them, 'Dry bones, hear the Word of the Lord!'"*

God has pressed those words on my heart, burning in me a fresh conviction to SPEAK HIS TRUTH OUT LOUD. He's whispered in my heart, "Say with your mouth, 'I will leave my Moab and lay all it held for me before the King, and I will be established in the House of Bread. I will get there. I will not die on this side of the mountain. I will not be robbed or mauled. I will not get trapped in a valley and starve to death. I WILL GO WHERE THE LORD SAYS I CAN GO. I will see more than I've yet known. The House of the Lord will be my dwelling, not the house of fear, disease, death and lack or despair. The Sanctuary of the Most High will be my home, and in Him I will be safe and blessed.

If I'm walking through something right now, it's just that—THROUGH something. It doesn't define the rest of my days. It doesn't mean this is it. It means the King has allowed a mountain to rise in my path to teach, mold and transform me, and in the end it will be counted as blessed because His hand was leading me and whatever He touches is blessed." *Speak faith. Speak Truth. Talk to those mountains out loud. Fiercely guard what comes from your mouth.*

Whatever mountain you're standing on, whether of trial or victory, let it do its perfect work. Let the Lord teach you on it and over it, and let it lead you closer to the King's harvest. *Let it become a mount of transfiguration.* What good is a mountain if it doesn't change you for the King? If Ruth and Naomi hadn't seen Moab become a valley of dry bones and sorrow, THEY PROBABLY WOULD NEVER HAVE DESIRED, LET ALONE SET OUT OVER THE MOUNTAINS FOR, BETHLEHEM. I believe the Lord dries up where we've settled sometimes, *so we'll desire more,* long for His House of Bread and do whatever it takes to get there—to BY ANY AND ALL MEANS, GET TO BETHLEHEM.

I imagine by the time their trip was over, Naomi and Ruth weren't the same women who started out. They probably screamed in anger at God over a few things and then let them go. *The Lord can take your outbursts of rage and questioning fits.* He may or may not choose to explain His actions at the moment, but He does choose to hold you, sing over you and whisper to your aching soul, "Hold on. Trust My heart for you. Don't stop here. Bethlehem's fields hold so much more. Come with Me, I know where the green pastures and the quiet waters are. I will shepherd you; I will lead you to the table I have prepared. I will overflow your cup, and absolutely give you rest. I will command goodness and love to follow you. I will anoint and bless you, and My house will be your home." (See Psalm 23.) Thank You, Lord.

As Ruth and Naomi topped the rugged hills surrounding Bethlehem, their arrival didn't go unnoticed. Their presence excited the women of the city—at least, they were the ones who talked about it. "Can this be Naomi?" they questioned. Time and trouble had changed her, but they saw a glimpse of the young woman they once knew. The Bible says, "the whole town was stirred because of them." That short phrase burns a desire in me for people to be *stirred* because of what of God does in our hearts, along our tough, mountain roads and by the way He leads us past ourselves. Not because we want anyone to know OUR names, but so they can see *HIS* with fresh eyes.

People were talking. Naomi had their attention. She had a perfect opportunity to give praise to the King who had brought them safely out of Moab, set their feet on fresh soil, ordered their days, led them to the Holy Land, brought them to ripe fields and landed them in the city of her kinsmen. She was given a wonderful platform to express faith in what God had done, and could still do; to recount His faithfulness to His people and to her. *She had much to be thankful for. She lived through what could have killed her.* Yet, instead of falling on her knees in praise to the God who had escorted her all the way, she expressed bitterness saying, "Call me Mara...Bitter is my name."

By what name do you want to be called? How do you want to be identified? Bitterness is blinding, but often has a lot to say. And here "Bitter" spewed out a completely self-focused lack of appreciation for where she was now. Faith was drowned out, and Bitter was locked into what she had lost instead of onto what the Lord was stretching before her. "The Lord didn't do what I asked Him. He didn't work things out like I wanted. I begged and begged, but He wouldn't let me stay in Moab. He emptied my hands. He took away my fullness..." *Oh, but He was about to give you His, Naomi.*

How many times have we had the same temper tantrum, accusing the Almighty of slighting us when things didn't go as we thought they should? How often have we dared judge the Lord by our situation rather than by His heart? Have you ever asked yourself, "How can He be good when...?" *IT'S CRITICAL THAT WE SEPARATE HIS GOODNESS FROM OUR CIRCUMSTANCES.* He's always and forever good, no matter where we find ourselves. I pray that we'll come to the point before the King where we so passionately love and crave His presence that the circumstances He allows don't sway us. May the cry of our hearts be, "Heal me, or slay me. Use me, or silence me. Honor me, or lay me low. My desire is YOU. Whether my situation on earth is a struggle or not, whether my flesh is pleased or not, doesn't matter. I MUST HAVE THE KING!"

I plead forgiveness for the times I've judged His heart according to my situation. Ever been in a hard place, and then judged Him to be hard? *He is good all the time*, even when you can't quite trace it out. Even when "why?" echoes through your heart. He knows the "whys," whether He reveals them to you or not. I believe when we arrive at the point for which He's been patiently preparing us, it will all blend together into a thing of great beauty that brings Him much glory. In this life, we'll understand all He knows we need to, and the rest will unfold in heaven. *There's sweet peace and satisfying rest in that.*

How often does Scripture present circumstances that don't look very good and could easily cause those experiencing them to doubt the goodness of God? A lot. To name a few: Joseph in Egypt's dark prison, Daniel and the lions, Shadrach, Meshach and Abednego thrown into a blazing furnace, Mary and Joseph fleeing Herod's wrath, Jesus going to Calvary and Paul chained in prison, shipwrecked or snake-bitten. None of these, or scores of other biblical accounts, appeared very promising to human eyes, but the Almighty was weaving them together for GLORY, just as He desires to do in our lives. Everything we experience, understood or not, will become subjects of excellent praise to the King of Kings, as we ask Him to make Himself known through our lives.

Verse 22 says, *"So Naomi returned..."* which I interpret as, "And, so, in that condition of mind and heart, in that place of bitterness, she returned..." It describes God's great patience and longsuffering, and inspires great hope and love for the Father in me. He didn't wait for Naomi to get it together, to get over her bitterness or to have her heart in perfect condition before He'd bring her to fields of harvest. He didn't condemn her and block Bethlehem's gate. She wasn't cast out, overlooked or left behind, but led to her redeemer.

That excites my soul, because it means God will extend the *same grace and mercy* toward my own imperfect heart—that He won't demand I have everything "together" before He'll bless me and that His longsuffering will suffer long for me, too. How grateful I am that when bitterness has spewed from my mouth instead of faith, He hasn't cast me out either but has taken my hand and led me to the Redeemer. I desperately want to be pure before the Holy One of Israel, the Mighty, awesome Lord, and am *so* grateful for His patience.

I earnestly pray that Colossians 3:1-2 will begin to define my life, that my heart and mind will be set "on things above," not earthly things. That my soul will be rid of the things mentioned in verses 5-8, *"whatever belongs to your earthly nature: immorality, impurity, lust, evil desires, idolatrous greed, anger, rage, malice, slander, filthy language..."* I believe bitterness would fit nicely into that list. Naomi had a banner of bitterness spread over her life as she arrived in Bethlehem. *As you stand before the King today, what banner flies over your heart?*

The Lord invites us to trade banners. He is Jehovah-nissi, "The-Lord-My-Banner." His Word declares that His banner over us is deep, passionate love that renames and redefines us; a banner that declares us free, pure, redeemed and claimed for heaven's glory. It's a banner that should cause our hearts to tremble and pound with love for the King. Imperfect as Naomi was, she was covered by the mercy of the Lord, accompanied by a faithful, determined Ruth and protected on the long, hard path she'd walked. The Almighty was directing her steps. Whether she recognized it or not, His banner over her entire experience was love.

The Lord knew when the fields would be ripe and planned their arrival JUST IN TIME. He knew the perfect moment to set their feet in Bethlehem, among croplands that swelled with abundance, and how to set their soul free and restore more than they'd ever lost. He stretched a table of plenty before them, and whispered in their heart, just as He does in ours, "GLEAN FROM *THESE* FIELDS, MY CHILD." In John 4:35 we're told, *"Lift up your eyes and look at the fields, for they are already white for harvest!"* Help us do it, marvelous Lord. *I want to arrive at Your harvest fields right on time.*

Questions & Applications

1. **Look back over the years and thank the Lord God for all the evidence of His movement in your heart and life.**
2. **Thank the King for His longsuffering and patience with your heart, and ask Him to set you in His harvest fields right on time.**

12

Our Kinsman Redeemer

Now Naomi had a relative on her husband's side, from the clan of Elimelech, a man of standing, whose name was Boaz. And Ruth the Moabitess said to Naomi, "Let me go to the fields and pick up the left-over grain behind anyone in whose eyes I find favor.

So she went out and began to glean in the fields behind the harvesters. As it turned out, she found herself working in a field belonging to Boaz, who was from the clan of Elimelech, **Ruth 2:1-3.**

Ruth 2:1 gives us some family background. The scene is set: a kinsman lives in Bethlehem, a relative of Naomi by marriage—and he's no average guy, but a man of standing, a man of position and honor, a highly respected, well-loved man called Boaz whose mercy could change the course of their lives—a man *more than able to redeem.*

There are two definitions for "kinsman" in Hebrew, "yada" and "ga'al." The first represents a familiar friend, one you know well and have knowledge of, a famous one. The second is defined as, "one who is the next of kin, who could redeem, avenge or give a ransom for." He was life insurance and Social Security all in one for a widow. His responsibility was to purchase a widow's property, and even marry her. He extended grace, favor and the covering of his name and home not because the widow was beautiful, talented, deserving, charming or a good cook, but *because she was in his family line*. In other words, he was responsible for "preserving the integrity, life, property, and family name of his close relative and for executing justice on his murderer."

That stirs my heart for Christ Jesus, my Kinsman, who's stepped in to avenge the one intent on murdering the call of God on my life, the Enemy bent on stealing, killing and destroying all the Lord has planned. Christ alone is able to buy back the stolen and confiscated property of our souls and pay the required ransom. By His sacrifice on the Cross, Jesus became our closest "blood relative." There's a great price on your head and mine, a tremendous debt accumulated that we can NEVER repay, which the Bible tells us brings eternal death—pain, suffering and anguish—a sentence only His blood could satisfy. *"Bless the Lord, O my soul, and forget not all His benefits...who redeems your life from destruction..."* (Psalm 103:2,4).

Boaz was called a kinsman-redeemer. The Hebrew definition for "redeemer" excites my heart, too. (*Who ever thought a DICTIONARY, let alone a Hebrew or Greek one, could excite you?* I remember this really brainy guy in 6th grade who used to read the dictionary for fun. I was appalled, and thought he must be a total nerd. He probably scored a perfect SAT, but I just couldn't see the appeal. So who's the nerd now? Some might say I need to get out more, but I get out plenty. It's just sheer pleasure to have a deeper understanding of God's Word. Get yourself a *Strong's Concordance*. You won't know how much fun you're missing if you don't have one!) In Hebrew, "redeem" means, "an intervening, substitutionary action effecting a release from an undesirable condition." Everything the Enemy has for us is undesirable—no matter how pleasant it may appear. We know that, but how often do we still fall for his lies? I've fallen many times for the devil's condemnations and accusations (among other things), curling up in a ball of insecurity and fear. We all have some point of vulnerability that our foe will try to weasel in to. *How desperately we all need The Redeemer.*

Naomi and Ruth had been trapped in a very undesirable situation, a place of desperation crying out for intervention. As sinners saved by grace, we should all be able to relate to those ladies as we recall all we've been redeemed from—and who our Redeemer is. The Greek definition of "redemption" is, "to rescue from loss, to improve opportunity, purchasing a slave with a view to his freedom...to purchase out, implying a new master—the slave knows he will not be sold again—to buy up for oneself..." THE FACT THAT CHRIST IS CALLED THE REDEEMER IS *GOOD NEWS*. He rescues us from loss, improves our opportunity (I'd say so!) and purchases us back from hell itself with a view to our freedom, so we'll never be sold back again. *Bless His Name!*

Out of the rivers of His great love, Christ has chosen to stand in that position for you, adopt you into His family line, utterly fulfill the ransom on your head, completely take on the role of your Kinsman-Redeemer, become "responsible for preserving your integrity, life, property and family name, and to execute justice on the one who seeks to steal, kill and destroy," (*Strong's*). Christ holds His hand up against the Destroyer and says, "Enough. My blood covers this soul. I have given her My Name and called her by it, and SHE IS MINE," (See Isaiah 43:1). "I redeem her Myself. None other is worthy or able." *My soul bows in worship before my Kinsman, Emmanuel.*

The King has not only ransomed us, but made us children of the Living God and joint heirs of heaven with Himself, members of a holy nation and a royal priesthood. We're not some far off, distant relative with no contact or inheritance.

We're seated at His table in a place of honor, given His wine and bread, dressed in the beauty of His righteous robes, cared for by Him personally and completely, utterly satisfied.

I for one am desperate for the Lord to reclaim and redeem the property of my heart. There's plenty of ground I've handed over freely to the Enemy's hands through sin and rebellion, many areas he's been able to march into and steal because I let him. There's MUCH I've given away out of ignorance and lack of vision. *You don't have to be an Old Testament widow to desperately need a kinsman's intervention.* What do you need redeemed and restored? Is there a lack in your life? Have parts of your heart and soul been stolen away? What's broken deep within you? As I've searched my own life and heard many, many prayer requests from others through the years, I believe it boils down to this: *we all need the things we're called to love the King of Kings with—our heart, soul, mind and strength—redeemed from destruction.* Let's take a little deeper look at those things, then.

HEART

In Hebrew, it's described as the motives, feelings, affections and desires; the will, the aims, the principles, the thoughts and the intellect of a man. It embraces the whole inner man, the central part of a person (the head never being regarded as the center of intelligence); the source of all action and the center of all thought and feeling—the seat of emotions. Our hearts must be redeemed! If not, all our motives, affections, feelings and thoughts will be inwardly focused. It'll be all about *us.* What we *feel.* What we *want.* What our *goals* are. What will make us *happy.*

Scripture says our hearts are deceitful above ALL things. Your heart will absolutely LIE and tell you that *you* are #1, that *you* need to be stroked and catered to, that what *you* think is most important, that *you* are entitled to *your* rights, that *you've* got it together and can get it done, that *you* are ALL

THAT AND MORE. Or it'll spit out the opposite message: that you lack what others have, that you'll never amount to anything, that you're not smart enough, pretty enough, driven enough or loved enough; that you're unworthy, unable and inadequate, that you deserve what you've got and will never get out of that pit you've been in for so long...on and on. MORE LIES.

If Christ isn't seated on the throne of your heart, then you're sitting on a lie. You're being ruled by deception that centers on self. And self-centeredness will always produce either pride or bitterness, neither of which is productive and both of which oppose Jesus' lordship. *I don't want any part of my life to be in opposition to the Lord of Lords.* Since they often flow from a seat of emotion, relationships easily fall into the heart category. ANYBODY NEED A RELATIONSHIP REDEEMED? No comment necessary. Our hearts desperately need the power of the Kinsman-Redeemer, Christ Jesus. However, to become His rightful dwelling place, they must be purchased and set free.

SOUL

In Hebrew, it's "the essence of life, all that is within, the inner self, the part that moves into the afterlife and needs atonement to enter into God's presence after death." The Greek word means, "the spirit, an essence which differs from the body and is not dissolved by death, the seat of feelings, desires, affections and aversions." It is of UTMOST importance—a matter of eternal life or eternal death. WE WILL NOT DWELL IN THE HOUSE OF THE LORD WITHOUT A REDEEMED SOUL. We can never do enough good to earn a place in the presence of the Holy King. Stepping into heaven is absolutely dependent on accepting Christ's redemption. Does this knowledge cause a fire to burn in our hearts for the unsaved? I pray so. I don't want to care only about my own soul to the exclusion of others.

MIND

Hebrew says it's similar to the heart—wisdom, understanding, imagination and deep thought. In Greek, it's "the seat of reflective consciousness, perception, understanding, judging, determining, the faculty of knowing, to think, moral interest and reflection, counsels and purpose." *What track is your mind going to be on outside of redemption?* Studying ancient civilizations while homeschooling, I've been amazed at how far from Truth unredeemed thinking can go. In our culture today it doesn't often take the form of idol worship, human sacrifice or strange rituals, but comes in sophisticated (even religious) mind-sets, like secular humanism, New Age thought or denying the validity of the Word of God. *It's that self-focus, once again,* believing what you come up with instead of what's established in the heavens through the Word of the Most High King of Kings.

Along with obvious roads of deception and perversion, the mind can also lead you down subtle trails of independence. It'll tell you things like: Love the Lord, but just leave that one, little area to yourself. Go to church, just don't get overly involved and become some Bible-thumping fanatic. Don't let the Lord interrupt your schedule too much. You don't want to stand out, just blend in. You don't have to share your faith; it's personal, and you certainly don't want to offend anyone. After all, who are you to speak God's Word to others?

The mind is also very good at rationalizing. "Oh, well, it's just a little thing. Not as bad as my friend's thing. I'm doing pretty well. Why, I'm involved in this, serving here, I'm in a Bible Study..." whatever. HOLINESS IS NOT RELATIVE! In college, I fell hard into the trap of relativism. "Well, I'm not doing what *they're* doing. I'm a pretty doggone good girl. I'm not getting drunk, doing crack or sleeping around, blah, blah..." How pitiful. Our minds like to rank and compare sins, justifying our own and condemning those of others. They excuse addictions, greediness, unforgiveness, bitterness, judgments, criticisms, self-centeredness and all manner of stuff in OUR lives. They run from the Beatitudes, where Christ calls "blessed" the poor in spirit, the meek, the merciful, the pure; the ones who hunger for the King, mourn their sin, seek peace and endure persecution for righteousness' sake. *If He calls you blessed, you're blessed, indeed.* But I doubt that most of our minds find meekness, humility, purity or mourning over sin naturally desirable. Nor is holiness legalistic. But your mind will tell you it is. I despise legalism, because it puts chains right back on what the Lord has set free, and promotes major self-righteousness.

OUR MINDS DESPERATELY NEED CHRIST'S STRONG ARM OF REDEMPTION. We need to be set free from our own way of thinking. Check yourself—what's the main focus of your thought life? Your own needs? Those you love? What you want for the future? What happened in the past? Fears? Obsessions? Trying to please people? What is it? I view the mind as the Enemy's primary target of his attempts to weave us into his captivity. If he can control your thoughts and cause you to doubt God, he's got a stronghold going. If he can just whisper lies in your mind that you fall for, he's on his way.

It's critical, of absolute urgency, that we focus our minds on Truth, on Christ crucified and risen, so our minds can be full of the knowledge of God instead of Satan's deceptions. They need to be renewed, transformed and pressed into Christ's image. They need to be trained in true wisdom and understanding from the Lord. I believe we do that by asking Him to lead us through His Word and imprint it on our souls; to show us where we've embraced a lie and help us know the Truth. I have Ephesians 1:17 stuck on my refrigerator: *"I keep asking that the God of our Lord Jesus Christ, the glorious Father, may give you the Spirit of wisdom and revelation, so that you may know Him better."* I cry out for

Lord to make His Word active in my and my family's minds. I'm just smart enough to know that *I know nothing* and must completely rely on Christ for wisdom, revelation and knowledge. I have nothing to say, nothing to boast in—*but He has everything*. The purpose of wisdom is *to KNOW HIM BETTER. Him ALONE.*

I believe the Lord intends our minds to be filled with the overwhelming, absolutely thrilling, depths of His wisdom. We have to lay ours down and take His up through the Scriptures and the guidance of the Holy Spirit. I open the sweet Word of God every morning and say, "Holy Spirit, DO YOUR THING. Teach me. Change me. Kill me, then breathe new life into me. I MUST HAVE CHRIST. Show Him to me, and exalt Him in my life." Allowing the Lord to renew your mind with His Word will bring peace to your wave-tossed thoughts. It'll drive out fear and anxiety, doubt and despair and highlight the deceptions you've fallen for and drive them out. *"He will keep in perfect peace Him whose mind is fixed on [Christ]."* The old mindset will begin to peel away, and the very mind of Christ will take its place. *Hallelujah!*

Whatever you've been counting on to renew your mind besides the Word of God will fail you. Knowledge and education can't do it, no matter how prestigious or who teaches you, or how many degrees you have—even seminary degrees. I homeschool because I want my children's minds filled with the knowledge of God and the power of His perfect Word from which all wisdom comes. *But I can't redeem those impressionable minds.* I can make sure they're able to spit Scripture back to me, but I can't change them from the inside out or make them passionate for the Lord. I can control a certain amount of *head*-knowledge, but *the Holy Spirit gives true heart-knowledge. We need to surrender our brains to the Kinsman, and let Him fill them with Truth.*

STRENGTH

In Hebrew: "power, might, ability, substance, vigor, fruits, gifts; leads to wealth and property." The Bible warns us not to tolerate self-sufficiency and pride in ourselves, but says that God is to be our strength. Zechariah 4:6 says, *"Not by might, nor by power, but by MY SPIRIT, says the Lord of hosts."* I NEED MY STRENGTH REDEEMED. For so many years I relied on my own strength. How stupid was that?—thinking I could do it all and feeling responsible for everything. Praise God for stripping away my personal strength and showing me His own. Stuck in my own weaknesses, He's rolled up His sleeve, exposed His mighty arm, and said, "Look at THIS, Child." How strong He is!

I pray now for increased strength from Him to walk from *"glory to glory and strength to strength,"* as Scripture says. I don't ask just for the sake of being strong. I desire the incredible might that springs from the joy of the Lord in order to use that supernatural power to serve HIM ALONE. Nehemiah 8:10 states plainly, *"the joy of the Lord is your strength."* A few verses later it says the people were rejoicing greatly, *because the Word of the Lord had been made known to them, and they understood it.* Grasping the Word of God will cause joyfulness to spring from deep within your soul and lead you straight to the feet of the Almighty in pure, passionate worship.

You have no true strength without the joy of the Lord. You can have health, vitality, wealth and every earthly thing imaginable, *but it has no real power if it's not soaked in His joy.* You can be healthy and miserable and wealthy and miserable. Real power isn't found in numbers, abilities, money, power, friends or fame, it comes from the Almighty. "I look unto the hills, from whence comes my help? My help is from the Lord, the maker of heaven and earth," (Psalm 121:1). Humbly looking to Him will be your greatest delight and source. As you draw from the deep wells of His joy and become strong in Him, every earthly blessing becomes not the root of your happiness but a tool in your hand to help build the kingdom of Christ. Instead of blessings being your goal in life, they become instruments of praise to the King.

It doesn't matter what you need redeemed, Christ is more than able. It doesn't matter where you've been or how long you've been there, whether it's a deep place of woundedness and pain or of pride and self-righteousness, He's able to bring you out. He's big enough. Our mighty Kinsman has paid the price and is more than willing to buy you back from that fear, that obsession, that overwhelming compulsion, that addiction, that sorrow of soul, that hardness of heart, that pride and self-reliance, that co-dependency, that thing that's plagued your heart and troubled your life. Not as an escape, but as THE answer. He's it—the One and only Redeemer, the Satisfier of your soul. *Run to Him.* His arm is outstretched to welcome you home, and that arm is MIGHTY.

I love Job 19:23-27, which says, *"Oh, that my words were recorded, that they were written on a scroll, that they were inscribed with an iron pen on lead, or engraved in rock forever! I know that my Redeemer lives, and that in the end He will stand upon the earth. And after my skin has been destroyed, yet in my flesh I will see God; I myself will see Him with my own eyes—I, and not another. How my heart yearns within me!"* Oh, that our hearts would cry, "I know that I know that I know that my Redeemer LIVES, and that He's grabbed my heart, blown my mind and ransomed my soul. With all my heart, I KNOW HIM. He's not just THE Redeemer, HE'S MINE."

Yet, I don't deserve a Redeemer. In no way have I earned the covering of such a famous Kinsman. I have nothing with which to charm or woo Him, and there's nothing I can do to make His redemption worth His while—except to pour my whole heart, mind, soul and strength into loving and serving Him.

Questions & Applications

1. **Your Redeemer lives. Search your heart, soul, mind and strength. What do you need Him to redeem?**

13

Where the Harvest Begins

Just then Boaz arrived from Bethlehem and greeted the harvesters, "The Lord be with you!" "The Lord bless you!" they called back. Boaz asked the foreman of his harvesters, "Whose young woman is that?" The foreman replied, "She is the Moabitess who came back from Moab with Naomi," **Ruth 2:4-6.**

Before they even came close to Bethlehem, *a harvest was being prepared.* Boaz was already there ahead of them, tilling the soil and raising a crop. The fields meant for Naomi and Ruth were already prospering, even before they set foot in them. It wasn't their sweat that watered the dirt, nor their seeds that were sown. It wasn't their work that opened up the fields, *it was their relationship to the kinsman-redeemer.* He was the lord of the harvest, and, as we'll see, he offered to them not just leftovers but *all he possessed.*

One so much greater than Boaz has set the scene for you, whose mercy won't only change the course of your earthly life but your eternal path, as well. He's a Man of the highest honor and greatest position in heaven and earth, whose feet stand not only on Bethlehem's soil but on glory's ground—Jesus Christ Himself. *He's already in the fields awaiting you, preparing the way for your feet and positioning you for the greatest harvest, whether you realize it or not.*

Ruth was looking for mercy and leftovers, yet we don't see her complaining. She was grateful for the barley she was able to glean, not bitter that she didn't own the field. *Do you despise the day of small things?* Are you content with the portion the Lord has put in your hands today, or do you pout because someone else has more? Are you gathering all you can with each step, trusting the One who owns it all to provide the supply you'll need tomorrow? YOU'RE WHERE YOU ARE RIGHT NOW FOR A REASON. *Determine in your heart to gather everything the Lord has to show you everywhere He takes you.* It doesn't matter if it looks like you thought it would or if it pleases your flesh, TRUST the Lord of the Harvest. I wonder if we've ever missed something the Lord had for us tomorrow, because we weren't satisfied with what He gave us today—because we slipped on jealousy, anger or self-pity, instead of abiding in contentment and faith, or because small portions appeared to be leftovers, and we were too good for that?

While I don't want to stay where I am, I don't want to despise this day either because *there's something the Lord has for me here He wants me to discover and gather.* His fields contain more than barley. There's always pure gold to be found in them. There's a harvest being prepared for every one of us. We're all invited to step in and begin to reap. *And these aren't just any fields. They belong to the KING.* He's the One tilling the soil, preparing the ground, planting the seeds and watering with living water. It's His voice that rings in your soul, "GLEAN FROM THESE FIELDS, CHILD!" If you've been trying to harvest from somewhere else or attempting to gather something for your life from any other source, it's time to step onto new ground.

How do you glean from the holy fields of the Most High God and gather His harvest? *HIT YOUR KNEES* and

BOLDLY ASK for all He has for you. As I've sought the Lord concerning what the harvest is and how to receive it, He's answered me in a way I never expected. (The Holy Spirit is so faithful to illumine the Word of God in our hearts when we ask Him to. I hate to think what absolute joy I've missed by not seeking and studying more.) The Lord showed me that we need to come to Him FIRST. We're not to depend on anyone else to glean for us, but to receive from Him *first-hand*. He's more than able and so incredibly willing to pour out all He's planned and provided, even to (maybe *especially to*) poverty-stricken Moabites. We need to come to His feet believing He wants us to gather, no matter what we were or did yesterday, that He and His plans are always good and that He's equipped us well with every gift and tool we'll ever need. God is absolutely and forever our supply and portion, and His Word is meant to be powerful, even in our trembling hands.

Neither depend on someone else to harvest for you, nor settle for their leftovers. No man can give you what the Holy Spirit wants to provide Himself. Of course, we learn from, encourage, love and inspire each other; we teach what we know and use the gifts we're given. *But we gather for ourselves alone in the Secret Place,* where it's just the King and us. That's where we hear His voice for ourselves as we silence ours; where we cry out to the Master, and He responds; where we ask for wisdom and receive it; where we give Him our hearts, and He holds them to His chest as precious treasure and where we give Him deep praise, and He inhabits it.

IN YOUR CLOSET ON YOUR KNEES (or better yet, on your face) IS WHERE THE HARVEST GROWS. There, you'll cross the threshold of the Holy of Holies through the blood of the perfect Lamb and glimpse the very storehouses of glory. You'll find the source of provision for your own soul, receive an overflowing abundance from the King of

Kings and find bread and drink for every soul to whom you're called to minister.

There's no other source. You'll be filled from no other well. His presence *is* the harvest. Everything else is mere blessing, a side effect of His touch meant to inspire pure praise. For so long I thought it was up to me to gather everything I could with my own hands and that God's goal for my life was to do His will. He's corrected that thought, showing me that the goal of my life is to LOVE HIM WELL—to be in love with Him—and that He'll then use that passion to bring in souls. Several summers ago, I was walking on the beach alone, just talking to my King. I felt so grateful for His presence and that He'd dare bend His ear to me, and asked Him with every ounce of strength, "Oh, my Lord, what can I do for You?" I expected some sort of "church answer," like, "Go get busy doing something for Me. Go preach on the street. Go teach all the children single-handedly. Go to Africa immediately. Go do this or that." Instead, His answer was simply a short but firm, "LOVE ME."

LOVING HIM IS YOUR PURPOSE. EVERYTHING ELSE FLOWS FROM THAT. The work of my hands is not my life's purpose, the work of His heart is. *He's* the goal, and *He's* the fullness of the harvest. The Psalmist cries out, *"Lord, You are the portion of my inheritance and my cup,"* (Psalm 16:5). The presence of the Lord Himself is our amazing heritage and lot. His astounding presence in you will cause others to crave the depths also, and then comes the harvest of souls as you become equipped to "Go and make disciples..." Who could ever do that effectively if they haven't first fallen to their knees in passion before the King?

How can you draw the lost, wounded or weary to the abundance of the King if you haven't tasted it for yourself? How do you expect to spark love for Him in others if you aren't madly in love with Him yourself? If you stand proudly in the fields and say, "I've got it together, and I'm bringing it home," how can you reap anything but flesh? You don't glean spiritually by formulating a new plan or program, *but by finding a new position—ON YOUR KNEES*. Any program stands in danger of becoming a "man-thing" if it's not absolutely inspired and led by the Lord of Hosts. I want no part of something that isn't birthed on well-worn knees. Harvest is always a *Holy Spirit-thing*. As we faithfully step forward and venture into *His* fields, the outcome is *His*.

In Matthew 9:35-38, as Jesus was going about teaching, preaching and healing, He saw the pitiful, harassed and helpless crowds and said to His disciples, *"The harvest truly is plentiful, but the laborers are few. Ask the Lord of the Harvest, therefore, to send out laborers into His harvest field."* If you view the harvest as the manifest presence of the Christ saturating your soul and drawing others to Himself, then *it would make sense that the laboring part would happen on your knees*—in the abiding place, the "be still and know" place, the place by the quiet waters of His heart. It seems to me the real work happens as we wrestle in prayer, pouring our hearts out like a river for the harassed and helpless. That's where pure motives rise up and passion overflows.

Unfortunately, our flesh likes to be seen and heard, not hidden in a prayer closet. But what good are our words or works if they don't begin there? How well will they be received by desperate souls if their purpose didn't originate in the Secret Place beneath the shadow of the Almighty? Several years ago, the Lord spoke this word to my heart in prayer: "Nothing happens in ministry that does not stem from what happens on your knees. Authentic ministry comes from an authentic love and passion for Christ." I immediately thought, "Who am I supposed to give this to?" It didn't occur to me that He was speaking to ME. I absolutely didn't see myself in ministry. But the longer I walk with the King, the more I understand that ministry is not a title, position or job, but a spilling out of His heart through ours, in whatever manner He desires. *Every one of us is called to that!* No one is excluded from laboring in this way for the Kingdom.

I don't want to gather in the King's field on my own terms, with my own ideas, agenda or strength. I want to worship at His feet and from there receive my commission, purpose and harvest. *I believe when we do that, we won't be able to stop what the Holy Spirit pours out. We'll see what Ruth eventually saw—ownership of the entire field, not just what someone dropped.* How I want to see that. And, regardless of how spiritual they may be, no man or woman can produce it for me or give it to me.

As I pondered prayer itself being the place of labor and harvest, I was led to Luke 2:36-38, two short little verses that I've read over quickly countless times. This time, however, they filled my heart. The verses concern Anna, a prophetess who worshiped night and day, fasting and praying and never leaving the temple. In one sweet moment, all she'd been crying out for was fulfilled as she watched Jesus come through the door, cradled in Mary's arms. Ah, sweet fulfillment, salvation and redemption. She went over to Him, and began to praise and prophesy. *Beautiful.*

SHE SAW THE KING. As the Christ Child was brought into the temple, I believe the Holy Spirit spoke to Anna's spirit, "Look, My faithful daughter. THERE HE IS. Your cries are answered, beloved child. GO SEE WHAT I'VE DONE." Why else would she rush over to Mary and begin to speak to *"all who were looking forward to the redemption of Israel"*? Why else would the sight of a babe in arms stir her very soul?

Here's a question for you: *How critical was Anna's labor of prayer?* Did an old woman's intercessions play a role in ushering in the birth of Messiah? Did they rock the heavens and pave the road for the King of Kings to step into the world of men? Did they, in a slightly different way, help prepare the way for the Savior much like John the Baptist? If so, how critical is prayer to ushering in the kingdom of God on the earth now; in paving the way for Christ to come for a prepared Bride and giving the Holy Spirit a vehicle to move through? *How incredibly urgent is the labor of our knees*?

And what about fasting? Anna fasted. She turned away from the things of the flesh and fed on the fullness of the Holy Spirit. In the Greek, the definition of fasting is just what you'd think: "to abstain from eating." However, the Hebrew root word for it means, "to cover over the mouth." *How many of us need to cover our mouths?* Could fasting be a way of quieting our mouths, so we can receive from God's? How important is this discipline to the body of Christ? What's accomplished in us as we seek Him completely, even to the point of abstaining from things? What do we desperately want to see happen on earth, and do we need to fast as well as pray for it to be done?

Are we, like Anna, crying out in our "temple" night and day for the King to come to us, or is our intercession sporadic and frequently interrupted? Does prayer continually spill out of our hearts—and sometimes our mouths? As we cry out for Jesus, will we, too, hear the Holy Spirit say, "Look, My faithful child. THERE HE IS. Your cries are answered. GO SEE WHAT I'VE DONE. Then give Me praise and proclaim Him to all who have ears to hear." Oh, Lord, let it be.

The Lord has led me to a pattern of prayer that's been so powerful in my life. First, of course, is the way Jesus taught us to pray in The Lord's Prayer. He's also led me to pray based on the example of the Old Testament tabernacle, stepping from the altar to the very Holy of Holies, the sacred place behind the veil in deep intimacy with the King. (That's a whole study in itself!) Praying like this has lifted me into God's presence as never before and shown me things I never imagined. *He is good, and He wants you to come to the place with Him where you catch a glimpse of His splendor and become equipped to display it. You'll leave there like Moses left the mountain—radiant!* And what comes forth will be laced with pure, passionate LIFE. You'll sow an abundant crop, one I doubt you'll see the full depths of until you step into heaven. *Go there and labor. The harvest awaits you.*

Just mentioning seeing the ultimate harvest of our prayers when we stand before the King of Glory makes my mind drift there. I once heard a precious lady picture heaven as a perpetual tea party with butterflies and stingless bees. Sweet picture, especially if you're partial to tea parties. But what stirs my soul and makes me yearn for the courts of heaven is to think about the harvest of souls being fully revealed—of people of every tongue and tribe bending the knee—and of an atmosphere charged, energized and illumined by the King's radiant presence, absolute Truth and wisdom. It's a place where hearts and eyes are wide open and no question remains unanswered. I want to experience pure, unhindered worship from the spotless Bride, to hear angels' songs and see for myself the glory of the Lord shining 'round about them, to kiss His feet and hear, "Well done." I want to look deep into the eyes of the One I've loved so long, see face to face what my spirit's only glimpsed and feast forever at His banquet table in Redemption's perfect beauty.

Amazingly, Jesus says to ask that the Lord's kingdom come and His will be done ON EARTH as it is in heaven. So, I request every divine thing earthly eyes can see to be seen with these little eyes and for my flesh to behold all it can of Him and His kingdom without disintegrating before His glory. I pray for as much wisdom as finite minds can grasp, for His splendor to be the feature of the day, for the Enemy to have no part or say, for Christ's kingdom, power and glory to blast through all we've ever known and arise in loveliness upon the earth, for every heart to bow and every knee to bend and for the Lord of Lords to reign.

Oh, King Jesus, make us laborers on our knees. Let us gather from Your glorious fields, taste and see Your harvest and proclaim it out loud. Help us hear Your voice whisper, "You be about the loving, and I'll be about the gathering." Help us bow in Spirit and Truth and see Your kingdom come.

Questions & Applications

1. **Are you content with where the Lord has you today, or do you tend to "despise the day of small things"?**
2. **Ask the Lord Jesus, as the disciples did, to teach you to pray. Then expect some harvest to begin.**

14

Barley, the Bread of Life

So Naomi returned from Moab accompanied by Ruth the Moabitess…arriving in Bethlehem as the barley harvest was beginning, **Ruth 1:22.**

Another seemingly insignificant thing that stirs my heart is the *kind* of field Ruth gleaned in—barley fields. Seems like an incredibly minor detail, but as I looked deeper into its significance, I was washed afresh all over again with the beauty of the "small things" of our God. Barley was a major ingredient for bread, was used for food and offerings to the Lord and was a symbol of blessing and prosperity. It's listed in Deuteronomy 8:7-8 as part of the goodness of the Promised Land. Barley was the offering brought on behalf of an unfaithful wife. Land value was determined by how much barley seed was required for it. In 2 Kings 4, 20 loaves of it were multiplied to feed 100 men, and it symbolized God's power in Judges 7. It was barley bread that Jesus multiplied for the 5,000 in the New Testament. *It was significant.* Ruth was out there working with all her might in the fields of something that represented sustenance, the stuff of offerings to the King of Kings that symbolized blessing, prosperity, favor and might. In other words, *she was most definitely in the right field, and was diligently gathering in life itself.*

Judges 7 is the passage about barley that excites me most. It's the account of Gideon and the Midianite army. Israel was greatly oppressed by Midian, because, as Judges 6:1 tells us, *"Again the Israelites did evil in the eyes of the Lord, and for seven years He gave them into the hands of the Midians."* Their crops were subject to destruction, with their fields continually destroyed by a people whose numbers were likened to "a swarm of locusts." Only their impoverishment at the hands of these "locusts" caused Israel to cry out to the Lord. The wonderful thing to me is how He then rescued His starving, oppressed people.

As Judges 7 unfolds, God calls a weak, trembling, testing, least of the least kind-of-guy to step up to the plate and go out against that locust swarm-sized enemy. After reminding the Lord of his weakness, and laying some fleeces out to repeatedly confirm His call (ever done that?), Gideon finally gathered a few thousand men and set out. The Lord then sifted the army, reducing it to just 300. So 300 frightened but faithful men, led by Gideon, camped out near the Midianites. The part about barley (I'm getting there) happens next. The Lord said to Gideon, *"If you are afraid to attack, go down to the camp with you servant Purah and listen to what they are saying. Afterward, you will be encouraged to attack the camp."*

The Lord was saying, "If you're the least bit afraid, go listen to what the enemy is whispering. It's going to encourage you, stir boldness in your heart and convince you that the battle truly belongs to the Lord." I believe the same holds true for us. If we could just hear the whispers of fear the Enemy has of Christ in us, I believe nothing but boldness would rise up. Gideon must have indeed been afraid to attack because he and Purah quickly went out, arriving just in time to hear one of the Midianites share a troubling account: *"I had a dream,"* he was saying. *"A round loaf of barley bread came tumbling into the Midianite camp. It struck the tent with such force that the tent overturned and collapsed."* His friend responded, *"This can be none other than the sword of Gideon, the Israelite. God has given the Midianites and the whole camp into his hands,"* (Judges 7:13-14).

Just a *dream* about a barley loaf sent fear racing through the enemy camp! *What did the barley represent here?* The BREAD OF LIFE, the never-ending power of God and the absolute victory and dominion of the Lord of Hosts. The same One the barley loaf represented wants to tumble into your Enemy's camp and scare the life out of him, too! He wants to stir boldness in your "least of the least" heart, and give you victory—not the kind generated by your strength, but by His. That same Bread of Life wants to satisfy you in a weary land, a place of yearning. He wants to feed you not only from His table, but also from His heart. He wants to show you *"great and mighty things that you know not of."* He wants you to taste and see for yourself and to hear the whispers of fear spoken by the thick-as-locusts enemy.

Have there been any "locusts" in your fields? Any swarm coming against you large enough to make you want to hide in a cave somewhere? We know a battle rages against us, because Ephesians 6:12 states, *"For our struggle is not against flesh and blood, but against the rulers, against the authorities, against the powers of this dark world and against the spiritual forces of evil in the heavenly realms."* Indeed, there are locusts waiting to devour your crop, harvest thieves waiting to steal away your life, an Enemy bent on your destruction and a hierarchy of demonic power that's furious over your position in the King's household and determined to destroy your fields. *The Enemy wants your barley—your sustenance, your offering to the Lord, your blessing and prosperity and the very power and splendor the King wants to display in you.*

Yet, the Lord of Hosts is with you! Joel 2:11 says of Him, *"The Lord thunders at the head of His army; His forces are beyond number, and mighty are those who obey His command."* Psalm 97:1-6 tells us, *"The Lord reigns, let the earth be glad; let the distant shores rejoice. Clouds and thick darkness surround Him; righteousness and justice are the foundation of His throne. Fire goes before Him and consumes His foes on every side. His lightning lights up the world; the earth sees and trembles. The mountains melt like wax before the Lord, before the Lord of all the earth."* Mighty is He!

In Joel 2:25 the Lord goes on to say, *"I will repay you for the years the locusts have eaten, the great locust and the young locust, the other locust and the locust swarm..."* That's awesome news—a Word to make the Enemy tremble. All those locusts sent into your fields will be devoured by the Word of God and swallowed up by Calvary. Everything they meant to destroy in you will become a testimony to the Lord's grace and power instead. You'll neither fall, nor be destroyed. Whatever was taken from you, THE LORD HIMSELF WILL REPAY. There have been plenty of locusts in my life, and I'm counting on that promise!

Moses stretched out his staff and asked the Lord to remove the plague of locusts from Egypt, and I do the same. I lift the staff of God's Word and cry out to the living Christ, "Remove the locusts and restore what they've devoured, Lord! Let my heart no longer be their feeding ground and prey! Let Your hands gather from my heart, mighty King, not the Enemy's!" One morning I prayed before the Lord feeling weak and defeated. Tears fell freely, and I cried out to the King until I heard His reply in my heart, "I will pay you back for those tears." How I praise Him. I felt He was saying, "Yes, the Enemy has come against you, but I am building you through his assault. You are going to be a stronger vessel for My Spirit because of it. I have allowed this sifting and weakening because it will ultimately bring Me glory, and you will be blessed also. You will one day count it all joy." I suddenly began to realize how Paul could rejoice in the great suffering he experienced. *He knew he was in the hand of Almighty God, who would work it out and bless him for it*. That encourages me so greatly to never despair when locusts crouch nearby, but to draw the Sword, wait on the Lord and expect to see His wonders.

Thinking about how the locusts are described in Joel 2, I began to ponder what they represented. The Lord categorized them, which tells me there are different kinds of attacks on our fields. Follow along with me here. The "great locust": could that be something deeply rooted—a generational stronghold, a problem tormenting many in your family line or a negative predisposition? Could it be something disabling and tormenting that's seemingly always had you in its grip and that you seek to deny and hide? Could the great locusts represent addictions, obsessions, dependencies, serious illness or deep-seated rejection and insecurity? Could they rise up as fear, jealousy, a self-defending, critical, nagging spirit or as bondage wrapped so tight that deliverance from it could come only from the Lord?

The "young locust": perhaps these are new things coming into your fields to which you open the door through sin and rebellion. They may not yet be strongholds in your life, but could easily become one—a lustful image that keeps coming to mind, a dabbling with something that might become an addiction or a tempting thought that has not yet become an action. Maybe it's an affair of the heart, but not yet of the body, hateful thoughts toward other people to whom you still smile and speak, unforgiveness toward someone, pride about your good behavior or other things easily justified but still rooted in sin. Young locusts like these, if not taken captive to Christ and renewed by His Word, have the potential to grow up and destroy. I think this is why so many times in the Old

Testament the Lord instructed Israel to utterly destroy the enemy—even the young ones. *He knew those young ones would grow up to destroy.*

The "other locust": I believe these represent assaults that come from *others*, like abuse, neglect, verbal attacks and undermining, gossip, slander or judgmentalism (*how many of our fields have this kind of locust in them disguised as "accountability"?*). Perhaps persecutions due to our love for the Lord should be listed here, that name-calling and labeling the world wants to slap on us, or the rejections that sometimes occur when you alone stand for righteousness. In some nations it might involve physical persecution and even death.

Who is naturally equipped to deal with these kinds of attacks? Many times I've had to remind myself that it's not flesh and blood I battle, but evil forces working through someone that are attempting to destroy me. When a personal attack occurs, it's so tempting to grow bitter toward those who let loose on us, rejected us or spread a bad report about us. It's so easy to let anger fester in our hearts and allow a desire for revenge to set in. Dwelling on the offense comes naturally, but as we do *we're giving it ground.* The Lord has many times spoken in my heart, "YOU STAY PURE BEFORE ME. Vengeance is Mine." Reacting with an impure heart invites destruction.

The "locust swarm" is a huge, overwhelming thing. It's wave after wave of oppression, a seemingly endless attack so great it has the potential to utterly destroy all you've ever planted in your life. It threatens total annihilation, a complete and thorough stripping of all you hold dear and makes the great locust look like a little lamb. It might be something like the governors coming against Daniel, Haman scheming to destroy the Jews or Pharaoh's army charging the children of Israel at the Red Sea. I believe that corporate attacks on the body of Christ by those who hate Christianity fall into this category. But it's also discouraging to see the Body falling prey to Enemy swarms like chaos, compromise, division, confusion and hatred; to see popular culture invading the Church instead of the Church invading the culture, and to see many in the Body of Christ deviate from Scripture and reject its inerrant Truth.

I expect opposition and attacks from the world; however, what's shocked me most is finding that locusts can put on church clothes and blend right in. They can fill pew or pulpit. They can talk church talk, all the while tearing down the Body instead of building it up (after all, Judas was one of the Twelve). These assaults, coming from the very ones you expect to support you, it seems to me, have the greatest potential to harm the Church and to send unbelievers running away with all their might. How that causes me to beg the King of Kings to never let ME be a locust in someone's life! May I build the Kingdom, not tear it down. May I speak Truth in love, not with a destructive, condemning spirit, and be a planter and waterer of all that's of God, while not being afraid to resist what is not.

SO, LOCUSTS CROUCH AT OUR DOOR AND DESIRE TO HAVE US, BUT WE'RE TOLD NOT TO FEAR. We're told to gear up, to put on the full armor, to resist and stand firm, pour out prayer and let praise continually fill our hearts. We're to let the hand of the Almighty plant and protect our fields and let Him, not the Enemy, open the doorways of our hearts. Psalm 27:1-2 says, *"The Lord is my light and salvation—whom shall I fear? The Lord is the stronghold of my life—of whom shall I be afraid? When evil men advance against me to devour my flesh, when my enemies and my foes attack me, they will stumble and fall."* THE LOCUSTS WILL STUMBLE, not us.

We're told not to sit down and give up, but to keep pressing on and moving forward in Spirit and Truth, as it says in Hebrews 12:1-2, *"Let us run with endurance the race that is set before us, looking unto Jesus, the author and finisher of our faith."* When we focus on and moan about the locusts, endurance dies right there. Instead, we need to look to the Bread of Life—*that round loaf of barley tumbling into the camp*—that can send the Enemy into confusion and utterly destroy his every scheme. The Enemy wants to control our attention. He wants our eyes to dwell on his attacks on ourselves and our fields. At times like that I ask the King to take my tiny cheeks in His massive hands and TURN MY GAZE UPWARD, to take back what the Enemy stole and redeem and restore what was lost.

Don't despair if your fields have been invaded. We've been given all we need for victory through the blood of Christ and the power of His Name—mighty weapons—which 2 Corinthians 10:4-5 tells us, *"are not carnal, but mighty in God for pulling down strongholds, casting down arguments and... bringing every thought into captivity to the obedience of Christ."* We need to hide ourselves in Him (He IS the armor), lay our hearts bare in His hands and then do as Philippians 3:14 says, *"forgetting those things which are behind and reaching forward to those things which are ahead, I press toward the goal for the prize of the upward call of God in Christ Jesus."* HE'S THE GOAL, and His fields are the prize. *May they forever be locust free.*

Don't bend under the condemnation of the Accuser of the brethren if locusts do make their way through. Apart from Jesus, not one soul has completely avoided their fields being invaded by sin. We need to go to the Secret Place with the King and let Him wash us with His Word and stand us up straight again. If we abide in the flesh, every little attack has the potential to become a great threat. But if we stay rooted, grounded and established in the Spirit through the Word and the cries of our heart before the Lord, then small assaults will remain just that: minor threats immediately handled and given no ground on which to settle. *It's not locusts invading your fields that destroys, it's their SETTLING there.* Don't let the sun go down on them. Deal with them at once!

Another thing that's become amazing in my heart is that JOHN THE BAPTIST ATE LOCUSTS (Matt. 3:4). I've always read this verse and thought, "SO? How gross was that?" But think about it: John dined on something meant to destroy. He consumed the stuff of plagues. He was nourished by the very things that degrade life and washed them down with sweet honey. *Instead of being devoured, he became the devourer,* a living example of how the Lord can turn things around! The King of Kings can take those locusts swarming around you and cast them onto your plate, saying, *"Dine on the victory of the Lord! Delight in the spoils of the Lord of the Harvest!"*

We're called to act in Spirit and Truth, and to be about growing, gathering and shielding our fields with faith. We're to build as Nehemiah did, with a tool in one hand and a sword in the other. *When we do, I believe our fields will yield supernatural crops, planted and raised by God Himself—the kind you just can't explain, grown not by or for men, but as offerings of praise to the Lord—beautiful, abundant barley. Let it be, our King.*

Questions & Applications

1. **Ask the Lord to show you the fields of your heart and to reveal any locusts settled there, waiting to devour.**
2. **Repent of giving them ground, and ask the Lord to cleanse your heart and fill it with the Bread of Life—His sweet barley.**
3. **If there are places in your past that locusts have already devoured, ask the Lord to restore them and then trust Him to do it.**

15

Watching and Working

"She said, 'Please let me glean and gather among the sheaves behind the harvesters.'

She went into the fields and has worked steadily from morning till now, except for a short rest in the shelter," **Ruth 2:7.**

Ruth humbly stepped into the fields of Boaz, requesting permission to gather only what the harvesters left behind. There's a subtle but important lesson the Lord pointed out to me here. "Watch the harvesters," He whispered in my heart, meaning workers who've been gathering much longer than us. There are men and women who've walked through life with the Living God longer than you've been alive. They have great experience in tilling ground, planting seeds, pulling weeds and driving away locusts of all kinds.

Much can be gleaned from following behind and watching them work—by observing the tools they use, their patterns and schedules and how they protect and tend their crops and daily receive their bread and wine from the King's table. By watching how they lace up their shoes and faithfully run the race set before them to the glory of the Lord alone, how His sustenance keeps them from growing weary and how they mark their rows (set up their spiritual markers), the reminders of what God has taught and done. (I keep mine in the form of a written record of what the Lord shows me in prayer and the Word. Most of it is never shared, it just fuels the fire in my soul when I read it again.) By seeing them work in the field, according to Zechariah 4:6, "*'Not by might, not by power, but by My strength,' says the Lord,*" and, as Galatians 6:9 describes, reaping the due season harvest of God. *There's great benefit in watching mighty souls bringing in the sheaves.* Not only do you receive inspiration and training, but also enough of their gleanings to sustain you until the Lord places you in your own harvest field.

I occasionally watch old Billy Graham crusades that air on Saturday evenings. (Twenty years ago, if you told me I'd be watching preaching on Saturday nights, I'd have said, "Get a life!") It never ceases to amaze me how that man pours out Truth so simply but powerfully, and how the masses respond. I watch them press up to the altar to receive Christ and I can't stop the tears, praying for them wherever they are now and asking the Lord to help my little life bring some souls to His feet also. *I'd say Billy Graham definitely qualifies as a harvester!*

Others from whom I've gathered a few sheaves include Beth Moore, my old pastor in Banner Elk, N.C., my youth minister from many, many years ago and some Titus 2 women, who may or may not be much older than me. *Watching these harvesters and their lives lived purely before the Lord has inspired me.* There's also much to be gathered from those who've toiled in the past and now inhabit heaven, souls whose lives have left us a rich trail from which to glean. As we've studied history in homeschool, I've learned so much from reading great biographies of lives lived for the Lord, like Henrietta Mears, George Muller, Charles Spurgeon and many others.

There are thousands of great examples to follow, but be cautious. Test everything against the mighty Word of God, and work it out in the Secret Place with the King. Make sure the harvester you observe is bringing in the wheat, not the tares. Never be charmed or led by flesh and blood, and never put a mere man or woman on some holy pedestal. Christ alone is worthy of that. At the end of a women's conference a few years ago, as I watched the speaker leave the stage, I felt the Lord speak a word in my heart about serving Him. The tears started flowing, and I whispered back, "I'm not worthy, Lord." His sweet response was simply, "Neither are they." *Grace abounds for us all.* Unfortunately, I've also learned a few things *not* to do from harvesters walking in the flesh and gathering trouble, like seeing pride sneak in and wreak its deadly havoc or the Word watered down and ears simply tickled. Those are lessons I wish weren't true, and ones I NEVER want to teach! *Protect us from ourselves, Lord!*

Learn from souls bent on following Christ at all costs, but don't *depend* on them for your own harvest. It's not their responsibility to mold you, establish your path, equip you and open doors for you. Your life isn't in their hands. They don't hold the number of your days, nor do they know how to order your steps. Set them free from any unholy expectations and never require of them what only God can do. Ruth didn't sit back and wait for the harvesters to bring grain to her, *she went out herself and worked.* We should never expect to be spoon-fed, but need to march boldly into the fields ourselves and labor in Spirit and Truth.

The harvesters I've observed, and still observe, will probably never even know it, which makes me realize that others coming up may also be observing our lives "unawares." *How I pray that anyone watching my life will see deep-rooted, authentic passion for the King flowing out of my heart, along with faithfulness, obedience and much fruit.* May the Lord keep my flesh on the Cross so it never rears its ugly head and sends people away from Him, instead of drawing them to His sweet presence. Have you ever been around someone who seemed to glow with the joy of the Lord and the thrill of toiling in His Word and fields, with a deep radiance that only time on one's knees in the Holy of Holies can bring? I'm sure they don't even know the fire in their heart is burning on their faces. I pray that when those in the world look at us, they'll see the same glow—the very light of Christ in us—and want to step onto holy ground beside us.

This verse also informs us that as Ruth followed the harvesters she worked "steadily." That word speaks to my heart, because so often we grow weary with what seems to be a little harvest and are tempted to give up. We become jealous when someone is gathering more than us, or get discouraged by the behavior of another harvester and want to pack up our tools and go home. If results don't come fast enough to suit us, we want to quit. The fields may be hot and dirty and involve humiliating work our flesh doesn't like, not to mention our pride. How many people want the Lord to give them the ministry of scrubbing the church floors, or better yet, the toilets—or sitting in the nursery every Sunday? How many of us are satisfied with where the Lord's placed us? Are we doing everything as unto Him, thankful for the portion He provides in this season? Do we work steadily, learning, growing, building and rejoicing in Him alone and seeking no praise from men?

We need to guard ourselves against a spirit of discontentment with where the Lord has us. Jesus warns in Luke 9:62, *"No one who puts his hand to the plow and looks back is fit for service in the Kingdom of God."* If you're not willing to work steadily where you are now, find your heart yearning to go back to Moab, pridefully think you deserve more or complain about the day of small things and seek to make a name for yourself, THEN YOU'RE NOT READY TO GATHER FOR THE KING. The Lord has convicted me sharply about times of complaining in my life: "Why this, Lord...why that...why here...when are You going to do something...I'm not doing very much for You here..."

Written to the Israelites following their exodus from Egypt, Leviticus 19:23-25 contains insight into those dark, silent, seemingly small times of gathering: *"When you enter the land and plant any kind of fruit tree, regard its fruit as forbidden. For three years you are to consider it forbidden; it must not be eaten. In the fourth year all its fruit will be holy, an offering of praise to the Lord. But in the fifth year you may eat its fruit. In this way your harvest will be increased. I am the Lord Your God."* As Christians, we're a planting of the Lord, trees meant to bear much fruit and display His glory. *"They are the shoot I have planted, the work of My hands, for the display of My splendor,"* (Isaiah 60:21).

We're absolutely meant to produce an *abundance* for the King's glory. Yet, how many of us have accepted Christ and thought we could skip right to the fifth year, the time of great fruitfulness? Or how often have we received a call or vision from the Lord, believing it all needs to unfold tomorrow? The Lord planted a word in my heart 20 years ago that I'm just NOW beginning to see come to pass in little pieces. In spite of this, how frequently is the body of Christ guilty of taking a brand new believer and sticking him or her in a position of leadership or teaching?

The years of not plucking fruit are critical. How can we truly produce and gather for the King if we're passing out all our little buds of promise before they have time to ripen and mature? How often do we think that because we've accepted the King's salvation, we can by-pass the maturing time and immediately get out there and do something? In Paul's life, we see some real ripening time. Following his conversion, he says it was three years before he *"went up to Jerusalem to get acquainted with Peter..."* (Galatians 1:18).

Then he writes, *"Fourteen years later I went up again to Jerusalem..."* (Gal. 2:1).

I've underlined those verses to remind me that *the Lord doesn't bring forth all our fruit in one day.* He's the Lord of the Harvest, and a full, abundant yield isn't produced in a single season. The most excellent fruit comes from the fullness of seasons, the times of plowing ground, planting seed, pulling weeds, watering, fertilizing and guarding the crop and letting it ripen. I've been very impatient at times with the seasons of the Lord, wanting all He's shown me to take place NOW. But looking back, I'm convinced even more that His ways are so absolutely not my ways for His perfect purposes and glory. My ways would destroy the fields every time. My impatience would kill the fruit.

The greatest commandment has nothing to do with works or fruit. It's to LOVE THE LORD. As you draw farther into that quiet place of knowledge and passion for Him, your little fruit tree starts growing. As the roots of your heart dig deeper into His heart's ground, you begin to bud and sprout in Him. As you remain still and at rest in that place, the fruit starts maturing. And as you water your heart, soul, mind and strength with the Word of God, it starts bursting at the seams. It becomes an offering of sheer delight before the Lord of Lords and something He can then pour out through your life in great measure to all you come in contact with, and yet never run dry yourself. *"In this way your harvest will be increased..."*

The "fourth year" mentioned in Leviticus 19 is so exciting to me. It represents the time when you've been seasoned in His fields and finally come before His throne to offer Him your whole, grown-up life. The marinating time, the silent time, the time when it doesn't appear you've gathered much, has caused you to let go of jealousy and selfish ambition. It's no longer about the fruit—what you will produce and do for Him—it's just about HIM. It's about yearning for His presence, seeking His face and the beauty of His temple, desiring to minister to the King of Kings, offering Him the fullness of all you are and somehow bringing joy to His amazing heart. You're no longer proud of your branches or impressed by the little buds on them. YOU'RE JUST THRILLED TO BE CONNECTED TO THE VINE. Any fruit is just an offering to the King, something through which He can make His glory known.

If you belong to Christ, you've got some buds needing to mature. You've got some sprouts He wants to water and feed. There's some Kingdom building He wants to do through you, but IN HIS TIME. How I pray He'll help me love, and not resent, His timing. I want Him to have the freedom to bear much through me. Impatience, pride or premature harvesting won't let that happen. I beg Him, through the power of His mighty Holy Spirit, to help me work steadily in every season He takes me through and to faithfully glean everything He has for me in every stage.

The next part of this verse tells us Ruth worked steadily, *"except for a short rest in the shelter."* That stirs my heart, too, by telling me that the Lord doesn't expect us to labor so much that we kill ourselves. Indeed, His Word commands a Sabbath rest. He knows how desperately we need to come into His shelter and rest awhile in His arms, to lay down our tools for a day and just sit in the shade at His awesome feet and let His Spirit restore our weariness, energize our resources and impart strength. (As I was writing this, my son climbed up in my lap and wanted me to read his Bible to him, then he snuggled in and fell fast asleep in my arms. I looked at his sweet face and listened to his deep breathing and saw a picture of Christ holding and delighting in us as we just *rest.*) *We don't always have to be doing something to delight the heart of the King.*

Some of my most intense prayer times over my children have occurred as they slept. I wonder if some of Christ's deepest intercessions for us don't come during times of rest also, those periods He provides in which to relax, grow and gain strength, knowing what we'll face when it's time to go back to the fields—the training we've yet to master, the battles we've yet to face, the labor we've yet to accomplish, the heat of the day we'll face tomorrow and the necessity of His shelter and shade. HE IS THE SHELTER, what the Hebrew describes as, "a place of refuge, hope and trust." Psalm 61:1-4 says, *"Hear my cry, O God; attend to my prayer. From the end of the earth I will cry to You, when my heart is overwhelmed; lead me to the Rock that is higher than I…For You have been a shelter for me, a strong tower from the enemy. I will abide in Your tabernacle forever; I will trust in the shelter of Your wings."* How sweet is the shelter of His wings!

What good are we in the fields if we're exhausted? I've witnessed this firsthand in my own life. One evening my son woke me up at midnight because of a bad dream, then thunderstorms rolled in which sent my daughter to my bed, too. The storms lasted the rest of the night, and I got very little sleep. In addition to the fibromyalgia I battle, it greatly affected my strength. By the next night I was hurting, exhausted and, on top of that, a hormonal mess. I felt like there was a key in my back winding me up WAY too tight. I was no good to anyone. I finally took a bath and went to bed, telling myself, "OK, what's truth here? Truth is that I'm not a crazy woman, just an exhausted, hormonal one. God is still on His throne and will hold me tonight. He still loves me, even though right now I'm a wreck. He wants me to rest in and trust Him. Greater is He...greater is He." I was reminded of David saying, *"Why are you so downcast, O my soul? Put your hope in God."*

I believe weary harvesters are prime targets for locust swarms. The Enemy NEVER plays fair; he'll not back off because you're tired. In fact, he'll take full advantage of those times. It's *critical* that we find our rest in the temple of the Lord. There's no peace sweeter than that which comes from resting in His presence. He alone *"gives strength to the weary and increases the power of the weak. Even youths grow tired and weary, and young men stumble and fall; but those who hope in the Lord will renew their strength. They will soar on wings like eagles; they will run and not grow weary, they will walk and not be faint,"* (Isaiah 40:29-31). Awesome.

God's Law even established that the fields *themselves* should be given a rest. He instructed His people to sow, prune and gather for six years and then allow the cropland a year of rest, gathering only what came up on its own. In Leviticus 25:21, He promised such a blessing in the sixth year that they'd have enough stored for THREE. *Obedience to God brings blessing, rest and overflow—more than enough.* We need to obey Him, working when He says "work" and RESTING WHEN HE SAYS "REST." The Bible also describes the Year of Jubilee in Leviticus, a counting of seven times seven Sabbaths. The Hebrew for "jubilee" actually means, "the blast of the trumpet, the sounding of the shofar." Every 50th year the Jews were to blow a trumpet and proclaim a time of liberty, when land was to be given back and fields returned to their original owner. Debts were to be cancelled, and any Israelite who'd fallen into bondage was to be set free, for it was a holy year of release.

I believe this is a shadow of what Jesus would accomplish on earth, *"to proclaim freedom for the captives, the year of the Lord's favor..."* (Isaiah 61:1-2), as He quoted in the synagogue, boldly declaring, *"Today this Scripture is fulfilled in your hearing,"* (Luke 4:21). He was announcing Himself as our freedom, redemption, rest and ultimate Jubilee. Christ is eternally and solely our Year of Jubilee—our peace and strength, our Redeemer, our harvest and the only One who can cancel our debt. As the book of Revelation tells us, His own voice thunders like a trumpet blast. At His mere whisper men fall as though dead and demons flee. The Words of His mouth flash as a perfect, all-powerful, double-edged Sword that nothing can withstand. HE'S THE KING! *And He'll absolutely sound the blast of jubilee again,* as He promises in Revelation 22:20: *"Yes, I am coming soon."* Come, Lord Jesus. May we work steadily and rest when necessary until then.

Questions & Applications

1. **Do you have any seasoned harvesters in your life who serve as vivid examples of a godly life that you can follow? If not, ask the Lord to point some out to you.**
2. **Thank the King of Kings for those walking ahead of you on this journey. Pray for them, bless, encourage and learn much from them, but never put them on an impossible pedestal.**
3. **When the Lord calls you to a time or season of rest, REST, don't resist. He's growing and preparing you for the next season.**

16

Listen to Me, Child

So Boaz said to Ruth, "My daughter, listen to me. Don't go and glean in another field and don't go away from here. Stay here with my servant girls," **Ruth 2:8.**

Ruth finally comes face to face with her kinsman-redeemer. She's been in his field and is now in his presence. He's close enough to talk to, interact with, smell, look into his eyes and study the features of his face. I wonder what was racing through her mind as he approached her? Here she was, a Moabite, a foreigner—a tired, poor widow with nothing to offer but a plea for mercy—working in the abundant field of an Israelite. He'd noticed her, but she didn't know if he'd greet her with grace or wrath. She'd probably heard the other girls whispering about him in the fields. He was, after all, a very eligible man, known in town as a man of standing. She'd heard that he was good, but would that goodness embrace *her?* Would he be angry at her boldness? Would he send her home empty-handed? A thousand thoughts must have gripped her mind as Boaz drew near, and her heart must have pounded furiously as he began to speak.

What relief his first words must have brought to her troubled soul, "My daughter..." He was calling her by a term of endearment that expresses relationship and responsibility, a label identifying her with the family line, as part of the household and one who'd inherit blessing. *Your Redeemer calls you the same.* His thunderous voice whispers, "My child," and those two little words hold enough meaning to bless your soul for a lifetime. The fact that the King of Glory turns His face to you and calls you MY...*anything*—let alone family—is a miracle too powerful for words. That the King of Kings has claimed you and grabbed your heart, no matter how poverty-stricken or unfaithful you've been, and has said of you, "That one is MINE," should set your soul to *dancing*.

One of the first times I spoke to a group the women's minister called to ask for the title of my message. It hadn't occurred to me that I needed one, but what the Lord was giving me to share was all about stepping into the Holy of Holies and letting Him thrill your soul. So I said, "Well, maybe I'll call it, 'Dance With Me.'" There was dead silence on the other end of the phone. Then she said, "We don't dance." I changed the title, but in my heart still thought, "Sometimes, when you sense the presence of the King and He woos you with His Word and you finally begin to get a clue of how deeply He loves you, you just can't help yourself. *You dance.* Maybe not with your feet, but absolutely with your heart." *I believe the Groom of all grooms may just dance Himself!*

Song of Solomon 2:16 echoes here, *"My beloved is mine, and I am His."* May we never lose the joy of being called *His* and of knowing He's breathed the word of adoption over us, that His hand has sealed the deal and old records are forever closed. *When the King gives you His Name, you'll never be the same again.* The Greek word for adoption means, "the placing as a son, the condition of a son given to one to whom it does not naturally belong." *Thank God, our condition has changed because of Christ.* In Romans 8:15, we learn that it's the Holy Spirit who produces in us the realization of sonship and the attitude belonging to children.

I visited Charleston, South Carolina a few years ago, and as I thought about our adoption by the King of Kings an image of the old slave market there came to mind. Picture yourself standing on that auction platform in chains, destitute and desperate. Your head is hanging low and you're expecting the worst, hoping for a kind owner at best, when suddenly the ruler of the land comes forward and pays full price for you. You're released to him and step toward him with much gratitude, but also with much fear of the power in his hands. You bow and say, "I'm your slave now." He smiles, lifts your chin, takes your hand and says, "No, beloved. You are my *child.* I am bringing you into my household as a precious heir, with the same benefits and inheritance as my other children. You will sit at my table, take my name and share my wealth and the wonders of this land. You will no longer be what you were. Chains will never again bind and cut you, and you will no longer be forced to places of horror. You were a slave because of what you were born into. You are a child because of what you have been bought into." *Hallelujah.*

Jesus instructs us to pray, "Our Father," confirming our adoption right off the bat. He wants us to approach the Throne of Grace knowing first of all, and acknowledging with our mouths, that we're a blood-bought child of the Most High God, called by a new name, planted in His royal bloodline and heirs of grace and glory. He wants us to know that He's building His house and establishing us in it, that He's Abba and that He's for us, that we're not left to our own defenses or devices and are never abandoned or forsaken. He wants us to realize that we're cradled by perfect, holy hands of strength—hands that will never tire of teaching, soothing, lifting our chin, pulling out His finest for us and pointing the way we should go—that Almighty God, Jehovah, the Holy One of Israel, the mighty Lord of Lords, is *our Father*, knowledge far too wonderful to fully grasp. *But let's try.*

Romans 8:14-17 speaks of our adoption by the King. Paul informs us that as God's children, we're led by the Holy Spirit. We're told that we shouldn't be in bondage to fear because we have the Spirit of adoption that cries out from within us, "Abba, Father," and that the Spirit, Himself, *"bears witness that we are children of God, and that as His children, we are heirs—joint heirs with Christ."*

Can you wrap your mind around that? Have you ever stopped and camped out on that fact until your heart trembles before the Lord and the wonder and depths of His love blow you away? The Almighty, the God in the smoke and thunder on the mount of Moses, the Holy One of Israel before whom priests would fall down dead if any sin dwelt in their hearts, the Lord who had to hide Moses in the cleft of a rock to let him catch a mere glimpse of the *back side* of His glory, the brilliant Face no man could see and live to tell about, the One who led Israel with cloud and fire, who parted the waters and later walked on them, who swept Elijah up in a blazing chariot and sweeps up our hearts with the same brand of passionate fire, *wrapped Himself in flesh.* He covered His glory with mere skin and stepped into our fields so that we too could hear the words, "My child, listen to Me."

You're the King's child, and He has a Word for you. That's nothing but *scandalous glory.* The fact that the Ruler of Heaven, the Alpha and Omega, the Morning Star, the beautiful Lamb of God, would even dare draw near to us—foreigners and Moabites—let alone single us out, claim us and speak Truth to us, is absolutely amazing. This One that calls you "child" is pure, passionate and perfect in every way. He's staked His claim on our hearts and promised that He'll never leave us and will come and fill us with His precious Holy Spirit. Oh, there's no one like our Abba.

I've been forsaken by ones I expected to love me and have seen others forsaken also, but this Father is here to stay. Psalm 27:10 reads, *"When my father and my mother"* (or grandparent, friend, pastor, mentor, spouse, child, co-worker or anyone else on the face of this earth*) "forsake me, then the Lord will take me up."* THANK GOD. He's absolutely, eternally worthy of our trust. He's not going anywhere, but is ours for keeps. An old friend of mine called me one night, terribly hurt and upset. This 50-something-year-old man was speaking like a child, telling me his mother said she hated him. It pained my heart to hear him, and I could almost picture him lying in a fetal position as he mourned his mother's hate. I tried to encourage him with Psalm 27:10, but his hurt was so deep I don't know if he even heard me. I couldn't help but think, "How many messed up, dysfunctional lives are there as a result of rejection or being forsaken as a child?" The Spirit, once again, powerfully drove home the point to me that *we're all desperate for the Father's deep, unchanging love. In this life, there's no guarantee of any love but His.*

And this One whose faithfulness you can count on for all time says, as did Boaz, "listen to Me." He whispers, "I'm going to instruct you. I'm going to give you My Word. I'm going to drop some vital information in your ears. LISTEN. Take note. Take it to heart. Ponder it. Treasure it. Meditate on it. Then don't be a hearer only, but a doer of what I tell you. I know more, see farther and have a good plan. Listen to My voice as you seek My face. Come close in Spirit and Truth, and I will instruct you. Draw near and gain a heart of wisdom. I want to bless you. Come, listen to My Word."

Do you remember where you've been: that trip across those rugged, dangerous mountains, the aching in your heart and feet, the emptiness of your soul and all the futile things your flesh turned to? *Do you remember what Moab felt like?* Sometimes a helpful spiritual marker is remembering the feel of it, the taste of the darkness you once knew and the pain that gripped you. Then recall God's Word to you. Here's how I've paraphrased it:

"LISTEN TO ME, the time has come for your spirit to soar, for your Redeemer stands before you with open arms and widespread wings. You are face to face with the Man of Standing, the Lord of the Harvest, the Maker of the Fields. Bend your ear, child, and I will do as Isaiah 42:16 says, *'I will lead the blind by ways they have not known, along unfamiliar paths I will guide them; I will turn the darkness into light before them and will make the rough places smooth.'* I know the rough places of your feet and the hard places of your heart, and I am more than able to smooth them before your astounded eyes. You will go out with joy and be led forth in peace, for I am the One escorting you. You have been poor and blind; I will now give you My own storehouses and vision. You will eat until you are full, and then you will feed others. I will do as Song of Solomon 4:16 describes, *'I will blow upon your garden, that its spices may flow out.'* Morning will bring you word of My unfailing love, for you have put your trust in Me. I will show you the way you should go, because you have lifted your soul to Me (Psalm 143:8). You have heard and believed My Word, and will see My glory."

HEAR WHAT THE WORD HAS TO SAY ABOUT THE WORD. *"Let the Word of Christ dwell in you richly in all wisdom,"* (Colossians 3:16). *"How sweet are Your Words to my taste, sweeter than honey to my mouth!"* (Psalm 119:103). *"The unfolding of Your Words give light; it gives understanding to the simple,"* (Ps.119:130). *"You are my refuge and my shield; I have put my hope in Your Word,"* (Ps.119:114). *"Your Word, O Lord, is eternal; it stands firm in the heavens,"* (Ps.119:89). *"Your statutes are my delight; they are my counselors,"* (Ps.119:24). *"I run in the path of*

Your commands, for You have set my heart free," (Ps.119:32). "Your promise preserves my life," (Ps.119:50).

Continually throughout Scripture, the Lord urges us to listen to Him. He longs for us to hear and receive instruction, direction, promise and covenant. Dive into His Truth and ask for open ears. Record and remember what God says to you. Be extreme if you have to, radical if you must, crazy-looking if necessary, BUT REMEMBER THE WORD OF THE LORD. Get into it early in the morning, ponder it through the day and let it sing you to sleep at night. Keep it flowing in study, music, tapes and conversation. Do what Deuteronomy 6 says: impress it on your children, talk about it wherever you are, tie it around your neck and write it on the door-frames of your house. Make every effort necessary to hold onto and treasure the Word of the Living God. Continually drink in its pure, sparkling, living water. *Whatever comes from the Lord of Hosts is living, active, powerful, sharper than any two-edged sword and absolutely essential for life.*

TEST YOURSELF! Do you have selective hearing? Children are masters of it. We can be, too. Do you hear the promises of God, but not the call to holiness? Do you want His blessings without any sacrifice or letting go on your part? Do you ignore the quiet conviction of the Holy Spirit? Do you overlook the call to repentance, unless it concerns someone else? *WE NEED TO HEAR THE WHOLE COUNSEL OF GOD'S WORD, NOT JUST SELECT PASSAGES.* And we need to be on guard against anyone who teaches that way.

TO WHOSE VOICE ARE YOU LISTENING? In Deuteronomy 6:15 we're told, *"the Lord your God, who is among you, is a jealous God..."* He's jealous for your ears! He wants Truth to resonate through your soul, not some deceptive ploy of the Enemy. He wants you to hear divine wisdom, not worldly whims, and things beyond this world's comprehension (*"...My ways are not your ways nor My thoughts your thoughts...")*. 1 Corinthians 14 says,

"The natural man does not receive the things of the Spirit of God, for they are foolishness to him; nor can he know them, because they are spiritually discerned." We must ask the Lord for SPIRITUAL EARS.

Have you ever tried to hear from God while stomping around in a fit? Ever sought discernment in a situation, while unwilling to lay down your own thoughts and opinions, or looked for a Scripture to justify what your flesh wants? *Have you ever accused God of refusing to speak, when you were actually refusing to listen?* Deep calls to deep. If you want to hear the Lord's voice, you need to lay down your flesh and climb into the strong tower of the Spirit. Leave that state of frenzy and enter the place where you can be still and know—and hear. I like to call it the "Knowing Room." For me, the place where I sit and pray and open the Word is a chair in my dining room. Somehow, in that spot more than any other, I can sense my flesh falling away and Spirit and Truth rising up. I think it's because it's my appointment place, the spot where I know I'll encounter the King. I go expectantly, and He never fails to speak. (It's not always what I want to hear, mind you, but He speaks.) Except when company comes for dinner, I do nothing in that chair but seek the face and voice of Jesus.

The Lord isn't hiding His voice. He's given us His Word and invites us into His inner chamber. He *wants* to speak to and be known by us. But if we won't go to the Holy of Holies with the King of Glory, take the time to sit still before Him and search out His voice and heart through His inerrant Word, how can we expect to hear Him? Sitting quietly before Him isn't a natural state. In fact, it's foolishness to our flesh. But in the spiritual realm all things are possible—*even hearing the voice of GOD!* In Matthew 13:16, Jesus said, *"...blessed are your ears because they hear,"* and calls such hearts *"good soil"* that will yield a hundred, sixty or thirty times what was sown (Matt.13:23). He also said, *"What I tell you in the dark, speak in the daylight; what is whispered in your ear, proclaim from the roofs,"* (Matt. 10:27). He expects what He gives us not to merely remain with us, but to produce a harvest out of us.

Jesus said, *"My sheep listen to My voice..."(*John 10:27). His voice brings me to my knees, causes tears of amazement to well up within me and fills me with joy and wonder. The King of Kings wants to speak to the depths of our heart, soul, mind and strength. He wants to exhort, counsel, convict, instruct and absolutely astound. LET HIM!—"MY DAUGHTER, LISTEN TO ME."

Questions & Applications

1. **Do you have an "appointment place" with the Lord of Lords? Do you go expecting to hear His voice through His Word? If not, GET ONE! You're missing life's greatest thrill.**
2. **Ask the Holy Spirit for a fresh revelation of your position as a blood-bought child of the Most High God, then celebrate your adoption by the King of Glory.**

17

Don't Go

"Don't go and glean in another field and don't go away from here. Stay here with my servant girls," **Ruth 2:8.**

The first two words of this sentence, "Don't go," grab my heart. I hear the Spirit's voice in them saying, "There are plenty of places your heart can wander off to, *don't go*. Multitudes of fields exist out there where you can try to find a harvest, *don't go*. Many voices and worldly things urge you to come to them, *don't go*. Numerous philosophies, prideful, blind reasonings of men and scores of books full of men's thinking call out to you, *don't go*. Lots of emotions and experiences will attempt to deceive you, *don't go*. There are even people in the body of Christ who'll lead you astray, *don't go*."

In Deuteronomy 6:14 the Lord instructs, *"Do not follow other gods, the gods of the peoples around you."* Our culture is absolutely immersed in the worship of other gods. They don't look like the mythological deities of old and they're probably not carved from stone, but they're everywhere. Some are blatant, some more subtle. But they all want your attention and devotion. They're also tools of the Enemy who's bent on your destruction. Meanwhile, in the depths of our souls the voice of Christ cries out, "Don't go and glean in another field and don't go away from Me. STAY HERE." Stay here…

The "produce" of the field of Christ's presence is *matchless* on the earth. No other relationship can fill your heart and cause it to tremble and swell within you like the one He offers. No other promise is as faithful. No one else is capable of reaching into your soul and rescuing it. No other living thing can caress, nurture, nourish and empower you with absolute Truth. None other can cleanse and satisfy. If you expect anything or anyone to provide what's found in Him alone, you'll be disappointed every time. Jesus told a parable in Matthew 13:44 about a man who found a treasure hidden in a field who sold all he had to buy it. There's ONLY ONE FIELD containing *real value*. You can search your whole life but until you seek holy ground, you'll come up empty. Have you tried other fields? THEY'LL KILL YOU. They reap nothing but a harvest of destruction—things that steal, kill and destroy. RUN!

I know what it's like to visit the wrong field, trying to dig up something that doesn't even grow there; to seek a harvest from relationships, things, pleasure, personal strength, legalism, "to do" lists and self-righteousness. If that's where you are, let me save you some time: *change fields!* Consider 2 Corinthians 1:3-4, *"Praise be to the God and Father of our Lord Jesus Christ, the Father of compassion and the God of all comfort, who comforts us in all our troubles, so that we can comfort those in any trouble with the comfort we ourselves have received from God."* Allow me to comfort you with the comfort I've found.

Your Redeemer wants you to stand amid His glory, where His Word illuminates, His splendor grows and radiates and Spirit-produced fruit and pure love abound. He wants your life to be as Hosea 14:5-7 describes, *"he will blossom like a lily, like a cedar of Lebanon he will send down his roots, his young shoots will grow. His splendor will be like an olive tree, his fragrance like a cedar of Lebanon. Men will dwell in his shade, he will flourish like the grain, he will blossom like a vine, and his fame will be like the wine from Lebanon."* God wants that to be *us*—and to define all that's happening in our fields.

In Hosea 14:8, God says, *"...your fruitfulness comes from Me."* It's all from Him. HE IS the field of blessing and life, and He wants you in it—living in, hidden in and sowing in Christ alone. He alone is worthy, mighty, holy, powerful, faithful, righteous and glorious. His hands satisfy uniquely. The God-Who-Was knows the fields you've been in, and only He is able to redeem the time you wasted there. The God-Who-Is knows where your feet stand now and beckons, "Come to Me," or "Don't go." The God-Who-Is-To-Come wants to lead you into more than you've ever imagined. He wants you to experience the fullness of His harvest and the beauty and pleasure of His presence HERE ON EARTH. He wants you to see, as Psalm 27:13 says, *"the goodness of the Lord in the land of the living."* Go to His field and STAY THERE.

Be on guard against thinking that because you attend church or Bible study you're living in the right fields! Church membership isn't your Savior or the source of your life, Jesus Christ is. The best-laid plans and policies don't produce life in and through you, Christ alone does. No person or program can take on the role of the Holy Spirit in you. Don't expect them to. I'm not saying you should forsake your church or don't need corporate worship and sound biblical teaching. Just don't let church replace the Holy Spirit.

Have you learned, as I have, that we can have one foot in God's field, but another in sin—in pride, jealousy, fear, unbelief, bitterness...anything outside His Word and will? *That's unstable ground, a tottering place on the fence and a danger-*

ously lukewarm position. The Holy Spirit has convicted my heart about this, saying: "Don't you dare think that because you're in the right place with the King you're immune to the temptations of foreign fields. Adam and Eve lived in the ultimate field, the Garden of Eden, exactly where the Lord positioned them, a place of natural prosperity and perfect beauty, of satisfying work and the pleasure of walking with God Himself in the cool of the day. Yet, Eve was tempted. She changed her focus from the face of God to the face of deception and slipped right into fleshly reasoning. Can't you imagine her thinking, "Yeah, why *can't* I go there? Why *shouldn't* I have that? Sure looks good to me. God's denying me something." In fact, God *was* denying Eve something—trouble and heartache—but fleshly deception caused her to long for what would kill her.

The Prodigal Son was raised in a righteous, prosperous home. Yet, he, too, removed his gaze from the fields of home to those of the world, and off he went. I can just picture him, pockets stuffed with cash, running and shouting down that road he'd all too soon come trudging back on. Israel saw plagues fall on Egypt, Jehovah part the swirling waters and manna rain down from heaven, yet still stumbled into the foreign field of unbelief at every test. It's so easy to read of their wandering unfaithfulness and judge them, but how often have we also seen the mighty hand of God move on our behalf only to shrink back in fear and unbelief at the very next trial? Don't think that because the King has done something in your life, you couldn't step into sin in a New York minute.

Foreign fields surround us on every side. They're magnetic and want to draw us in. Why did Jesus teach us to pray, *"Lead us not into temptation...,"* if He didn't know we could absolutely fall headlong into it? ALL OF US. 1 Corinthians 10:12 says, *"So, if you think you are standing firm, be careful that you don't fall!"* That causes me to grab the feet of my King and ask Him to cement my prone-to-wander feet on holy ground, call out the troops, bring in the big guys, cover me in heavenly armor and draw His Sword. *I want Him to take my feet in His hands and hold them still unless He alone chooses to move them.*

When I was a teenager, I decided I wanted to marry a pastor because I thought they were SAFE, faithful and trustworthy. (Although I never actually dated someone who showed the slightest promise of being called to ministry—some weren't even Christians! There's flesh in action for you.) There was nothing spiritual about my endeavor, like wanting to be a helpmate to a Kingdom builder, I just wanted a man I could count on. It was all about me, myself and I. But I've learned that even clergy can venture far afield. *"All have sinned and fallen short of the glory of God,"* (Romans 3:23). How many men and women in ministry have fallen because of stepping into pride, lust, money, power or whatever the Enemy dangles before them to tempt their flesh? *That puts a holy fear in me. I remember that I'm dust and that my soul is just as feeble as Eve's, the Prodigal's, the Israelites' or anyone else who's stepped off the track.*

Don't dare judge someone by the "foreign field" they're in, as if you've never stepped in one yourself! Which one of us is without sin and worthy to cast stones of judgment? NONE. NOT ONE. *We may not all have tried the same field, but we've all tried something.* God forgive us for criticizing one another. I heard a well-known Bible teacher tell of a church where she was supposed to speak asking her not to come because the pastor found out she had a sinful past. HELLO! And he didn't? Seems to me that man was standing in a foreign field right there, one called judgmental, critical, legalistic and prideful. How quickly we can fall into those things ourselves!

The Lord has posted "No Trespassing" signs over all foreign fields throughout His Word, because He knows the land mines hidden in them, their empty promises, the fruitlessness of their crops and that we're open game for the Enemy there—we're exposed, easy prey, sitting ducks. God warns us, as He did Cain in Genesis 4:7-8, *"Sin is crouching at your door; it desires to have you, but you must master it."* Cain chose to dwell in the field of sin (in his case, jealousy and anger), and destruction came. All too often, we choose the same. We trespass, consciously or unconsciously in sampling "the deadly," thinking it's our right.

I find it interesting that Cain's judgment was to be a restless wanderer, and that his fields wouldn't yield crops. SIN WILL LEAD YOU FROM FIELD TO FIELD TO HOPELESS FIELD. Try this, try that, maybe here, now there's a plan, but it will never give you rest or fruit. You can't grow a righteous harvest on unholy, selfish, angry ground. *But thank God that, like the Prodigal Son and any who've wandered or run away, we're welcomed back to the field of feasting with the Lord through Christ.* He calls us home with mercy's bread, not condemnation's stones. Even if we go to distant places, He pursues us and waits for our return with a robe of righteousness ready for our shoulders, a ring of sonship fitted for our finger and a feast of celebration ready to begin.

As it says in Ephesians 2:4, *"God, who is rich in mercy, because of His great love with which He loved us, even when we were dead in trespasses, made us alive together with Christ."* How good is our God. How good! Psalm 103:10 states, *"...He does not treat us as our sins deserve or repay us according to our iniquities."* Thank God. Christ takes our unfaithful feet, cleanses them Himself from all the mud and filth of those foreign lands, and then establishes us in a field we could never buy and certainly don't deserve. That's the beauty of mercy and the glory of grace. I'll say it again, *He is good!*

Thanks to Christ, we don't have to hide in shame because of all our missteps. In Genesis 3:8-9, Adam and Eve tried to hide from God as He called out, "Where are you?" I believe He's still asking that question today. "Where are you?" Look at your feet. Where are they standing? You know the Lord; you've walked with Him in the cool of the day, *but have you walked somewhere else in the heat of it?* Has the pressure been turned up and sent you packing to the first field you could find? Are your feet being muddied by pride, legalism, self-righteousness, lust, materialism, fear, doubt, unbelief, unforgiveness, jealousy, self-pity, selfish ambition...? Or are they being bathed in the rivers of living water of God's Spirit and Truth, and washed in the wisdom and knowledge of God and the Word-made-life in you? Be honest and bare your soul before the Lord here; be as naked in your heart as Adam and Eve were in their flesh before they sinned. *Where are you?*

While the Lord always gives us a choice of fields, He desperately wants us to choose His. He wants us to stay because we're convinced in the depths of our soul that His is best, the ideal one for which we've been designed and destined. One morning I went to the table with the King, feeling utterly downcast and unworthy. I felt like Paul, declaring himself the chief among sinners. I bowed my head before the Lord, but really just wanted to hide in shame. I just couldn't fathom that He'd speak to me in that state, let alone whisper something through His Word that He wanted me to share. I began to pray, apologizing for my weakness. He then spoke a Word I've heard and spoken over and over that He then drove home with power in my soul: "IT'S NOT YOUR RIGHTEOUSNESS. IT'S MINE." *How I thank Him.*

Even after that, I came to Him another morning praying, "Lord, I feel so unworthy, so weak, so unsure of myself." He interrupted my thoughts with, "It doesn't matter how you feel. It matters what I say, what I have done and established and what I'll do. Don't give in to those same old emotions. I AM THE KING. I AM NOT ASHAMED TO CALL YOU SISTER, FRIEND and THE LOVE OF MY HEART. *Get out of your shame. It's not the field I have called you to walk in."* Blessed be Jehovah-tsidkenu, the Lord-Our-Righteousness!

In John 15:4, the Lord calls us to stay in His fields, to believe they're meant for our feet and to abide in Him, and He promises to remain in us. He reminds us that we can't bear fruit apart from Him, that we—the branch of the Lord—MUST remain in the Vine. The pull toward temptation is never stronger than the pull toward Truth. The Word promises that there's always a way to avoid the lure of those foreign fields. 1 Corinthians 10:13 puts it this way, *"No temptation has seized you except what is common to man. And God is faithful; He will not let you be tempted beyond what you can bear. But when you are tempted, He will also provide a way out so that you can stand up under it."* That's good news. That's news that should build confidence in our feeble hearts, lift our heads and steady our feet.

I love the picture in Genesis 24 where Isaac goes to meditate in his field. There he was, walking over ground the Lord had prospered, focusing his praise and thoughts on the King and pondering the things of God, when he heard someone coming. He looked up, *and there was Rebekah.* In the field of the Word and the place of praise, the Lord sent the answer to his prayer straight to him. He didn't have to go wandering around looking for what he desired. He just pressed into the Almighty, and blessing marched right up and found him. *Beautiful.*

As an old man giving his blessing to his son, Isaac said, *"Ah, the smell of my son is like the smell of a field the Lord has blessed...."* (Genesis 29:27). I WANT TO SMELL LIKE THAT!—like the fragrant field of Christ, not the stench of sin. When the Lover of my soul comes to meet with me, just as Rebekah came to meet with Isaac, I want to be found in

His rich harvest, in a field free of thorns and tares. I long to meet Him while meditating on Truth and blessing His Name, in earnest intercession and Spirit-produced fruit, in the divine instead of the temporal and on holy, established ground. I want Him to find both of my feet on His property. *And I want to stay there.*

Questions & Applications

1. **What field are you standing in—Christ's or the world's? If you find yourself with one foot in each, or both feet running headlong toward the pull of temptation, repent and run home to the open arms of the Father.**
2. **Thank the King of Kings for the amazing grace that has received you back from every foreign field you have run to. He is good, His mercy endures forever.**

18

Watch the Fields

"Watch the field where the men are harvesting, and follow along after the girls. I have told the men not to touch you. And whenever you are thirsty, go and get a drink from the water jars the men have filled," **Ruth 2:9.**

Before, Ruth was watching the harvesters, now Boaz is telling her to WATCH THE FIELDS. Look at the fields of the Lord. Something's happening, something's stirring beneath that soil. The Lord has set in place everything necessary for great harvest. WATCH THE FIELDS.

Psalm 65:9-13 beautifully describes the King tending them. Turn to this one and drink it in: *"You care for the land and water it; You enrich it abundantly. The streams of God are filled with water to provide the people with grain, for so You have ordained it. You drench its furrows and level its ridges; You soften it with showers and bless its crops. You crown the year with Your bounty, and Your carts overflow with abundance. The grasslands of the desert overflow; the hills are clothed with gladness. The meadows are covered with flocks and the valleys are mantled with grain; they shout for joy and sing."*

As I think about that, the Holy Spirit stirs my heart in response! The Lord has drawn us to His field, welcomed the prodigals home and is BUSY drenching the furrows of our hearts, leveling out those rough ridges and watering the seeds He's sown. His voice goes forth as the sound of many waters that calls out to our dry, thirsty souls. When the King's in the field, it can't remain the same! It can't help but shout for joy and produce spiritual growth, because wherever He plants His feet becomes holy ground. He's the One filling us with such harvest the overflow spreads to all with whom we come in contact; the One speaking, tilling, tending, watering, filling, smoothing, protecting and quenching the deepest of our thirsts. He is beauty and glory, and He's standing beside you. He wants to crown you with His bounty, clothe you with His goodness and make the fruitfulness of your heart obvious. He wants your desert places to bloom, and for praise the Enemy can't penetrate to surround you as the hills. Whether in the valley or on the mountaintop, there's cause for joy if the King is there. Wherever He stands, LIFE RISES UP.

Let the meadows be covered with flocks, the precious sheep of His pasture. Let all run to the Word of God and let revival winds shake the fields. Let's wear the mantle of Jehovah, the cloak of His anointing and favor. The King's busy in our fields, and fresh showers are falling. Praise Him! *Watch the field.*

I want to watch the harvest of God spring forth in my life, beginning in my heart and my home. Of course, I want to see Him move in our church, community, nation and to the uttermost parts of the earth, but I'm believing Him for a mighty crop in my family, lineage and seed. I'm trusting for salvation to cover those who don't know the Lord Jesus, and for my husband, children and I to walk in the power of the Holy Spirit. There are obvious attacks and attempts to discourage me in this, but I KNOW WHO'S GREATER,

AND I KNOW WHAT HE SAYS. So I plant my feet in the Word and prayer and bank everything on the faithfulness of the King. *And faithful He is.* I continually cry out to the Lord for my family, always sowing the power of His mighty Word through prayer, as well as through opportunities that arise in conversation. AND I EXPECT TO SEE SOMETHING STIR IN THE SOIL OF THEIR HEARTS.

Who knows what prayer sets in motion in our loved ones? With all my heart I believe our cries to the Lord on their behalf will cause life to stir in, and spring up out of, their hearts. My Dad's gotten interested in tracing the family tree, which could be fascinating or very scary! He told me about a relative who used to lead revivals in our hometown. He said he remembered him preaching at the local college when he was just a child. That moved me and made me wonder if that man cried out for his seed, of which I'm a part. Did he ask the King for every generation following in his family line to have a passion for Christ? Did he pray for revival not just for that college in that moment of time, but for a shaking of hearts down through the decades? I don't know, but *I'm sure going to ask for it!*

I used to think I had to search out some righteous soul to pray for my family and me because James tells us, *"The prayer of a righteous man is powerful and effective."* Well, I liked the "powerful and effective" part, but never grouped myself in the "righteous" category. THAT'S UNBELIEF. God has given all who have accepted Him the righteousness of Christ and says He's clothed us in it. Wear it well, and let it empower your prayers. I have several tangible ways to remind my heart daily of the position and purity the Lord Jesus brings our hearts. When my daughter was about 8 years old, she drew several precious posters for me. One is a sweet picture of a lady in a dress, and on the skirt of the dress is inscribed, "I am Jesus'Bride!" I have that, as well as the others, pinned to my closet wall to continually remind me who I am in Christ, and that He will absolutely move in the hearts of my children. When I pray and study in the mornings, I wrap a cozy afghan around my shoulders. If you drop in, you'll see it on my chair where all my books and papers are spread out. I wear it not just to keep warm, but to remind me of how the King has dressed me. It's a physical symbol of what the Lord says He's given us to wear—a mantle of anointing, a royal robe that glistens with the righteousness of Christ Himself. When insecurity and self-doubt arise, that little blanket reminds me who I am in the heart of the King. I wrap it around my shoulders, even if I'm having a "personal summer" and sweating bullets, because I need to remember. It's a spiritual marker to myself that I possess no goodness, except what the Holy One's given me. The Enemy wants to steal it away, but it's fastened, zipped, wrapped, sealed tight and forever mine. Wrapped up in the righteousness of Christ, I seek His face. *And I watch the fields.*

While pondering this subject, I heard the Holy Spirit so clearly in my heart ask, "What do you want to see rising up in your fields?" There was a sense of, "Let's talk about this. What is it you're really looking for?" I believe He poses that question to all of us. Pray carefully over your reply! Consider your motives and what drives your requests to God. Are the things you ask Him for rooted in the flesh or the Spirit? I cheated. I cried out, "OK, Holy Spirit, what do I need to ask for? Purify my motives, and let them reflect God's will!" I then read 1 John 5:14 that states, *"...if we ask anything according to His will, He hears us,"* and these things began to fill my heart:

> I want to see the King walking in the fields of my heart, sowing, reaping and having His way.
>
> I want to have "the spirit of wisdom and revelation in the knowledge of Him..." (Ephesians 1:17)

I want "to be strengthened with might through His Spirit in the inner man, that Christ may dwell in your hearts through faith; that you, being rooted and grounded in love, may be able to comprehend with all the saints what is the width and length and depth and height- to know the love of Christ which passes knowledge; that you may be filled with all the fullness of God." (Ephesians 3:16-19)

I want the Holy Spirit to produce His Galatians 5:22-23 fruit (love, joy, peace, longsuffering, kindness, goodness, faithfulness,gentleness, self-control) in great supply in me and my family.

I want my family and I to tremble before the Word of the Lord, and be continually astounded by it and passionate for it.

I want Christ alone exalted and glorified, and for anyone who looks at my heart to be able to say, "The King lives there and is great and glorious—and she smells like a field the Lord has blessed."

I want everyone I touch to gather MUCH from my life that causes them to hunger and thirst for the Lord and His Word, and to yearn for Him like never before.

I want fields free of tares, chains, strongholds, bondages and locusts—no devouring going on.

I want a passionate love for the Lord to rise up in my heart and in the hearts of those I love.

I want to spread everything the King's given me before Him, so that His hand can bless and multiply and feed many with it.

I want to walk in the "exceeding greatness of His power toward us who believe..." (Ephesians 1:19)

I want healing. Miracles. I want to be healed and to lay hands on the sick and see them recover.

I want everything and anything that will show forth the resurrection power of Christ.

I want LIFE abundant in Him, full of His strength and wisdom.

I want the living Word to be living and active in me.

I want every ounce of Him I can have on this side of glory, and I want to worship Him like I'm already on the other side.

(As soon as I wrote this, a whisper of doubt rose up as, "Well, aren't you going to look stupid asking for things like that? Aren't you quite the freak?" THAT MAKES ME WANT TO ASK ALL THE MORE!)

The Lord's reply? "THEN WATER IT." Soak the ground. Are you watering the desires of your heart with Scripture and cries to the King? Are you asking according to His will and Word? Are you hoping your fields will spring up because you're trying awfully hard, or because you're asking Him to cause it to be so? *Believe with all your heart that the Lord wants to cause something new to spring up in your life and wants a harvest to break through. Give Him a mustard seed of faith to work with, and ask for it all.*

I found a scrap of paper in the car one day on which I'd scribbled a question the Lord had planted in my heart, and it amazed me all over again. It was dated 9-14-05, and simply said, "Do you believe My power? Do you want to see it?" I had replied, "Yes, Lord! Holy Spirit, intercede and show me how to ask for its manifestation. I tremble before You, Lord Jesus." It was as if the King was wooing me, romancing me as a Groom with a Song of Solomon-kind-of-love. Like He was saying, "I'm so strong! Do you want to see my strength? Do you want a glimpse of what shakes all of heaven?" Yes, Lord. Yes. Stir something EVEN IN THIS SOIL, even here on my little plot of ground. *If you want this for yourself, then ask Him for it. Ask Him to rain His Word down on the soil of your heart and show you the power of His.*

There can be no harvest without rain! In the very beginning, in Genesis 2:5, we're told that *"no plant of the field had yet sprung up, for the Lord God had not sent rain upon the earth."* Nothing is going to sprout from dry ground. Just as land needs a soaking from heaven to produce, so do our hearts. In Exodus 16:4 the Lord told Moses, *"I will rain down bread from heaven for you."* He promises not just water, but sustenance—food delivered from His hand—the Bread of Life broken and showered down upon us freely with enough for all. Later, the Lord fulfills His promise to Moses as the Bible tells us, *"when the dew was gone, thin flakes like frost on the ground appeared on the desert floor."*

The bread fell gently in the night, quietly, softly, barely noticed. Don't think the Lord can't rain His Spirit and Word on you quietly. He's heard in whispers as well as rushing waters. Do we only think we've seen a move of God if it's a huge, everybody-talking-about, majorly obvious, shake the world kind of thing? While I do pray for that, I also pray for the soft falling in the night, for tender flakes waiting for me in the morning light, His daily bread, the just right portion for the day. I want to see Him move powerfully in coliseums, stadiums, churches and huge revivals, but also in the sweet dew of dawn, sitting at His feet.

How I pray for the Lord to rain HIMSELF down on us sweetly and softly, as well as powerfully, like He did with Paul on the Damascus road or Constantine, the Emperor of Rome. Constantine received a vision from God of a flaming cross in the sky and heard the words, "With this sign, you will gain victory." He then ended the brutal persecution of believers begun by Nero. That moves me to pray for all the leaders who oppose the Lord, to ask the King to give Muslims, Communists, secularists, atheists—whomever—VISIONS,

DREAMS AND LIFE-CHANGING EXPERIENCES OF HIMSELF and to release whole nations through them.

1 Peter 5:8-9 says, *"Be self-controlled and alert. Your enemy the devil prowls around like a roaring lion looking for someone to devour. Resist him, standing firm in the faith..."* Be forewarned: as we begin to see movement in our fields and little buds of promise start to blossom, we need to soberly watch for the Enemy's attempts to get his destructive hands on them. If he can't entice you to step out into foreign fields and wander restlessly through them, then he'll attempt to enter yours. BE ON GUARD. SUIT UP. Put your armor on, hold your Sword high and stand firmly beneath the banner of Christ. Isaiah 59:19 says, *"When the enemy comes in like a flood, the Spirit of the Lord will lift up a standard against him."* THE ENEMY WANTS TO RAIN SOMETHING DOWN ON YOUR FIELDS ALSO! He wants to flood your life with discouragement, opposition, persecution, fear, strongholds, insecurities, addictions, pride...whatever he perceives as a weak spot in you.

Attacks will come, but we know the hand of the Almighty is lifted forever against our Foe! A standard is raised on our behalf! I looked up the original meaning of "standard," because I never really understood what it was. In Hebrew it means, "a signal, a banner, a flagstaff." In this particular verse, however, it implies, "to vanish away, to chase, to take flight, to deliver." AT THE SIGN OF CHRIST OVER YOU, THE ENEMY MUST TAKE FLIGHT! He must flee! There's a sign posted over you that tells him, "NOT HERE, YOU DON'T! THIS FIELD IS PURCHASED. IT'S SPOKEN FOR. IT'S HOLY GROUND. IT'S ALREADY FULL AND FLOODED WITH GLORY! THERE'S NO ROOM FOR YOU HERE!"

It's time for us to look up and watch for the King to pour holy rain on our hearts and stir up our fields. We need to do what Elijah did in 1 Kings 18, where he stood his ground before the people of Israel, asked the Lord to show Himself strong and waited expectantly for rain to come and end the famine. He told King Ahab, *"Go, eat and drink, for there is a sound of a heavy rain,"* when there was nothing yet in sight (or hearing). Elijah heard it in his spirit before it hit the earth and spoke in faith. *Can you hear it?* Next, the prophet went to the top of Mt. Carmel, bent down, put his face between his knees (sounds like intercession to me) and told his servant to go and look toward the sea. SIX TIMES the servant returned reporting that nothing was happening. Yet, Elijah didn't give in to discouragement; he just kept praying and waiting on the Lord. Finally, the seventh time, the servant said, *"A cloud as small as a man's hand is rising from the sea."* IT'S COMING. It may look tiny, small enough to fit in a man's hand, but there's a downpour big enough for God's hand alone on its way, something no man could produce or take credit for. GET READY. WATCH.

Then it came. The sky grew black with clouds, the wind arose and a *heavy rain* fell—a drenching rain, a filling-up rain, a soaking, big-enough-for-desert-soil rain. BRING IT AGAIN, LORD. WE'RE WAITING EXPECTANTLY IN THE FIELD. I don't know if we're in the seventh watch or not, but we might be. In any case, don't give up. Put your head down and cry out for the rain. Keep praying and expecting. Be like Naaman in 2 Kings 5, keep dipping in the river, seven times if you have to, watching for God's hand to move. Naaman obeyed God in what seemed foolish to him and saw His power. May we also. Let it rain, blessed King, as your Word declares:

> *"You gave abundant showers, O God; You refreshed Your weary inheritance. Your people settled in it, and from Your bounty, O God, You provided for the poor,"* (Psalm 68:9-10).

"He will be like the rain falling softly on a mown field, like showers watering the earth," (Ps. 72:6).

"He will also send you rain for the seed you sow in the ground, and the food that comes from the land will be rich and plentiful," (Isaiah 30:23).

"...as the rain and the snow come down from heaven, and do not return to it without watering the earth and making it bud and flourish, so that it yields seed for the sower and bread for the eater, so is My Word that goes out from My mouth; it will not return to Me empty, but will accomplish what I desire and achieve the purpose for which I sent it," (Is. 55:10-11).

The Word of the Lord is on a mission in your heart. He has something for it to accomplish in you, a purpose in sending it your way. It's not by chance when a particular passage comes to your attention. Receive it as a planned shower from the Lord, a scheduled rain, a powerful truth meant to work its wonders in your soul. WATCH FOR THE CLOUDS. Soak in the rain of His Word. Dance in it, sing in it and delight in it. It will do exactly as He intends. It's living power and holy rain poured out. Celebrate, and *watch the fields*.

Questions & Applications

1. **Ask the Lord of the harvest for eyes to see and ears to hear what He is stirring in the fields of your heart.**
2. **Ask Him for faithfulness and endurance to watch and pray in Spirit and Truth, and then look up with expectation as the showers of heaven's mercy begin to fall.**

19

Favor for Foreigners

At this, she bowed with her face to the ground. She exclaimed, "Why have I found such favor in your eyes that you notice me—a foreigner?" **Ruth 2:10.**

Ruth was overcome with gratitude and astonishment at Boaz—amazed that someone like her could obtain favor from someone like him. SO AM I. My face is on the floor in astonishment and I'm forever overwhelmed to be allowed in the field of the King of Kings, gathering the inheritance of the royal priesthood. I'm continually astonished that I, a foreigner to everything holy, am permitted to hear His incredible voice, be wrapped in His compassion, sense the wonder of His attention and receive His consuming love. Why should the King of Glory notice me, much less shower *favor* upon my life? It's the sacrifice of the Redeemer's blood alone, not one thing I've ever done.

Ruth's amazement turned her face to the ground in humility and gratitude, and so does mine. When you feel God move in your heart, hear Him whisper through His Word and sense Him so near in the throes of intercession, where else can you go but to your knees? My time with the Lord and studying His Word begins face down in prayer and ends face

intercession- to plead or make a request on behalf of another down in the Word. Sometimes my face is literally on the table, bowed to God's voice spoken in Scripture. I bury my face in that precious Book, thank the Living God for piercing my heart with it and ask Him for all of it. It's precious—He's precious. *"To you who believe, He is precious,"* (1 Peter2:7). There is nothing more costly, valuable or astonishing than Him. *We're to bow to no other.*

The Lord knows that bowing to another will produce death in us. He wants to amaze us and establish our feet on holy ground. Over and over throughout the Word, we're told to forsake our idols and worship the true King of Kings alone. When the Law was given to Moses, God clearly commanded, *"You shall have no other gods before Me...you shall not bow down to them or worship them; for I, the Lord your God, am a jealous God,"* (Exodus 20:3 & 5).

The King of Kings wants you. He's jealous for your heart, because He wants to fill it with glory and passion and display His splendor in it. Bowing to other things crowds your heart, muffles your hearing and dims your eyes. *God has so much more for you than that.* There's no lack of "idols" seeking your worship. Fear wants you to bow to it, addiction calls your name, relationships, lack of relationships or envy of other relationships all want to be worshiped. We can idolize insecurity, jealousy, slander, pride, legalism and self-righteousness, or worship things in our culture, home and family, even our own plans and opinions. We can bend the knee to experiences, pleasure, discouragement, condemnation, defeat, anger or rejection, and can venerate the words of men, or a crowd mentality— whether good or bad—instead of the Word of God.

We can even wrongly revere good and holy things. In Revelation 19:10, when the Apostle John received a word from an angel, he fell at *the angel's feet* to worship him and was told, *"See that you do not do that! I am your fellow servant, and of your brethren who have the testimony of*

Jesus. Worship God!" If John, the beloved disciple of Christ, could bow before something in error, surely we can too. We may or may not receive a visitation from a divine messenger, but we can certainly elevate people in ministry (or a ministry, itself) to dangerous heights. Or we can worship a dream the Lord has given for our lives more than the Lord Himself—or a godly vision, program or goal. Yes, even we who desperately love the King are very capable of committing idolatry.

As the children of Israel were being led toward the Promised Land, God said, *"Do not bow before their gods or worship them or follow their practices. You must demolish them and break their sacred stones to pieces,"* (Exodus 23:24). The Lord makes it pretty clear here how He feels about the influence of false gods and cheap worship. We're to leave *no room* for such deceptive things in our lives—to have absolutely no tolerance for them. The Enemy is looking for any little thing he can grab onto that he can use to overwhelm you. Is there anything in your heart not of God, no matter how small, that you refuse to utterly and completely destroy or release? It'll trip you, deceive you and give the Enemy a foothold from which he'll try to condemn and defeat you. *Break it to pieces with the mighty Sword of Truth.*

Jeremiah 23:29 speaks of the power of that Sword: *"Is not My Word like a fire?" declares the Lord, "and like a hammer that breaks the rock in pieces?"* I've had to let His Word break many things in my life to pieces and I am sure there's more to go. I've had to grab the Sword of the Word of God and break down fear, doubt, insecurity, jealousy... many things have needed to be demolished by Truth.

We need to ask for discernment, for eyes to see what we're bowing to. Just because you attend church doesn't mean your heart's right. Ask for truth in the innermost parts of your soul. Whatever you find, the Sword is strong enough to handle it. God's hammer is big enough. His blazing fire is hot enough to melt whatever hard thing you have to face, and no matter how deeply rooted or how long you've bent low before it, it can't stand before heaven's flame. Thank God, Christ is still all about destroying yokes and setting captives free—to be free, indeed.

In 2 Kings 17, Israel falls into the worship of false gods as they began to follow the practices of the nations around them. Verse 35 says, *"They feared the Lord, yet served their own gods—according to the rituals of the nations from among whom they were carried away."* The scary part of this account is that, while they were falling before false gods, they still claimed to fear the Lord. That sends me to my knees, asking Christ to guard my heart for Him alone and never let me be so brazen as to say I worship Him, while bowing to some politically correct trend (even in the Church), like an ear-tickling word or being entertained instead of challenged with God's Truth. Do we say we love the pure Word, but then try to make it mesh with the world? I've seen a lot of entertainment in the Church and much designed to make us feel good, but none of it thrills my soul and brings me to my knees like *the Word itself.*

The Word of God is holy, inerrant and glorious. It is power breathed from the very mouth of God, our only weapon, victory and life. And, yes, it's sometimes offensive as it confronts our hearts. God forgive us for cherishing any other "word." If you're bowing before anything but the Risen Christ, your face will find the floor all right—but in defeat instead of worship. Don't do it. The King wants all your heart through which to bless, prosper, fill, thrill and bring a harvest. It grieves Him when you withhold any part of it from Him. Give it up. He'll replace it with glory.

I saw news coverage recently of a New Age festival somewhere. It looked so utterly ridiculous, so reminiscent of ancient false god and pagan worship that I thought, "How in this day and age can that kind of thing still be going on?" I felt the Lord respond in my heart, "The Enemy has the same old tricks up his sleeve—the same ancient deceptions—he just tries to repackage them for each generation. He's still desperate to steal My worship." The Enemy hasn't changed. He wants to deceive until you bend the knee to him. He's after your heart, craves your attention and worship, and ultimately desires to take the place of the Most High in your life. Don't bow to his whispers. Ask the Lord Jesus, echoing His own prayer, to lead you far away from temptation and deliver you from every evil scheme. Don't bow to shame, condemnation or guilt. Don't bend to unbelief, doubt, fear or insecurity. *Don't worship anything but the King.*

Continually renew your mind in Truth so it's strong enough to stand before anything the Enemy wants to dangle before you. I need the Word to renew my thoughts *daily*, or I quickly slip into fleshly thinking. As you dig into Scripture, it begins to burn in you like a mighty fire, and wisdom and revelation well up within you through the power of the Holy Spirit. As your eyes open to Truth and the Word starts coming to life in *you,* instead of a pastor or someone famous, you can't help but bow before the Lord of Lords. Your knees will hit the floor with sheer wonder at being in the presence of the King. Gratitude and amazement that He'd dare send a glimpse of glory *your* way will leave you face down before the Holy One.

Then, you need to ask God for something else. Yes, we must open our hearts, examine what they're worshipping and get real before the Lord, but then we should ask to see His glory, His face, His heart—all of Him we can take in. *And as He answers that prayer, you'll bow again at His precious feet.* He wants to be known by us, and I've found that when we start earnestly asking to know Him better, He won't deny us. He opens up His Word and makes it come to life. He'll meet you as you cry out His Name and unveil wonders to your heart. To me, freedom from all that used to bind me is a wonder. Joy in the Lord is a wonder. Knowing the Holy Spirit is doing His mighty thing in my heart is a wonder. To sense His presence in my prayer closet is a wonder. To see Him work miracles is a wonder. Salvation itself is a wonder to top all wonders! *No wonder Isaiah calls Him "Wonderful."*

Ruth was amazed at Boaz welcoming a foreigner into his barley field. According to the Law, she could have been rebuked and sent away. How much deeper should be our amazement that Jesus brought the Gentiles into His Jewish bloodline, as it says in Ephesians 3:6, *"that the Gentiles should be fellow heirs of the same body, and partakers of His promise through the Gospel."*

In Acts 10:34 Peter states, *"In truth I perceive that God shows no partiality,"* meaning He makes no distinction between Jews and people from other nations who believe in Christ. Verse 43 says, *"through His Name, whoever believes in Him will receive remission of sins."* In Isaiah 49:6 the Lord God declares of Christ, *"It is too small a thing that You should be My servant to raise up the tribes of Jacob, and to restore the preserved ones of Israel; I will also give You as a light to the Gentiles, that You should be My salvation to the ends of the earth."* Isaiah 45:22 says, *"Look to Me, and be saved, all you ends of the earth! For I am God, and there is no other."*

Foreigners (sinners) are welcome in God's house! Now, that's something to BOW over! That's enough to send you to your knees in gratitude. Awareness of the beauty and miracle of salvation should stir our hearts every day and never be taken for granted. Christ is the King who rescues us with His own hand, saying to the prisoner, "Go forth," and to those in darkness, "Show yourselves" (Isaiah 49:9). I can't remain standing in the light of that knowledge.

Do we really grasp the beauty of being welcomed into the intimate field of the King of Kings, a place we absolutely don't deserve to be? Are we continually celebrating that in our souls and letting the joy of it be our strength? *How I ask the Lord to keep me rejoicing in His salvation.* While we *should* rejoice in the glory of our salvation, we WILL bow before the power of His mighty Name. Philippians 2:9-11 says, *"Therefore God has also highly exalted Him and given Him the Name which is above every name, that at the name of Jesus every knee should bow, of those in heaven, and of those on the earth, and of those under the earth, and that every tongue should confess that Jesus Christ is Lord, to the glory of God the Father."* Let that sink in. No matter who you are, when Jesus returns at the Second Coming, *everything and everyone* is going to hit their knees. He's the King of Glory, and nothing can stand before Him.

Picture this scene from the Word: the Name is spoken, and praise immediately goes forth. Knees fall and worship rises merely at the power of Jesus' name. From the earth to the Pit to the far corners of heaven, Christ is exalted, lifted high and worshiped. His Name is like the sound of rushing waters, like streams on dry ground, like a shelter, a shade and a shield. Psalm 72:9 & 11 tell us, *"Those who dwell in the wilderness will bow before Him...yes, all kings shall fall down before Him; all nations shall serve Him."* No name will ever rise above His. In every place and circumstance, every knee will fall to the floor at the sound of His Name. I pray we'll be wise enough to tremble and bow before it *now.*

Do you realize just to Whom you're bowing? We're told over and over in Scripture that when the risen Christ appeared to men, they dropped like lead weights. In Revelation 1:13-18, John describes the King of Glory who stood before him, *"...His eyes were like flames of fire, His feet were like bronze, His voice thundered like the sound of rushing waters...a sharp, double-edged sword came from His mouth, His face was as bright as the sun in all its brilliance."* John's response? *"When I saw Him, I fell at His feet as though dead."* That one little Scripture has become the cry of my heart. I want to see Him!—in his Word, in prayer, in my heart, in my home, in our church, in our nation and in the ends of the earth. I long to remain at his feet, bowing in worship and intercession, letting Him speak over me and exalt Himself, with my flesh and all its selfish desires falling as though dead.

PRAY FOR EYES TO SEE THE KING! When you enter the Holy of Holies through the blood of Christ and catch a glimpse of His passion for you, or soak your heart in the Word of God and find Jesus revealed and glorified to you *personally,* how can you not fall before Him as did John? When you hear Him whisper in your spirit and experience Him moving in your life, how can you not tremble in awe? IT'S NO SMALL, CASUAL THING TO HAVE CHRIST, THE KING, DWELLING IN YOUR HEART! IT'S THE STUFF OF TREMBLING, FALLING FACE DOWN AND FOREVER BENDING THE KNEE. *Forgive us, mighty Lord, for when we've approached Your holy throne in pride, self-sufficiency, casualness and even with the boredom of religion and tradition. YOU'RE THE GREAT I AM, THE KING OF KINGS AND LORD OF LORDS, THE FIRST AND LAST, THE BRIGHT MORNING STAR. Help us to see You and bow in true, deep worship.*

Many times in the book of Revelation John is told, *"COME AND SEE."* And over and over he responds, *"So I looked...and I saw..."* We, too, are invited to COME AND SEE. No matter how long we've walked with the King of Glory, there's always more to learn of Him. Our two little, earthly eyes haven't even *begun* to drink in all of Him. *You're meant to see the King. LOOK, LOOK, LOOK!!!* He isn't hiding Himself. He's spread Himself out on the Cross and throughout His Word, and repeatedly urges us to come see Him, draw near and listen, drink in living water and let Him astound. And I, for one, want to go.

Questions & Applications

1. **Are you rejoicing in and bowing before the unspeakable gift of your salvation? If not, ask the Lord to restore to you, or maybe give you for the first time, its joy.**
2. **Ask for expanded vision to see greater and greater glimpses of the King of Glory through His perfect, living, powerful Word.**

What your thoughts on:

① Intercession — to plead or make a request on behalf of another —

② Forgiveness —
How can I know that I have truly forgiven another?

Tell God you forgive & every time thoughts start working on you again — stop — say it again

Don't have to be best friends anymore Just move on

Don't have to like them

20

Stepping Out and Stepping Under

Boaz replied, "I've been told all about what you have done for your mother-in-law since the death of your husband—how you left your father and mother and your homeland and came to live with a people you did not know before. May the Lord repay you for what you have done. May you be richly rewarded by the Lord, the God of Israel, under whose wings you have come to take refuge," **Ruth 2:11-12.**

Have you ever had to LEAVE ANYTHING to enter the fields of Christ? Have you had to let His fire burn away a few things? Has the hammer of His Word had to break bits of your heart to pieces? Have you had to pick up and walk away from something, no matter how settled in it you were? Have you been stretched and challenged as your feet were put in motion? Did you have to venture away from the familiar? Did you have to leave a few folks behind who were encouraging and enabling you to stay in a wrong place? Did you "come out and be separate," when you weren't sure you wanted to? The Hebrew for "leave" means, "to let go, to relinquish, to put distance between." Has the Lord called you to do that with anything in your life?

Through the years, the Lord has called me many times to walk away from something I was settled in—some earthly things, some spiritual things and some patterns of thinking—for something new. Slowly, surely, step-by-step, He's admonished me to STEP OUT AND STEP UNDER; to step out of me, and step under His wing. He's called me to step out of some relationships, out of a college sorority and out of self-reliance and independence. He's urged me to step out of guilt, shame and condemnation; out of bondage and unbelief; out of strongholds and deceptive thinking; out of some worldly entertainment that I saw no problem with for years; out of rationalizing, excuses and my own shallow reasoning; out of a pair of earrings; out of working outside the home and out of plans made by me. *And I've never regretted a single step.*

He's never called me to leave anything without replacing it with something SO MUCH SWEETER AND BETTER—namely HIMSELF, and Truth, and fire, and passion and satisfaction I didn't know existed on this earth. No matter how huge the decision to obey and step away from whatever it was appeared at the time, looking back it was really *nothing*. How pitiful it would have been to stay where I was in rebellion, and what glory I'd have missed. I'VE NEVER REGRETTED STEPPING OUT WITH THE KING. Neither will you.

Scripture presents numerous examples of divinely appointed people who stepped out in faith, not knowing the outcome but trusting the One who was urging them forward. In Genesis 12:1, the Lord said to Abram, *"Leave your country, your people, and your father's household and go to the land I will show you."* The Lord promised His blessing, but Abram had no map, no itinerary and no hotels to book along the way. He didn't even know what country he'd wind up in. *But he left. He trusted the King and packed up.* He moved where and when the Lord said and set up altars along the way to express the worship of his heart. Still, he must have had some fear about the whole thing, because the Lord comforted him by saying, *"Do not be afraid, Abram. I am your shield, and your very great reward,"* (15:1). The very same God calls us forward in faith and, when it scares us to death, consoles us with His mighty, active Word. I'm also encouraged to know the Lord called Abram at the age of 75. When I start feeling sorry for myself over wasted years, that fact makes me feel very young and *right on time.*

In Genesis 19, when God calls Lot out of Sodom, he's told, *"Flee for your lives! Don't look back, and don't stop anywhere in the plain!"* Sometimes the Lord calls you away TO SAVE YOUR NECK! He knows, whether you do or not, what's about to come down! In Lot's case, it was burning sulfur literally rained down from heaven—complete destruction. It's critical that we shield ourselves with faith and not look back! Lot's wife let her guard down, gazed backward, was paralyzed and turned into a pillar of salt. She was the salt of the earth all right, but totally useless, hard, lifeless and frozen where she was. *"But we are not of those who shrink back and are destroyed, but of those who believe and are saved,"* (Hebrews 10:39). God help us to obey and never look back!

It may not be a physical place like Sodom, but the Lord will absolutely call us to leave other things we're settled in. It may be some dangerous habit that's about to destroy our lives, or something that feels right but is far outside His will for our lives. We may be settled in a selfish, stagnant or comfortable place. Moses was taken out of both the comforts of Egypt and his new life as a shepherd to lead the Exodus. *That was huge!* He was called to be bold when he didn't want to be bold, and to lead God's people when he didn't feel adequate. *We may be asked to do likewise,* but the

SAME POWERFUL KING that parted the sea and utterly destroyed the pursuing enemy leads us. He can do it for us, too. I'm banking on it.

In 1 Samuel 1, Hannah had to reject her concern about what people thought of her and cry out to the Lord in His temple. In verses 9-14, she stands up and begins to weep and cry out to God, begging Him for a son, then continues to pray in her heart. As she poured out her soul, her lips moved but she made no sound. Eli, the priest, thought she was drunk. *She was willing to step out of sophistication and into deep intercession.* And the Lord answered her cry with a little prophet named Samuel.

Are we willing to pour out our hearts to the King even when we might be judged or ridiculed for it? Hannah was crying out *in the temple*. She was praying to God *in sight of the priest*—and was still criticized! We have to put our focus on the Lord alone and spill our souls before Him, no matter what others think. At a Ladies Retreat a few years ago, the Lord spoke a direct word to my heart, and I began weeping before Him right there. Slobbering mess that I was, I found myself wondering what people around me were thinking. *Oh, Lord, help me not be directed by the opinions of people, but by Spirit and Truth alone! Help me not be ashamed to cry out to You even in the presence of others!*

Jonah was called to step out of himself to minister to people he didn't think deserved it. He wanted to see them get what they had coming. Reflecting on this reminds me of how the Lord has burdened me to pray for terrorists and people in darkness to receive dreams and visions of Christ. It would be very easy to wish evil for those who greatly threaten our nation, instead of mercy. But we're called to put away our judgments of others and do what the Lord wants us to do for them, worthy or not, just like Jonah. That "unworthy" person may not be a part of international terrorism, they may share your family name, neighborhood or church. We aren't called to pray only for those who pray for us or only bless those who bless us! One test of the heart is this question- Can you pray blessing for a person? Can you take that one whom your flesh resists to the altar and cry out for them? Do you join your prayers with those who pray corporately for them, or do you shrink back? Do you long to see them prosper, even as their soul prospers? Yes, even *that one*. Even that hard one. Even that one that let you down. Hurt you. Abandoned you. Gossiped about you. Rejected you. Can you honestly pray for their blessing? If not, check your love. Ask the Lord to give you His Holy Spirit produced fruit of divine love so that you are able to pray effectively and share the Word with even those hard ones. Even as I type this, the Lord is bringing to mind one I cannot love on my own- one that requires a holy infusion of grace to be able to step out of feelings and minister blessing. God help us to step out of our flesh and minister to the difficult ones, too. Put a missionary heart in us, Lord!

Paul had to leave behind his "good" reputation as a persecutor of Christians, an upstanding Jew and a student of tradition in order to step under the wing of Christ. He had to physically step out to spread the Gospel on journeys that involved GREAT difficulties. *We may have to leave behind our reputations according to the world's standards, too.* The disciples had to leave their family businesses to Daddy and depart from all they'd ever known. They had to leave behind their nets, their obscurity, the comfort of blending in and not causing a scene and their fear and faithfully follow the King, even before the Cross.

Peter had to leave guilt and condemnation far behind after he denied Jesus three times. He had to step out from under that heartache, accept forgiveness and let the Lord restore him. Jesus taught about putting away, or stepping out of, dead things in our hearts—dry, fruitless branches. *"Every branch in Me that does not bear fruit He takes away;*

and every branch that bears fruit He prunes, that it may bear more fruit," (John 15:2). Don't mourn over the dead things the Lord takes away, and don't squirm and twist when He prunes them off. HE'S NOT HARMING YOU. He's perfecting, strengthening and establishing you to flourish and bear His glory! Search your heart with Him and take part in the process. Is there anything dead you need to repent of and forsake, such as self-righteousness, tradition, pride or cherished sin? Is anything in your heart in need of a trim, like your priorities, relationships, appetites or desires? Any good thing that's grown wild? *Step out and let Him do His thing in perfecting you.*

Isaiah 5:1-2 presents a parable about a vineyard established in a fruitful place and good growing conditions, saying *"...so He expected it to bring forth good grapes, but it brought forth wild grapes."* As a result, the vineyard's hedge of protection was taken away, its walls were broken down, the land was laid waste and covered with briers and thorns, no rain fell and a deadly lack of harvest resulted. *The wild, unpruned, dead stuff in your heart leads to captivity, waste and drought. Let the Lord remove it—it's so WORTH IT.* A few verses down, examples of "wild grapes" are listed, including calling evil good and good evil, substituting darkness for light and light for darkness and bitter for sweet and sweet for bitter, being wise in our own eyes and prudent in our own sight, becoming intoxicated by the world, justifying the wicked, taking bribes, denying justice to righteous men and rejecting the Word of God. Sounds to me like pride, self-righteousness, opposing God's Truth by dictating our own, falling for the world's way of thinking and being bought off by its charms, looking the other way when injustice rages around us, being quiet and letting evil have its way, watering down the Word and seeking teachers who tickle our ears instead of boldly teaching Truth. *Are you on your knees yet?*

That picture of wild grapes convicts my heart and applies to the whole body of Christ. As Americans, the Lord has graciously settled us where we have His mighty Word readily available and are surrounded by godly teachers; where we have the power of His Holy Spirit and the privilege of coming together in deep intercession; where we can gather as a body without the fear of armed guards dragging us away or bombing our church and where so many resources are available we can't even read them all. *What do you think the King expects to see rising from our fields? Forgive us, Father, for producing anything apart from Your perfect plan! Cut us, prune us, revive us and let Your Name alone be glorified through us.*

The King won't stand among dead, defiled things! From the very beginning, in Genesis 23, we see the deceased are to be BURIED! When the Law was given, the Lord said to stay away from dead things and that a corpse is unclean. If the Lord has killed something in you, He's asking you to *step away from it!* Don't keep going back and touching it! Let the past be the past. Put it outside the camp of your heart. As Christ walks there and sheds His glory, He wants to make your heart HOLY GROUND. LET HIM!

Releasing the dead things you've held onto and stepping out of them will lead to GLORY. So how do you lay them down? REPENT. Acknowledge the sin—stop making excuses or rationalizing it—confess it and let the power of the Cross remove it from your heart. There's POWER in repentance and death in excuses. *If you don't come to the King in the blessing of repentance and forgiveness, you're choosing to hold onto a corpse.* That's graphic, but true. Give it to the only One who can handle it. The King doesn't come with condemnation to prune you, but with compassion and mercy because He has SO MUCH MORE FOR YOU.

Isaiah 40:4-5 says, *"Every valley shall be exalted and every mountain and hill brought low; the crooked places shall be made straight and the rough places smooth, the glory of the Lord shall be revealed, and all flesh shall see it together; for the mouth of the Lord has spoken."* Picture that verse written over your own heart—every humble thing lifted high, every hindering thing brought low, every crooked, rough and dark place made smooth, preparing a highway for the King of Glory to walk in your life—*that sounds like glory to me.* (Just because you're moving forward with the Lord doesn't mean you don't have things in your heart you need to leave behind! I've found the Lord so patient and longsuffering with me as He's helped me unpack my "stuff" one by one. As He has, and is still doing, I've not been overwhelmed, except by His great, amazing, unfathomable, endless MERCY.)

Like others throughout the Bible, Ruth had to leave much behind. Look at your own life. Would you withhold from the Lord of Lords something that needs to be brought low and left behind? Would you refuse to let Him work on that which is crooked, rough and piercing in your heart, or leave it so crowded with flesh He has no place to stand? Would you hold onto something good, even if it wasn't His best? Do you trust yourself more than the King of Kings? HE ALONE IS THE MOST HIGH AND WORTHY OF OUR TRUST AND PRAISE. HE'S WORTH SO MUCH MORE THAN ANYTHING WE HAVE TO LEAVE BEHIND.

Isaiah 40:25-31 says, "*'To whom then will you liken Me, or to whom shall I be equal?' says the Holy One. Lift up your eyes on high, and see who has created these things, who brings out their host by number; He calls them all by name, by the greatness of His might and the strength of His power; not one is missing. Why do you say, O Jacob, and speak, O Israel: 'My way is hidden from the Lord, and my just claim is passed over by my God'? Have you not known? Have you not heard? The everlasting God, the Lord, the Creator of the ends of the earth, neither faints nor is weary. His understanding is unsearchable. He gives power to the weak, and to those who have no might He increases strength. Even the youths shall faint and be weary, and the young men shall utterly fall, but those who wait on the Lord shall renew their strength; they shall mount up with wings like eagles, they shall run and not be weary, they shall walk and not faint."*

This is *your God*. Oh, that we'd see His glory, His awesome magnificence, His beauty, His holiness, His strength and His power! Look at His love abounding to us and at the salvation oozing from His wounds! This is the One who rescues us and calls us forward. THIS IS THE ONE TO WHOM YOU RUN. Leave all the dead stuff behind and RUN ON, THEN WALK WITH THE KING AND LET HIM LIFT YOU UP TO SOAR BENEATH HIS WINGS. That's where we find refuge, just like Ruth and all the other men and women in Scripture who stepped out of themselves and found strength and comfort in the Lord.

Questions & Applications

1. **Thank the Lord of mercy for every place He's led you to step out of yourself and under His mighty wing.**
2. **What are you still holding onto that you know the Lord wants you to step out of?**
3. **Ask Him to do a complete work in your life, and to lead you forward in His strength.**

21

Soaring Under the Wings of the King

"May the Lord repay you for what you have done. May you be richly rewarded by the Lord, the God of Israel, under whose wing you have come to take refuge," **Ruth 2:12.**

How awesome are the wings of the Lord Most High! Boaz spoke volumes with the simple phrase, *"under whose wing you have come to take refuge."* Ruth desperately needed a physical refuge, a place of safety in which to settle and call home, but she also needed a spiritual refuge, a sanctuary where she could find Truth. She'd been heartbroken, uprooted and devastated, had grown up under a cloud of lies instead of the cloud of glory and had seen everything she counted on fail her. *Yet, something about Naomi made her say, "I'm going with you. Your God is going to be my God. I'm going to settle on the same ground you settle on. I'm going to run to the same sanctuary you do."*

I pray that when others see my heart, they'll say the same thing, NEVER NOTICING ME, BUT THE KING WHO DWELLS THERE: *"I'm running to the same God she runs to, because He's powerful in her. I want to settle on the same ground she has and want the same refuge and strength. I need that same mighty Wing to cover my heart also."*

I don't care who you are or how strong you think you are, you desperately need the covering of the Lord. The first biblical reference to God's wings occurs in Exodus 19:4-6, when the Lord spoke to Moses on Mt. Sinai: *"You yourselves have seen what I did to Egypt, and how I carried you on eagle's wings and brought you to Myself. Now if you obey Me fully and keep My covenant, then out of all nations you will be My treasured possession. Although the whole earth is Mine, you will be for Me a kingdom of priests and a holy nation."* That's so powerful! Jehovah states that He *personally* carried His people out of bondage on His wings. He reminds them whose power set them free and makes a promise too amazing to fully grasp: *"You will be My treasure...a kingdom of priests"* (not just a select few!)... *"a holy nation."* He carried them out of Egypt's strongholds beneath His wings right to HIMSELF.

God's Word is eternal and prophetic. It reaches down through the generations to this moment and says to MY HEART AND YOURS, "Don't you see whose wing you're under? Don't you remember the bondage you were in back there, and how far I have carried you from it? Do you see My strength and power? Does it dazzle and amaze you the way it should? Walk on with the King, and I will make you My treasure, My delight, My priesthood and My holy, spotless Bride. I am for you, and I've got you covered." This is a good place to shout hallelujah!, even if you're not the shouting kind.

Wings show up again in Exodus 25, when the Lord is giving instructions for setting up His tabernacle. Because everything in the Old Testament is a foreshadowing of Christ, and we know there's nothing insignificant in the Word of God, we understand that these directions are powerful, significant and prophetic. Look at the description of the cherubim on the ark of the Covenant. Made of hammered gold, there were two of them, one on each end of the cover (also called the Mercy Seat). They faced each other and looked downward, with their wings spread toward each other, overshadowing the Ark. *And that's where the Lord promised to meet with His people and speak.* There's the reward for those, like Ruth, willing to leave Moab behind—stepping into the very presence of the Lord God Almighty and speaking with the King—the same one awaiting us.

This description really strikes me. Those cherubim weren't placed on the Ark just to be cute! There's purpose in what they represented and deep layers of meaning. For starters, they faced each other. We're called to do the same. When we come before the King, we're not to turn our backs on one another! We're to enter His presence in unity, as fellow members of a priesthood and holy nation, not pridefully thinking we've got it all together and can survive on our own. WE'RE A BODY AND NEED TO ACT LIKE ONE—no matter how different we are. Sometimes we'd rather look somewhere else, pretend we don't see each other and split ourselves up into comfortable little denominations or even groups and cliques within our church. I've wanted to run far away from people many times, instead of facing them, loving them in the Lord and serving together in His presence.

The eyes of the cherubim looked toward the cover, focused on the seat of mercy, and that's where we, too, should fix our eyes. Otherwise, we're going to be let down every time. *There's nowhere else to look but to the mercy of Christ.* The gaze of those angels was set. It was hammered out in pure gold and would never change. As we allow the Lord to break our prideful hearts with the hammer of His Word, He covers them in pure gold and transforms our worship until we can't help but keep our eyes on Him.

Picture the whole ark of the Covenant with me. It was a chest made of acacia wood, overlaid in gold inside and out (we need to model outwardly the deep truths inside, found in the inner sanctuary). God's testimony (the tablets of the Law) was placed inside, and a cover of pure, solid gold was set on top, called the Mercy Seat—not gold-plated wood this time! (Christ is the Mercy Seat. He's absolutely PURE.) Gold cherubim were on each side, spreading their wings upward and looking to the place of mercy. The Mercy Seat rested over the Word, and the Lord met the people there in power and intimacy and spoke Truth.

Just like the common wood of the Ark, we're shaped into a vessel to carry the very presence and Word of Christ. Through amazing grace, He puts His testimony securely inside our hearts. With His own blood and hands He shapes us and then covers us with the pure gold of heaven. He invites us to come, no matter who we are or what we've done, to the seat of pure mercy, promising to meet us there, purify and cleanse us and spread over us not angel's wings, BUT HIS OWN. And beneath those mighty wings He says we'll mount up and SOAR.

I don't know what you need to soar out of, but I know Whose wing to get under and where the seat of mercy rests: *in the Cross*. When you position your heart there, you place your life beneath God's eternal covering that will NEVER fail you or fall short. It ushers you into the presence of the King of Glory, the Lord of Lords, whose wings are big enough to extend over every area of your life—over every bitter wound, deep hurt, disappointment, regret, blatant or hidden sin, rebellious act or thought, puffed up, prideful way of thinking, self-righteousness, fear and doubt, questions of your heart and whispers and lies of the Enemy. *He's big enough*. Thank God, He's big enough.

This is the stuff heaven celebrates. The Bible says there's great rejoicing in heaven when every sinner comes to Christ.

When you bring your heart to the Cross, to that great seat of mercy, faces of angels watch and rejoice, all of heaven sings and the heart of the King pounds with delight. Did you ever think about how precious your one, little heart is to God's entire kingdom? Whether you're appreciated here or not, the celestial host celebrates your faith in the King. The Lord draws near to meet with and speak to you, angels wait to be commanded concerning you and the Lord Jesus, Himself, intercedes for you with passion and love that can't be grasped. *We should celebrate this stuff, too!* I pray the praises of my soul blend with the perfect worship of heaven, and that the Lord will build His kingdom through it.

I run every morning to that Mercy Seat. I ran to it first for salvation, but now go there daily for strength, wisdom and a fresh filling. *I can't imagine a day when I'm not desperate for Christ's mercy and don't need to be covered and sheltered by His mighty wings.* It's pure pride to think we can function apart from the King of Kings, and it's pure loss when we try. Have you gone before His feet and sensed Him pour out so much of His Spirit that you felt your puny physical body would burst from the fullness? Have you experienced His manifest presence so strongly in prayer that you couldn't find words to express it, and were afraid to open your eyes because you knew He was standing right there and you just might die from seeing His glory? *That's my prayer for us, and what I'm watching to see rise up in the fields of our hearts.* I believe when that happens, we'll see mighty waves of sweet revival in our own hearts, families, churches and far-reaching places. *Let's get beneath His wings.*

As I've thought about my own little heart at the Cross, God's put a picture in my mind of taking others there in intercession, too. I envision the Mercy Seat right in the center of the Cross, with its blessed arms representing the Lord's wings. Then, I bring my husband, children, unsaved family situations, friends and whole nations—even the entire body of Christ—to it in prayer. There, you can place failure, sin, dreams and every desire of your heart and cry of your soul. God's mercy is large enough to hold it all. I DON'T KNOW WHAT YOU'RE CARRYING, BUT I KNOW WHERE TO SET IT DOWN! *What do we miss by not going there or placing others there? The Lord says to ask of Him. How can we receive if we don't go before Him and ask?*

Put yourself and everything that burdens your heart on that seat, making sure you're under the right wings. Isaiah 30:1-3 says, *"Woe to the rebellious children," says the Lord, "that take counsel, but not of Me; and that cover with a covering, but not of My Spirit, that they may add sin to sin. That walk to go down into Egypt, and have not asked at My mouth; to strengthen themselves in the strength of Pharaoh, and to trust in the shadow of Egypt. Therefore shall the strength of Pharaoh be your shame, and the trust in the shadow of Egypt your confusion."* Take that as a dire warning from the Lord of Lords! If you're placing your life beneath any other covering, nothing will come but shame and confusion! Check your heart. Are you abiding in the shelter of the Most High, or trusting in worldly wisdom (what Egypt represents)? Consider these passages from the Word, and let them fall like sweet rain and water your heart:

> **Deuteronomy 32:11-12**—*As an eagle stirs up its nest, hovers over its young, spreading out its wings, taking them up, so the Lord alone led him, and there was no foreign god with him.*

> **Isaiah 40:31**—*But those who wait upon the Lord shall renew their strength; they shall mount up with wings as eagles, they shall run and not grow weary, they shall walk and not faint.*

Psalm 17:8-9—*Keep me as the apple of Your eye; hide me in the shadow of Your wing, from the wicked who oppress me, from my deadly enemies who surround me.*

Psalm 36:7—*How precious is Your lovingkindness, O God! Therefore the children of men put their trust under the shadow of Your wing.*

Psalm 57:1b—*...and in the shadow of Your wings I will make my refuge...*

Psalm 64:1-4—*Hear my cry, O God; attend to my prayer. From the end of the earth I will cry to You, when my heart is overwhelmed, lead me to the Rock that is higher than I. For You have been a shelter for me, a strong tower from my enemy.*

I will abide in Your tabernacle [where the Mercy Seat is!] forever; I will trust in the shelter of Your wings.

Psalm 63:7—*Because You have been my help, therefore in the shadow of Your wings I will rejoice.*

Celebrate with heaven! Malachi 4:2 says, *"But for you who fear My Name,"* which I picture as falling on my face before His holiness, *"the Sun of Righteousness shall arise with healing in His wings; and you shall go out and grow fat like stall-fed calves"* (NIV: *"you will leap like calves released from the stall.")*. As you worship King Jesus and cast yourself on His mercy, heaven is bowing and rejoicing. The Sun of Righteousness is rising over your life, carrying salvation and healing in His wings, and ready to lift you up and out, tuck you in and cover you—to say to your heart, *"Arise, shine, for your light has come, and the glory of the Lord rises upon you,"* (Isaiah 60:1.) In short, the Lord will shine upon you like the sun and show you glimpses of glory—what Moses, Isaiah and Ezekiel saw—*GOD, HIMSELF.*

You're safe beneath the Lord's wings. That's where our battles are fought and won. You're secure there, the place of perfect refuge. It's holy ground, from where you'll rise up in His strength. The King wants you to soar straight into His plan for you, the things He purposed for you before you ever took a breath. He spreads His wings over you and displays His will in beauty beneath them.

LET'S SOAR! *We get there through the Word, prayer, faith and praise that springs from the very depths of our being, and by abiding in Christ's presence, where we hear His whispers and grab His grace, where sick hearts are resurrected and we step into fullness and wholeness in Him.* This is *not* playing church. This is soaring in the Lord to the place He's prepared for you, *right now—not in the distant future or one day in heaven, but now.* Settle into, as Psalm 91 says, *"the secret place of the Most High."*

A SEED DIES IN SECRET, THEN BURSTS THROUGH EARTH'S CRUSTY SOIL AS SOMETHING NEW, BEAUTIFUL AND FULL OF FRUIT. I pray we'll let our hearts go to the secret place of Christ, and that He'll lift us up on His wings fresh, transformed and new creations bearing much fruit. I don't like heights, but His are BREATHTAKING. Don't be afraid of how high He may take you. You're soaring on HIS WINGS, not your own. YOU'RE SAFE THERE. *Enjoy Him, and savor the view.*

Questions & Applications

1. **You were meant for more than just getting by and getting through life. You were meant to soar beneath the wings of Christ and fulfill His purpose for you. Are you doing that?**

2. **Ask for new heights in Christ as you seek Him in His Word and in prayer. The results might just be labeled "lasting revival."**

22

The Bread and the Wine

"May I continue to find favor in your eyes, my lord," she said.. "You have given mecomfort and have spoken kindly to your servant—though I do not have the standing ofone of your servant girls." At mealtime Boaz said to her, "Come over here. Have somebread and dip it in wine vinegar." When she sat down with the harvesters, he offered hersome roasted grain. She ate all she wanted and had some left over, ***Ruth 2:13-14.***

COME OVER HERE. COME SIT WITH ME. The words spoken by Boaz to Ruth, a foreign woman he wasn't supposed to associate with, echo directly from God's throne to our hearts. WHO ARE WE TO TALK TO THE KING OF GLORY? WHO ARE WE TO ENTER INTO HIS HOLY PRESENCE? WHO ARE WE TO THINK WE SHOULD BE ABLE TO ASK ANYTHING OF HIM APART FROM *SHEER FAVOR?* It's nothing but the priceless blood of Christ that grants us the unspeakable grace of entrance to the very presence of God. It's MERCY that shakes our hearts and says, "Come sit with Me."

The Lord of Lords invites you to sit at His feet in the innermost chamber at the table of the King. It's not to shame you, heap guilt and condemnation on your head, size you up and remind you of all your failures or to compare you with another. He's bringing you there *to feed you.* HOW LIGHTLY DO WE TAKE HIS INVITATION? How half-heartedly have we regarded the privilege of entering His presence through the Word and prayer? *He's asking us to come, feast on His voice and be transformed and then to eternally affect our world for Him.* He's laying out an offer to step onto holy ground and be absolutely and thoroughly satisfied.

The Father knows every hidden desire of your heart. He knows your every thought, fear, need and longing. He knows how hungry your soul is. He hears it rumble and understands how thirsty you are for Living Water, even if you don't. Sometimes we live so long in a spiritual wilderness we forget how good food and drink taste. Even now, the Lord is saying to you, "Come sit with Me. *Come on!* I've got some things to say to you! There are critical, life-giving Words you need to chew on. There's holy bread I want to feed your soul. Ask Me questions. Dive into My Word. Seek Me in earnest prayer. My Word won't change. The gifts and call I speak over you are irrevocable. *Sit with Me.* I have much to say and many things to give you. *(And by the way, they're free.)*"

God's invitation could be put like this: Have you stumbled? Come sit with Me. Do doubts plague you? Come sit with Me. Is your heart heavy and burdened? Come sit with Me. Is some stronghold controlling you? Come sit with Me. Have your dreams not come to pass? Come sit with Me. Is life not working out the way you planned, or according to your schedule? Come sit with Me. Are you full of sweet joy? Come sit with Me. Have you allowed My Spirit to penetrate and My wonder to fill every nook and cranny of your precious soul? Come sit with Me. Bring whatever you're carrying, whatever joy or weight you hold. Bring it to My table, and sit with Me.

Does the Lord's call to enter His presence and sit with Him not absolutely thrill your heart? No wonder He despises lukewarmness. He's given us more than enough reason to celebrate the rest of our days, regardless of our circumstances. *His invitation and Word IS our circumstance—and it is good!* Our joy isn't meant to be determined by our situations! When I'm discouraged the Lord says, "That stuff is not to be your focus! I AM! *I AM!* Come sit with Me, child!"

I want to sit with the King of Kings above all else. I want to feast on the depths of His Word and be blown away by it. I want to taste and see for myself that He is good. I want to see a table prepared by the Lord Himself, set in beauty and in the very presence of my enemies. I want to feel the anointing oil dripping from my head, and have the cup He's put in my hands *running over* with His presence and glory—too much of His goodness and love to contain, too much of His joy and wonder to keep to myself (see Psalm 23)—enough of Him and His holy Bread to stuff myself completely, and still have more left over to pass along to everyone who'll take it.

Christ *is* the Bread of Life, the First and Last Supper, the ultimate Feast, the One to whom every prescribed feast of the Old Testament pointed. The Lord's Supper was a celebration of the Feast of Unleavened Bread, the Passover, where Jesus spoke words too beautiful for our finite minds to grasp: *"Take and eat; this is My Body,"* He said, tearing the flatbread in half. Then He passed the cup with the words, *"Drink it, all of you. This is My blood of the covenant,"* (Matthew 26:26-28). The Lord Jesus not only invites us to the feast, HE IS THE FEAST! You lay your life down before Him, and He lays out His own for you. Beautiful.

The Enemy is powerless as you feast with the King. The Lord spreads His table, and that Foe can do nothing but *watch you eat* (see Ps.23:5). As the Lord feeds you in

Spirit and Truth, you grow stronger and stronger. You go from victory to victory, strength to strength and sustenance to sustenance until your cup runs over. The battle belongs to the Lord, and I believe His table is where He passes out His armor and weapons. There's also *unity* at the Lord's table. I don't care who you are or how you've divided the church up, when we come together to feed on Truth and drink in His presence in prayer, barriers melt away. Those mountains we raise up melt like wax before the Lord of Hosts.

At the Lord's table simple babes in Christ can feast together with the most powerful evangelists alive. In Christ, the prostitute can sit beside the priest and eat the same sweet bread. No one is more or less worthy than another. All are invited to the feast, and, as the Holy Spirit guides us in the Truth and Jesus fills us with Himself, we begin to bear the fruit of love for one another and to become united as the body of Christ is meant to be. We don't even really know *how* to love apart from the Spirit. Committees can't enjoin our hearts; goals and plans won't bring lasting unity. It happens nowhere but on our knees and in the Word.

I'm so grieved by division in the body of Christ. It's such an effective scheme of the Enemy, because if the troops are divided how can the battle be won? When soldiers turn on each other, they lose. Judges 7:22 presents a story of the Lord giving Gideon victory by *confusing the enemy and turning them on themselves*. When the Israelites blew 300 trumpets, the Midianites took their swords and began killing *each other*. I see so many examples of the enemy of our souls imitating this battle plan in the Church! A deception is blasted like a trumpet, and the troops pick up their weapons and turn on each other, bringing defeat to the camp. They raise not the Sword of the Spirit, the Word of God, but the sword of deadly flesh. Spreading Enemy-inspired opinions of each another, love grows cold and fruit withers on the vine.

I believe if we'd repent on all sides of picking up the fleshly sword and would take up the trumpet of praise and the Sword of Truth instead, it would be demonic forces turning on themselves, not us. We know, as it says in Ephesians 6, that we're not battling flesh and blood but powers of darkness. Apart from Christ, we're powerless against foes like that. *We must come together in the blood of Jesus, position ourselves at the Mercy Seat of the Cross and join together—not just individually but corporately. We need to live on our knees, crying out to the King, break the bread of the Word as one body and FEAST, not nibble.*

If we don't feast on God's Word *daily*, we become spiritually anorexic with a distorted view of ourselves, and remain self-focused and blinded to Truth. In the same way that anorexics look in the mirror and think they're fat, even while their body is wasting away, those enmeshed with religious legalism, tradition and pride think they're full. But there's only one place to fatten your soul and get a true picture of your life and heart—sitting with the King. Of His goodness Psalm 63:5 says, *"My soul shall be satisfied as with marrow and fatness, and my mouth shall praise you with joyful lips."* Your cup overflows.

Let's feast with joy, then! Let's take the Word spread before us and the cup of the Lord with pounding, trembling hearts. 1Timothy 6:17 says, *"The Living God has given us richly all things to enjoy."* I believe there's nothing we'll ever enjoy more than sitting with Him. We were made to enjoy His presence and to allow Him to enjoy ours. His table is awesome, abundant and full. There's nothing you need that you won't find there. He's GOOD, and He "supplies your needs according to His riches in glory by Christ Jesus," (Philippians 4:19).

I don't know what you're hungry for, but *Jesus is the answer for it.* I've hungered for a lot of things in my life, but have found that *nothing satisfies like His table*. I've seen what money can buy, experienced good relationships and had hopes fulfilled—*yet, I've known NOTHING, no matter how good, that compares to the thrill of the Lord's presence.* I've discovered that the longer you sit with the King, the more you desire nothing but Him, His food and wine, and sweet communion with Him. As longing for His presence starts to override everything else and your heart melts into His, He plants His so-much-better-than-ours desires deep within, then steps back and says, "Ask, that you may receive and that your joy may be full."

What are you asking the Lord for? What's going on in your life that you're crying out to Him about? Do you need direction, healing, physical needs met or feel called to ministry? What is it? *Whatever it is, it's not the goal.* Healing isn't the goal. Blessing isn't the goal. Ministry isn't the goal. SITTING WITH THE KING OF GLORY, FEASTING ON THE WORD AND EXPERIENCING THE POWER OF PRAYER IS THE GOAL. *Everything else is a side effect of being with Him.* When you enter the King's presence, do you ever really stop to consider *exactly with Whom you're sitting?*

Scripture is full of greetings, closings, doxologies and songs spoken by people who realized Who Jesus is and couldn't help but express praise. Just as Jesus told the Apostle John to *"Come up here, and I will show you"* in Revelation 4, He wants us to come and let Him show us some things. He wants us to behold His glory and splendor, and then display it. He's holy and pure; righteousness and justice are the foundation of His throne. All who see Him fall in worship before Him. Beauty surrounds Him and spills onto all who feast with Him. His eyes blaze like fire, and His face is like the sun shining in all its brilliance. His voice is like the sound of rushing waters and fills our souls with strength and salvation. Through the ages it beckons every heart: *"Whoever is thirsty, let him come; and whoever wishes, let him take the free gift of the water of life,"* (Revelation 22:17).

Sitting with Jesus puts passion in your heart that expresses itself in prayer, worship, cherishing the Word and walking in love. *You can't be with Him and stay the same.* He's absolutely worthy of praise, and when you take a long look at Him you can't help but rejoice. The more you taste and see Him, the more you want of Him. You develop very picky tastes— anything less than Him just won't suffice. *His presence becomes your home.* You begin to live what Ephesians 2:6-7 says, *"And God raised us up with Christ and seated us in the heavenly realms in Christ Jesus, in order that He might show the incomparable riches of His grace, expressed in His kindness to us in Christ Jesus."* Sitting with Him is a whole different realm, unlike any place you've ever parked your heart.

Luke 10:38-42 gives the familiar account of two sisters, Mary and Martha. You probably know the story well. They opened their home to Jesus, and there was much to be done in serving the meal. Martha was flustered and busy, yet Mary couldn't resist sitting at His feet and hanging on His every word. I believe that preparing food, setting the table, putting out flowers, sweeping the floor and pouring the drinks—every preparation—simply faded away as Christ took center stage in Mary's heart. I have no doubt His words ignited the very depths of her soul, and that she couldn't bring herself to leave His side. The joy and wonder of Truth spoken by the Lord directly to her heart far outweighed any earthly concerns. Dinner was suddenly nothing more than a distraction. Hadn't He fed thousands with a little boy's fish and bread? Isn't He the One of whom David spoke in Psalm 23 that *prepares a table for us?* Who cared about physical food, anyway, when the Bread of Life was sitting in the living room? What was up with Martha? Was her last name Stewart? *Martha may have been trying to impress Jesus with how she could satisfy*

His hunger, but Mary definitely impressed Him by showing her great hunger for Him.

I think it's interesting that Jesus didn't respond to Martha's complaint against Mary by saying, "Oh, thank you, Martha, for wearing yourself out to impress me with your house and food. Thank you for putting on a good party and a great show. Thanks for displaying your best china. You're so busy for Me. Thanks. You're right about that sister of yours, she's just lazing around soaking up My Word. Shame on her. I'll tell her to jump up and get busy right away." No, He said the opposite. I believe His words to Martha penetrated deeply, piercing through the surface issues and cutting straight to her heart—to the fact that busyness was not just Martha's physical state, but also the state of her soul. Jesus said to her, *"Martha, Martha, you are worried and upset about many things, but only one thing is needed."* Skipping right over dinner, He addressed the "many things" in Martha's heart. Dinner was just the tip of the iceberg of her worries and cares, with Mary's lack of help being the last straw. How often have we been so stressed out by "many things" that one little thing sets us off in a rage? I wonder, too, if Martha's busyness could have been a coping skill. It's certainly been one of mine. When the Towers fell on 9-11, I cleaned out the fridge. When my daughter was told she needed surgery for scoliosis, I started cooking. Busyness can be a way to keep our hearts distracted when life closes in and presses hard. You may say to yourself, "I can't control that, but I can control THIS..." That sounds like the beginning of a stronghold. A control issue. Taking a thing in your own hands. Or maybe the opposite of busyness sets in, and you find your heart and life paralyzed, crippled, barely functioning and overindulging in a place or two. *Either way, we need to look up from our distractions and look into the face of the King. Sit at His precious, nail scarred feet, and ask*

Him to speak through His Word. Say, like Samuel, "Speak, Lord, for your servant hears."

Jesus told Martha that Mary had chosen the only necessary thing, and what had Mary chosen?: TO SIT AT HIS FEET, SOAK UP HIS PRESENCE AND FEAST ON HIS EVERY WORD, LETTING IT BATHE HER SOUL. The Lord said that Mary's choice wouldn't be taken from her. He was telling Martha that sitting with Him is the best thing possible in life, and that seeking Him first is our soul's greatest joy. He understood their need to eat and that preparations were required, but He also knew the Cross was soon to come and how precious this time was with His girls. He's the King of Kings, and could easily make sure they had dinner! *It was the feast of Himself He wanted to share with them, in order to satisfy and fill their hearts to overflowing.*

Mary chose wisely, and who knows the blessings she received that evening at the feet of the King. MAY WE CHOOSE IT, TOO, AND RECEIVE THE UNSPEAKABLE, INEXPRESSIBLE JOY OF HIS PRESENCE. It's the joy of truly knowing Jesus and being able to say with Peter: "He's Christ, the Son of the Living God," because we sit with Him, hear the voice of the Holy Spirit in the Word, live in prayer before Him and have seen His power. In response to Peter's confession, Jesus told him that he'd be a rock, a Kingdom builder and a tool the Lord could use to establish His church on earth. *We will be, too.* Peter isn't the only one called to build Christ's kingdom. In fact, Jesus tells us all to pray for this in the Lord's Prayer: *"Thy Kingdom come, Thy will be done..."* Learn of Him, let Him reveal Himself to your heart and reveal His identity and power, and you, too,—yes, even you—will become a rock in the Lord's hand with which He can enlarge His kingdom. Sit...listen...be fed...then go out and echo His voice. *He's the King. Take a seat and break bread with Him.*

Questions & Applications

1. **Search through the Word and see for yourself just who this Christ is who invites you—even you—to sit and feast in His awesome presence.**
2. **Bring everything you are, have, have been, and will be to the table of the King of Kings. Lay it all before Him and worship the only One capable of filling your soul.**
3. **Ask yourself honestly if you are more like Mary or Martha. Are you so concerned about and busy with "many things" that you don't take the time to do the one thing truly necessary- sit at the feet of the King?**

23

Gleaning Where You Are

And when she rose up to glean, Boaz commanded his young men, saying, "Let her glean even among the sheaves, and do not reproach her (NIV says, "don't embarrass her").

Also let grain from the bundles fall purposely for her; leave it that she may glean, and do not rebuke her," **Ruth 2:15-16.**

Ruth had been with the man of honor, the owner of the field. She'd looked him in the eyes, shared his table and been satisfied completely by his bread, and now the time had come to go back to work. She didn't complain, whine or beg to remain at the table forever, but gladly returned to her labor. *Ruth headed back to the same field, but she wasn't the same.* You can do something in your own strength for a season, but after you've been at the feet of Christ, broken bread with Him, tasted His sweet wine, talked one-on-one with Him and received comfort from His mouth, *you can't return to the same job with the same heart.* It might look similar on the outside, but in the depths of your spirit there's new fire, fresh passion and power and strength you didn't possess before you met the One who owns the fields—and it doesn't matter what the field is, i.e.:

You're raising the same children, but you're not the same mother. You're cooking the same dinners, washing the same clothes, doing the same household jobs, but you're different. You're still buying, selling, answering mail and keeping the books (whatever job is before you); the same hands put to the task, but with a changed heart. There's fresh power now, *because you've just dined with the King!* I'm absolutely overwhelmed sometimes by many things the Lord calls me to do. But as I daily sit at the King's precious feet and break holy bread with Him, I find refreshing and renewing. Somehow, He imparts exactly what I need. As I cry out to Him about the tasks He gives me, one Scripture that's quickly becoming a life verse for me is 2 Corinthians 9:8, *"God is able to make all grace abound toward you, that you, always having all sufficiency in all things, have an abundance for every good work."*

Notice again that after dining with Boaz, Ruth arose and returned to the same field. *Breaking bread with the King doesn't mean you suddenly have to change your job or desert the tasks you were doing before.* Intimacy with Christ doesn't automatically translate to heading off on a mission trip to Africa. You don't sit with Him and receive nourishment for your very soul and then stop everything you were doing before. Of course, there certainly are times when the Lord call us to completely change something in our lives, but Scripture often presents Jesus touching someone and then saying, "Go back"—go back to your hometown, to what you were doing, to your family...

In Matthew 8:1-4, Jesus heals a leper, instructing him, *"See that you don't tell anyone. But go, show yourself to the priest and offer the gift Moses commanded, as a testimony to them."* He didn't send the man out to the nations, but to the local priests. Christ healed him out of profound love and mercy, and sent him back to the same sanctuary where he wasn't welcome yesterday to testify to those who could declare him clean. In Matthew 9, Jesus cures a paralytic, saying: *"Get up, take your mat and go home."* Go back where you live, to the place you were before, but different—healed, whole and full of sweet bread—because the King of Kings has touched you. It wasn't "go find a pulpit," but "go HOME," perhaps *the most difficult place to minister.* Jesus said in Mark 6:4, *"Only in his own hometown, among his relatives and in his own house is a prophet without honor."* Sometimes people who knew you before you dined with the King are the hardest to convince. Those who knew what you were yesterday may not accept what the Lord is doing in you today. Learning to love right there may be your toughest training ground.

For me, it's so much easier to speak somewhere, then leave and never have to deal with those folks again, or to send a check somewhere or do a short-term mission trip and then settle back into life as it was. Not that those aren't wonderful, Kingdom-building activities. I've just found that ministry at home is much more difficult, and that long-term commitments are the toughest to live out. In Mark 5, Jesus healed a demon-possessed man who'd been living among the tombs. When the Lord asked his name, he said, "Legion." This was one troubled, harassed man! After being set free, he ecstatically begged to go with Jesus, but Jesus responded to his cries to with, *"Go home to your family and tell them how much the Lord has done for you, and how He had mercy on you."* That probably wasn't the answer he wanted to hear. Go back to the people who'd tried to chain him up time and time again? The ones who listened to him cry out for years among the tombs as he cut himself with stones? Those who feared him, ran the other way when they saw him and scorned him? Those who seemed to care more about the loss of their pigs than him? Yes, "GO HOME"—back to the field.

The Lord tells us to love our neighbors as ourselves. At times, I've discovered that "neighbors" can be absolutely the hardest to love! It's often the ones you're around the most who can get most on your nerves, irritate you, possibly persecute you, gossip about or judge you; who may have cheated you, lied about you, taken advantage of you, or bring serious issues to your back door, like drugs, abuse or alcohol. Sometimes it's the "neighbors" that sit in the same sanctuary with you week after week, who've disappointed you, broken a sacred trust, shared a confidential prayer request or whatever. *The call to love your neighbor, those in the same field with you, can indeed be the hardest*. In my flesh, I don't even *like*, much less love, some of them- and I'm sure you can relate. *Loving the difficult ones requires the power of the Holy Spirit.* As we sit with the Lord and let His mighty Word and pure Spirit fill us, I believe He changes our hearts so we can't help but love—*even those irritating "neighbors."*

While Jesus certainly calls us to go out to the world in the Great Commission, I believe He first wants us to affect the fields He's divinely placed around us now. I always assumed "going into all the world" involved planes, trains and automobiles, but the Lord's driven home the point to me that where I walk now *is* part of the world. Proclaiming Christ doesn't have to involve lengthy travel. We need to begin where we are. He'll lead us further out when He's ready.

Several years ago, the Lord planted a desire deep within my heart to serve Him. It was truly one of those life-changing, spiritual marker-kind of moments. I fully expected to be leaving town soon thereafter on a glamorous road trip to serve the King, off on an exciting path of proclaiming Him and bringing hungry souls to Jesus. *Instead, the Lord has taken me on a journey of learning humility, worshiping at His feet, sitting with Him and letting Him pour into my heart*. It's been a path of weakness in my flesh, battling in my mind and spirit and finding myself utterly dependent on

Him; one of accepting contentment with where He's placed me now, instead of in a whole new place—no matter how much I wanted to go. In essence, He's told me what He told others in Scripture: "Go back home, back to the same town, the same people, the same street and the same church. Go back and *live Me* where you were before, and I'll lead you from there." Glean in that same old field.

Be careful you don't mistake *looking* back for *going* back. There's a difference between looking back, wishing you were still taking part in some of the old lifestyle, and going back to the same place with a new heart. Jesus said in Luke 9:62, *"No one who puts his hand to the plow and looks back is fit for service in the Kingdom of God."* If you're *looking* back with regret at worldly things the King has called you away from, then you're not ready to be a Kingdom builder. We need to be able to GO BACK, as Jesus said, without LOOKING back with eyes of flesh.

We're called to evangelize where we are, not huddle around and pat each other on the back (though we're absolutely to encourage and pray for one another). And while we're not to be *yoked together* with unbelievers, we're not to avoid them like the plague, either. We're to go display the power of the Lord among them. We're to be the fragrance and light of the King to the lost and to live-out Christ before them as we go about daily life, gleaning and grinding the grain we're given.

In Luke 22:33, Peter says to Jesus, *"Lord, I am ready to go with You to prison and to death."* NO, HE WASN'T. And Jesus knew it. Jesus knew that within 24 hours, Peter would deny Him three times. Peter needed more growing time. Have you ever told the Lord, "Jesus, I'll go wherever You say," while you're picturing in your mind just where that will be? Has discouragement or doubt set in when He took you somewhere different, or perhaps even worse, LEFT

YOU WHERE YOU WERE, in a place far different than you imagined? It's certainly been true of me.

Peter was only *truly* able to go the place of genuine surrender with Christ after the Lord, and Peter's heart, were resurrected. The disciple boldly proclaimed he'd risk prison and death for Jesus, and eventually, after a fresh renewing, he did. *Maybe going back home looks like prison or a death of sorts to you.* Staring those same old fields in the face may look nothing like your glamorous, far-away dreams. But maybe they're exactly where the Lord wants to train you, mold your heart, "kill" you and then resurrect you.

The Samaritan woman whom Jesus approached as she drew water from the well in John 4 ran back to town, excitedly telling her neighbors, "Come see a man..." She was running back to share Jesus with those who'd gossiped about her escapades with men, who'd judged her for being married so many times and had made life so miserable for her she didn't even draw water at the standard social hour. She'd been avoiding those folks in her shame, but suddenly, in her freedom, she was heading right to them, inviting them to meet Jesus—the Man who'd named her sin but hadn't humiliated her, who'd confronted but not embarrassed her and who'd identified the deep need of her soul and given her sweet, Living Water to drink.

That "drink" must have splashed the beauty of forgiveness on her heart, causing her to run straight back to those hard-hearted town folks to urge them to, *"Come, see a Man who told me everything I ever did. Could this be the Christ?"* In her words I hear, "Come, see the power of this Man! His Word cuts right to the quick. He knows the very depths of your being and the entirety of your circumstances, yet He offers real, true life. Come look at Him with me! Come ask your own heart, as I've asked mine, 'Could this be the Savior?' Just look at Him and let Him look at you, and then tell me who you say He is."

The passage informs us that, *"Many of the Samaritans from that town believed in Him because of the woman's testimony."* Are you denying the treasure of your testimony to those around you? Have you taken it back to town? Did you ever go back to your field and let the Lord do His thing through you?

I AM THAT WOMAN. No, I haven't had five husbands, but I've been just as desperate to see the Man who knows every single thing in my heart. How I love to sit with Him, draw deep water with Him and be refreshed by His power. And I pray He empowers me to GO BACK TO TOWN and not be afraid to speak of Him, but to go where He's placed me with a different, renewed, amazed, overflowing and eager-for-all-to-see heart. I don't want to hide in the shadows fearful of anyone's opinion, or think I can only take His Word to distant places. I want to go back with the overcoming power of the blood of Christ and the testimony of what He's done for me. I've always pictured the harvest as somewhere "out there," but there's plenty of gleaning to be done *right here*.

For years I prayed, "Lord, show me Your glory." Then one day, I sensed Him urge me to ask, "Lord, show me Your power." Part of His power is the strength to take your testimony to those around you who despise you (or whom you despise in your flesh) and share the treasure of your salvation; to live Christ before people who may mock you, call you a fanatic, tell you to calm down or whisper the dreaded words, "Who does she think she is? I know all about her," behind your back. *The town may have seen your flesh, but the King of Kings has seen your heart, and has touched and changed it. As you walk among those old fields with a new heart, the people around you are going to notice.* You're not responsible for their reaction to you. You're just called to go and tell. May Jesus give us the grace to do this. May He fill us so full we can't help but run and share it, even if it's in the lace. And may many come to Him because of it. *"I the strength of the Lord God; I will make mention ighteousness, of Yours only,"* (Psalm 71:16).

We need to watch our own reactions to others who come to Christ, as well. We're told not to judge, lest we be judged and that we must receive those the Lord sends our way, even if they've hurt us in the past, or we know what they've done and seen their ugliness. We must be willing to rejoice with them over what the Lord's done in their lives today, not hang onto what they did to us yesterday. Through the Lord's forgiveness working in both of us, He can put us side by side in the same field, *the home field.*

Questions & Applications

1. **Is there a hard place the Lord is calling you to take your testimony back to? Ask for the power of the Holy Spirit to fill you and equip you for the task.**
2. **Ask the Lord to open your eyes to opportunities to share Him in your "home field." Pray for a passion for Him that sends your feet running to tell others what He has done.**
3. **Are you serving the Lord right where you are today, or are you waiting for some "grand opportunity"?**

24

More than Enough...

"...let grain from the bundles fall purposefully for her; leave it that she may glean, and do not rebuke her," **Ruth 2:16.**

I love that Boaz instructed his workers to pull out some harvest, some grain to glean, and let it fall *on purpose* at Ruth's feet. All Ruth had to do to pick up more than enough was to reach out and take it. Ruth, the Moabite born in a foreign field, was now being provided for by another. The woman who by birth didn't even deserve to be in the field, let alone pick up grain, was now being given armfuls of it. The fact that she had no right to be there is probably why Boaz instructed his crew not to embarrass or rebuke her. *Beyond that, I believe Boaz was taken with Ruth and had a plan for her. She'd already captured his heart.*

The King of Glory is likewise taken with you and has a plan of provision for your life. He knows better than you the daily bread your soul needs. It doesn't matter whether you think you deserve the bundles He drops at your feet (have I ever struggled with that one!), nor how much harvest you've passed over in the past, what your age, race, sex or sin is, or how long you hung out in Moab. The King has ordered holy gleanings placed at your precious-in-His-sight feet. *They're paid for with blood*, and holy hands have dropped them in front of you. *Pick them up*.

Jehovah-jireh, the Lord our Provider, knows exactly how much we need to thrive and prosper. He's absolutely aware of our condition, just as sure as Boaz was aware of Ruth's. He also knows every detail of the deepest desires of our hearts. *The great I AM is for us*.

In demonstration of His faithfulness, over and over in Scripture we see examples of the Lord God Almighty stepping into the lives of people with the exact practical and spiritual provision they required: Israel in the wilderness given bread from heaven, "the food of angels," as well as water, honey from the rock. Elijah in hiding fed bread and meat by ravens. The widow in 1 Kings 17, who had only a little oil and flour and fully expected that she and her little boy would starve to death furnished lasting provision as she shared her last meal with Elijah. Five thousand hungry people on a hill, Jesus blessed a little boy's lunch and they were fed. These things not only met a physical need, but also touched the deep, spiritual hunger of God's people to see His strength displayed on their behalf. Again and again, the Faithful One showed His faithfulness to His people, the passion of His heart.

Time after time in battle, the Lord made provision for Moses, Joshua, Gideon, David and others. *They didn't need troops and weapons, but worn out knees*. And as they cried out to God, He responded with victory. Have you ever had a physical, spiritual or emotional need or battle in your life with which you struggled to trust Him? A time when no solution appeared except to wear out your knees?

One huge time like that for me was the sum of events in 1995. My husband always says, "If I ever wonder if God has moved in my life, I just have to think about 1995." My father-in-law reached a crisis that year with a serious, ongoing addiction to a prescription drug. The Lord ultimately set him free from it and caused it to be a powerful testimony to those around him, but until then it rocked our family. I gave birth to our first child, my sweet daughter, and the medical personnel were predicting some potential problems. She was born with serious jaundice, and we were told that she could be mentally handicapped because of it. Thankfully, she is *not*, but the reports sent me to my knees. Then, as we were in the process of building a little house, the house we were renting sold. The Lord put it on the heart of a family in our church to rent us a house they had on the market, *and it sold, too*. (We were in the process of moving when I went into labor. My husband had to leave the hospital, an hour away, and go back to move furniture.) My knees quickly became well worn, believe me. The Lord provided another place to live through the generosity of yet another church member, but until then, I found myself questioning the Lord a LOT!

These things may seem slight and minor compared to the tragic difficulties of others, but that year was a testimony burned in our hearts of the Lord's faithfulness, despite our own wobbly faith. I could cite many other similar examples in the years since then, but '95 was a major stretch of our faith and hearts, and a sweet time of the Lord's divine intervention. In our need, He showed Himself strong. *Yes, the Lord provides for the foreigners in His field!* He'll do it for you, too. He's no respecter of persons.

A need is really a chance to see the Lord's merciful, miraculous provision. It's an opportunity to hear the King of Kings whisper in your heart, "Watch this," and to see His mighty arm flexed on your behalf. *Just ahead there's something dropped in the field waiting for you to pick up and be filled with!* But, whatever else it may involve, your foremost need is relationship with Him—His presence and intimacy in your life. All else pales beside that deepest-rooted hunger. *"Seek first the kingdom of God and His righteousness, and all these things shall be added to you,"* (Matthew 6:33). "These things" can stretch into a long list, but our greatest necessity remains the same: "seek first the kingdom."

It's critical that we seek the Lord's face, not just His hands or how He can bless us and do for us. *He's God, let Him do as He pleases*. He knows your needs better than you do and uses them to work out His purposes in your life. It's His kingdom He's building and establishing, not yours. It's not your whims, but His perfect will He wants to satisfy. Psalm 78:18 reminds us that Israel *"tested God in their heart by asking for the food of their fancy."* We need to guard our tastes and appetites, examine our cravings and walk-out Colossians 3:1-2, *"...seek those things which are above, where Christ is, sitting at the right hand of God. Set your mind on things above, not on things on the earth."*

Does your heart hunger for the things of Christ, or is it focused on *your* interests, *your* pleasure, *your* reputation, *your* wallet, *your* personal space, *your*...? What are you asking the King to plant in your life? Are you seeking provision for your flesh or your spirit? *When the King of Kings bends His mighty, precious ear toward this simple soul, I don't want Him to hear selfish whining and pleasure seeking, but something that blesses and delights Him, something He can answer and use to build His Kingdom.* When we get our focus right, I believe the rest falls into place as God directs. *And what HE directs is good—better than any future or hope we can devise for ourselves—plans of provision that may defy our ways and thoughts, but which are higher, purer and richer through Christ.*

I know what it's like to have an all-consuming need, but even that kind of thing is not to overwhelm our attention. God is. And faithful, faithful, faithful is the Lord who sees down to our innermost. Never will He leave or forsake, and mighty and awesome is He to provide. *God's ultimate provision, the Lamb of God, Messiah, is for our lost souls.*

Foreshadowed by the Old Testament sacrifices, no one but the Messiah Himself could provide the pure, holy blood, the priceless price, required to pay for our sins. Jesus shed that pure sacrifice on the Cross for us- oh, thank Him again today for that most miraculous, merciful provision!

When God provided a ram for Abraham on Mt. Moriah, Abraham called it, Jehovah-jireh, The-Lord-Will-Provide. It also means, The Lord Will See. *God is not blind to your need!* No matter what it is, and even if you brought it on yourself with bad choices and rebellion, His ever-open eyes are taking you in. He views those needs with tender compassion. He knows the depth and root of them and is ready to drop a bundle of answers in your path as you seek Him first. What are your needs right now? The most urgent for me are wisdom, strength, endurance, boldness, courage, discernment and direction. Of course, there are also personal, family, school, church, town and national necessities. All should be taken to the Cross and placed on the Mercy Seat. But they pale in importance to God's call to pray and worship, soak in the pure water of the Word and allow the Holy Spirit to fill our hearts. As we seek the Lord above all else, He'll take care of all those other things. *It overwhelms my heart to think the very Lord of Lords is pulling out provision for ME—a worn-out Moabite. He's good, and His mercy endures forever.*

Hebrew meanings for "provide" include: "to see, consider, examine, look after, regard, enjoy, prepare, execute, perform, accomplish, bear, bestow, bring forth, gather, grant, serve, appoint, furnish; to create, do, or make; to prepare a meal or banquet, to take action." *Strong's* says, "God's acts and words perfectly correspond, so that what He says He does, and what He does is what He has said." Look at what He says in His Word—*that's* what He wants to provide and perform in you! *Oh, mighty Lord, may Your Word be accomplished in us!*

As we seek Him, The King of Kings is ready to do everything for us the name Jehovah-jireh implies! It's an overwhelming thought that the Creator of the universe is creating and providing for little ol' me. The mighty Arm that stretched out the heavens and parted the sea is pulling out bundles from His storehouse and placing them at our feet! The King has laid down His own flesh and blood for you and placed the sacrifice for your Moabite soul right in front of you. What will you do with it? I pray the joy of salvation will continually flood our hearts, souls, minds and strength; that the Lord will give us fresh eyes to see the beauty of the Cross, the power of His blood and the wonder wrapped up in His sweet Name; that sheer, inexpressible joy will overtake us at His feet; that we'll pick up the Cross that's caused men through the ages to either stumble or rejoice and that our souls will swell before Him with passion and praise.

Look at the Cross. You ask for bread, there it is. You want healing and wholeness, there it is. You desire love and acceptance, there it is. You pray for cleansing and freedom, there it is. You seek overcoming power and strength, there it is. You hope for wisdom and revelation, there it is. You need Truth, there it is. The Cross is the line in the sand for your life. Step over the mark and you'll never be the same. The Cross stretches before you and shades your life, and sweet, holy fruit is found there. *"I sat down in His shade with great delight, and His fruit was sweet to my taste. He brought me to His banqueting house, and His banner over me is love,"* (Song of Solomon 2:3-4).

What else do you need? Everything else—every physical need, desire of your heart, longing and cry of your soul—is swallowed up in the Cross. You may still have the same life tasks to do, but, somehow, at the Cross, the pressure and stress of them melts away. Somehow, the details of life scatter down the ladder of importance at its foot. Psalm 63:5 says, *"My soul shall be satisfied as with marrow and fatness, and my mouth shall praise You with joyful lips."* It's a fattening up, a satisfying of the *soul* not the flesh.

As I've pondered the King of Glory looking down at my little life, I've asked Him in prayer, "How amazing, Lord, that with all of heaven at Your command and all of earth as Your footstool, You focus Your eyes and heart on our tiny lives. Jesus, Your Word says, *'How precious...are Your thoughts to me, O God! How great is the sum of them! If I should count them, they would be more in number than the sand on the shore...'* (Psalm 139:17-18). What do You think of when you think of us?" His reply to my heart has been: "You are My own children, precious, beautiful, redeemed by My own hand, blood-bought instruments of praise, My intimate friends and completed ones engraved on My palms in blood. How could I not think of you? You delight My heart, and I rejoice in your footsteps toward Me. I've been planning your future a long time. Leave fear and doubt far behind and celebrate the road into it. Come with Me. Come dance."

He's also impressed on my heart that we need "forward feet"—feet willing to step up to or fall down at the Cross, to walk past fear and embrace the call of the Most High God, feet that don't turn around and walk back toward the past, but press on in Christ and move ahead in faith. *What would happen if the whole body of Christ put on forward feet?* Look at Hebrews 11:33-34: *"...who through faith conquered kingdoms, administered justice, and gained what was promised; who shut the mouths of lions, quenched the fury of the flames, and escaped the edge of the sword; whose weakness was turned to strength; and who became powerful in battle and routed foreign armies."*

Just look at that bundle of different people with the same brand of faith, serving the same mighty God—COMMON PEOPLE WALKING WITH FORWARD FEET! *Could we also see those things take place in our hearts, homes, churches, towns and nation?* Why not? The Lord hasn't diminished in strength or faithfulness to those who walk in faith, not just to see what He can do, but that seek to know Him well. Beth Moore says, "Genuine faith walks steadfastly with God for the pleasure of His company, not just for His results." The cry of my heart for my life and for those I love is that we'd know the pleasure of the King's company and allow Him to do all He pleases through us to build His beautiful Kingdom.

We need to press on in faith with forward feet, enjoying the Lord as we go. There's fresh bounty from His hand every single day. It's so reassuring to me that the King will never be unable to provide for my soul, or to establish and equip me with all I need to serve Him. I'll never find Him unprepared to feed my starving soul or with a well that's run dry. He's always, forever and eternally able to deliver, do what He's promised, keep His covenant, redeem and turn stones to bread.

You can't look at the Cross and tell me He's unable to provide for everything your soul and body needs! THIS IS NO WEAK ARM EXTENDED TO YOU! Jeremiah 50:34 says, *"Their Redeemer is strong."* Isaiah 49:26 says, *"I, the Lord, am your Savior, and your Redeemer, the Mighty One of Israel, mighty to save"*—not wimpy to save, but "MIGHTY TO SAVE." It's the arm of the King of Kings, arms that nailed themselves to the Cross and made a public spectacle of the Enemy, scattered the stars, hung the moon, gave the sun its light and resurrected Christ from the dead.

THAT SAME ARM is pulling out stalks from holy, perfect bundles and dropping them at your feet—dropping salvation and pulling out love you can't produce, joy the world can't give, peace that passes understanding, patience to wait on His perfect timing, kindness toward what the flesh would rather despise, gentleness where you were once rough and hard, faithfulness in a once-unfaithful heart, self-control that self can't generate and wisdom that passes understanding. He offers Truth that's absolutely eternal and that puts the whims of worldly trends to shame, as well as overcoming power through His Spirit and inexpressible glory that stretches far beyond anything we can imagine.

I've had a deep-seated fear in my heart that one day as I sit before the Lord I'll hear nothing, receive nothing and come away with nothing. But He's almost shouted in my heart, "I WILL STOP POURING OUT TO YOU WHEN MY LOVE FOR YOU CEASES TO BE." *That's NEVER! If His love endures FOREVER, so too then, does His provision and sweet Word to us*. There's rest in that. *The Lord will never stop teaching and leading His children, the beloved of His heart. He'll never give a stone to those asking for bread. He knows our frame and remembers we're but dust. He understands our utter dependence on His power, mercy and Word, and is forever faithful to deliver all who call on His Name.*

So, pick up the fullness of everything the King has provided for you—but don't ever think you've accomplished something yourself, or that you've gathered any harvest on your own or by your strength. IT'S ALL HIS DOING. He just gives you the privilege of participating with Him. Boast in Him alone. All is the Lord's: strength is His, power is His, harvest is His and all glory, honor and power are His. He's the Shepherd, the Keeper of the Fields and the King of all Kings. GIVE HIM GLORY! LET NO BOASTING COME OUT OF YOUR MOUTH, EXCEPT FOR IN THE LORD'S POWER DISPLAYED AT THE CROSS!

How blatantly prideful we can be sometimes. When the Lord Jesus, like Boaz, purposefully drops bundles to feed us and rejoice in, how inappropriate it is for us to act as if we're somehow responsible. Where do we get the nerve to ever think we're so much more advanced and together or have more favor than someone else in the field beside us, much less that we deserve it? Get real! It's all Him. The entire harvest is His, and everything He puts in our lives is a pure gift. Let's receive what He offers with sheer joy, delight and gratitude, and then share it. When He gives us bread, I believe He expects us to break it with others. *It's awesome to think that as we take His provision, He might dare use "even us," the least of the least, to drop some sheaves in other hearts.*

Questions & Applications

1. **Can you recall a year like our '95? Look back through your years, and thank the King of Kings for the specific bundles of provision He has dropped along your path.**
2. **Ask the Lord for "forward feet," feet that move on with Him and dare to press on with faith and courage, even when life gets hard. Trust that your need will provide another chance for Him to drop provision in your path.**

25

Enough to Share...

So she gleaned in the field until evening, and beat out what she had gleaned, and it was about an ephah of barley. Then she took it up and went into the city, and her mother-in-law saw what she had gleaned. So she brought out and gave to her what she had kept back after she had been satisfied, **Ruth 2:17-18.**

Ruth gleaned so much that day there was enough to fully satisfy her own hunger with plenty left over to spread before her mother-in-law. There's such a beautiful spiritual application here: as we go to the Word and prayer and gather what will completely sate our own deepest hunger, we'll always have armfuls more for other starving souls. We're not blessed just for ourselves and our families. We're not loaded down with Truth for our souls alone. We aren't called to store up our blessings and gifts, but to share them with the ones the Lord leads us to and let them take their fill. *The Lord means for others to benefit from our bounty.*

Naomi couldn't help but notice the bundles Ruth held as she came walking through the door! The provision was obvious. There was no mistaking she'd found a prosperous field. *And Naomi began asking questions.* When you've been picking up blessings dropped for you in the King's field, it'll be apparent to others! When you accept those on-purpose sheaves the Lord pulls out with His own hand, the people around you can't help but see His radiance and abundance. Nothing on the face of the earth compares to it, and I believe the folks around you will begin to ask a few pointed questions, such as: "Where do you get your joy?" "Why aren't you stressed out?" "There's a love pulsing through you I just don't have." "I couldn't do what you do; how do you do it?" "Why are you so happy?" "Why aren't you following all the latest trends?" "What makes you different?" "There's a difference in the way you approach your circumstances, whether good or bad." "HOW DID YOU GET WHERE YOU ARE?"

How much more powerful is that kind of open door of inquiry than trying to force your testimony on someone! Not that we aren't called to take a stand even when it's uncomfortable, but what a sweet thing it is when an observer says, "I want what you have. How do I get it?" What an opportunity to say, "It's not in relationships, finding the ideal mate, having perfect kids, looking cute, having a good income or anything else you can think of in this world. *My fullness springs from holy hands. It comes from the Lord God Almighty, the Maker of heaven and earth, through Jesus Christ, the only One crucified for my sins—and yours—and risen for our new life in Him, and from the Holy Spirit, poured out to equip, guide, train and exalt Christ alone."*

Regret washes over me when I think of times like that where I dropped the ball by failing to give the King the glory due His name. I've wimped out and missed some good opportunities to lift up my Lord. Waitressing together in college, a girl from Vietnam asked me, "Why are you so happy?" I don't remember my exact response, but I know it didn't give praise to Jesus—and it still bothers me. I pray someone with more boldness than me at the time has come into her life and shared the Truth. Who knows how far-reaching her testimony could be, even to the nation she came from? Teaching school years later, a younger teacher commented, "I can't wait to be thirty, then I'll have it all together. You seem to have it all together." Little did she know, and LITTLE DID I SHARE. God forgive me.

When you bear the fruit of the Lord's field (love, joy, peace, patience, kindness, goodness, faithfulness, gentleness and self-control), His mercy and cleansing, His overwhelming gift of freedom, the blessings of the Holy Spirit and the thrill of His Word and Presence, it will be apparent to all. How can you *not* look different when all that divine nature is being freely poured out to you? Others will notice the fullness of the Lord overflowing your heart. I know this not so much because I see it in myself, but because I've seen it blazing all over others in the body of Christ. I've seen it in women I've attended Bible studies with, in people I've prayed with and in the faces and voices of many by whom I've been taught. I've witnessed the glory of the Lord radiate, maybe a little like Moses, in some very common faces.

That kind of bounty and radiance comes from the King alone. A happy childhood can't give it to you. A good spouse can't provide it. Everything going well won't cut it. How many people have those things anyway? How many people have such great circumstances that life is sweet all the time, putting a grin on their face all day long? I know of few. And even for the few who may appear to have wonderful situations, given time they'll encounter bumps in the road too. I used to look at people like that and think very critically, "Well, of course they're happy. Look at their family. Look at their good, functional relationships. Look at their bank account. If they're not happy, who is?" But that's not it.

The riches of the Lord are in Christ. The bounty He longs to heap on your sweet, little head can't be found at a bank. True prosperity has nothing to do with dollar amounts or family lineage. You don't gather that ephah of awesome grain by being smart or coming from the right crowd. It comes through humility—by falling on your knees in prayer and worship and trembling before the mighty Word of God. You don't acquire it in your own wisdom, you come as a child seeking His. You approach empty, asking to be filled. In my heart I know I'm the King's daughter. I know the poverty He embraced as He walked to Calvary has made me rich in Him. *That knowledge took a long time to travel from my head to my heart.*

One thing that keeps me continually childlike before the Lord of Glory is knowing there remains so much deeper, higher, richer, fuller and more amazing that I've yet to experience of Christ. Realizing there's such a great measure of Him beyond what I've tasted so far, that His field is endless and that new wonders wait to be gathered in Him until I draw my last breath, keeps me eager to know more of Him. It fills me with youthful anticipation for what He'll do next and the latest bit of glory He'll let me glimpse. *May we never lose that wide-eyed wonder over Jesus. May we never think we've arrived at some high place of knowledge and have a handle on Almighty God, no matter how many degrees we have or how many years we've walked with Him. He'll never be boxed in or tamed by our fences. He's the mighty King! May we always come before Him as a little child.*

As Jesus states in Matthew 18:3-4, *"Assuredly I say to you, unless you are converted and become as little children, you will by no means enter the Kingdom of heaven. Therefore whoever humbles himself as this little child is the greatest in the Kingdom of heaven."* Leave your grown-up sophistication behind and come to the King of the fields as a wide-eyed child. Go to your heavenly Father and let His mighty hand touch and heal every wounded place in your heart from the day you were born. Allow Him to set free not only the grown-up-you, but the child-in-you, as well, from all the strongholds and sins collected along the way, and then to heap the fullness of Spirit and Truth on your newly freed soul. You'll never be the same once the Son has set you "free, indeed."

And people are going to notice the change in you. They're going to want to know where you got that "ephah" and gathered such sweet fullness. *We need to diligently tell it*—to talk about the darkness from which the Lord freed us, as well as the battles, times of overcoming, defeats and victories we've tasted. We need to share about our time in Moab and our trip out, of how Christ restored and redeemed our long-lost innocence, gave us back the heart we so foolishly gave away and made it new and full with Himself—a heart that's dead no more, but pumps with Christ's blood, is nourished by living water and able to produce fruit through the power of the Holy Spirit.

John 15:8 says, *"It is to your Father's glory that you bear much fruit, showing yourselves to be My disciples."* All that bounty, that sweet ephah of grain, is meant to bring the King much glory! It's a wave offering, something with which to praise His Name. Pride should never enter the picture, as if your fullness has anything to do with you. IT'S ALL HIM. He owns it all. We're just called to faithfully carry and share it. *When the King fills you with His harvest, He gives enough to share. He doesn't expect you to pour out until you're exhausted and dry, but for you to be so continually filled at His feet that it's absolutely natural for the overflow to touch those around you.*

It amazes me to think that we can be so fully loaded with love and power from the risen Christ as to stand out with a blazing brilliance, like a city on a hill or a bonfire on a dark night. That possibility astounds this wallflower. How great is our God, who pours out His Spirit without measure and lights a holy fire within us. *All of us.* Not just a few, not only those with a "special calling," but to everyone who simply asks.

Speaking of asking, what if every believer started praying for the Lord's fullness and overflow everywhere they went—every shop, grocery store, entertainment venue, mall, restaurant, church, city, country...? What if we stopped criticizing and judging and started interceding? Instead of complaining about government, leadership, culture, media, advertising, etc., *why don't we begin to pray over them and claim them as the King's?* What might happen in the heavenlies that could flow over into the physical? Let's entreat God for the purple-haired, the half-dressed, the drugged-out, the self-absorbed, the hurting, the forsaken, the poor, the deceived, the blind hearts, the backslidden, the abused and the otherwise unlovely. I even found myself in the Mall of Georgia feeling compelled to pray silently over clothing I was going through on racks, asking God to cover the one who would buy them with not just fabric, but Himself. Nothing is too hard or impossible for our mighty God!

For several years, the Lord has burned an urgency in me to pray for every city I visit. I've cried out for San Diego, New York, Dallas, Orlando, Atlanta, Charlotte and others. *If we all did that, how might the Lord pour Himself out and shake us with His power?* In Joshua 1:3 He states, *"I will give you every place where you set your foot."* As the New King James Version puts it: *"Every place that the sole of your foot will tread upon I have given you."* What if your precious-in-His-sight, well dressed in sweet peace, forward feet began to claim every place they walked for the Lord? What if we did that all the time, praying for and taking territory for Christ as we go on our way?

What if we then started interceding not only for the places our physical feet take us, but also where our "spiritual feet" are led? That can be *anywhere,* locations our feet may never touch but which can be reached by our hearts. *What could happen? What harvest could result?* We need to dream big in the Spirit. Imagine the possibilities that could arise from focused prayer on entire regions by the body of Christ. How could the King resist? He never gives stones when His children ask for bread.

Do we want to see revival, but do nothing to bring it about? The battle begins on our knees. Are our arms so full with the things of our own lives that we forget to look up, look around and cry out to the Lord for more? Are we asking the Lord to give us every place we set our feet for His kingdom? Are we seeking His direction on how to pray, how to prepare the way of the Lord and how to pour out the holy measures He's blessed us with—how to take our bundle of grain back to the city and spread it before whomever the Lord leads us?

We have no idea how profoundly the Almighty can use our testimonies and prayers in the lives of others, or how deeply He can plant His Word in someone's heart through our boldness to share it. *Only God can measure His measure. It's far beyond the limits of our simple minds.* The Bible instructs us to *"prepare our minds for action,"* and that *"each one should use whatever gift he has received to serve others..."* (1 Peter 1:13 & 4:10). We might as well face it and ready our sometimes-tossed-about minds for this: we're not called to take the King's provision and devour it ourselves, but to "break bread" and pass it around.

That kind of breaking may first require some things being broken *in* you. Fear has to be broken. Doubt must be torn to shreds. Insecurity has to be ripped apart. Selfishness and greed have to be destroyed. Laziness, pride, rebellion, a desire to be approved or honored—whatever binds you—needs to be crushed to death. *Many things of the flesh have to be shattered so things of the Spirit can pour through.*

Every one of us who've accepted the Lord Jesus is filled with His Spirit and given rich gifts. We all have a basketful from the King, as surely as Ruth carried her bundle of grain back to Naomi—*and we're expected to do something with our measure, too! We're called to share our bounty with others.* In the Parable of the Talents Jesus told, the men who invested and multiplied their riches heard these words, *"Well done, good and faithful servant. Come, share in your Master's happiness."* We delight the heart of the King when we invest what He's given us in others. Our blessings aren't merely for ourselves. The part of the story that strikes holy fear in me is where the man who hid his talent was scolded, had his money taken away, was called a "worthless servant" and was put out in the dark. *The Lord seems to be very serious about this!!!*

We need to examine all the Lord has put in our lives, and ask Him how we can invest it for His kingdom and glory. We also need to carefully weigh this question: Whose measure is your treasure, the Lord's or the world's? Jeremiah says, *"the heart is deceitful above all things."* It's easy to fool ourselves by doing some good things for the Lord, sharing a small portion of His blessings, while simultaneously holding onto the world's stuff. You can check yourself on this by examining what your mind is most focused on. *"For where your treasure is, there your heart* [desires, emotions and thoughts] *will be also,"* (Matthew 6:21). Your energies are going to be focused somewhere, and you're given a choice where that will be. *"Choose you this day..."*

If the focus of your thoughts and prayers is continually yourself, your family, your own needs, how to get ahead and prosper, your home, that next trip—things that concern *you*—there's probably not much room left for Kingdom business, much less taking your grain to town and laying it at someone else's feet. May the Lord protect us from beginning in the Spirit and finishing in the flesh, as Galatians 3 warns against. This applies to any calling of the Lord's.

Ephesians 4:11-13 tells us, *"It was He who gave some to be apostles, some to be prophets, some to be evangelists, and some to be pastors and teachers, to prepare God's people for works of service, so that the body of Christ may be built up until we all reach unity in the faith and in the knowledge of the Son of God and become mature, attaining to the whole measure of the fullness of Christ."* Heaven's measureless measure, the powerful, unlimited Holy Spirit, is being poured into our little hearts for more than thrilling our souls. We need to open our arms, move our feet, allow others to see into our lives and lift up Jesus, letting Him draw others to Himself and building up the body and kingdom of Christ. May we let the King fill us through prayer and His Word, and to use our lives as poured-out offerings that touch other hearts. In Matthew 9:38, Jesus says to *"Ask the Lord of the Harvest, therefore, to send out workers into His harvest field."* Let's ask Him to stuff our baskets with such abundance, we can't help but share His bounty.

Questions & Applications

1. **Examine your thoughts and prayers today. Are they focused more on you and yours or others?**
2. **Ask the Lord for open eyes to see opportunities to share the bounty He has blessed you with, for a mouth ready to give an answer and speak grace and Truth and for a willingness to follow through. Get ready, then, to be astounded.**

26

What's in a Name?

And her mother-in-law said to her, "Where have you gleaned today? And where did you work? Blessed be the one who took notice of you." So she told her mother-in-law with whom she had worked, and said, "The man's name with whom I worked today is Boaz."

Then Naomi said to her daughter-in-law, "Blessed be he of the Lord, who has not forsaken His kindness to the living and the dead!" And Naomi said to her, "This man is a close relation of ours, one of our close relatives," **Ruth 2:19-20.**

Ruth had encountered the owner of the field. She no longer needed to rely on hearsay, somebody else's description or a second-hand account. She'd come face to face, engaged in conversation and been abundantly fed and blessed by him. In her brief experience with the man, she'd already learned much about him beyond merely his name. *But sometimes there's power in a name itself,* and as soon as Naomi heard it she praised and thanked the Lord God, who was keeping covenant with them. The fact that Boaz was a close relative meant he had the power to rescue them and redeem their land—and hearts. *Hearing the name of Boaz was good news. It was cause for hope and reason to rejoice.* As Naomi spoke those words of blessing over Boaz, I believe her heart was pounding with excitement and hopeful anticipation.

Does the Name above all Names do that for you? When the name of Jesus falls from your lips or someone else's, does it stir your heart with a fullness for all it means? Does it inspire deep hope within you that He'll bring His Word to pass in your life and keep covenant with you, that He's well able to redeem and restore, provide for you, produce a harvest and revive what's died in your heart? Do you allow His Name to pour over your fears, worries, doubts, and distresses and smother them with its power? Do you stand on it and know it's strong enough for whatever you face? Do you wrap yourself in it and know it's your tower of defense, refuge, fortress, shield, covering and great weapon? Do you bless the Lord for giving the name of Jesus to embrace and take as your own—for allowing you to join His bloodline at His expense?

Have we heard His Name all our lives, but never really treasured all it means? Have we sat in a pew since infancy and listened to teaching about Him, yet taken His precious Name for granted? Do we wait for crisis before we call out to Him from the depths of our being? Does the name of Jesus fall from our lips with casual affection, or with an overwhelming, heart-soaking, desperate kind of adoration and pure amazement? Does the mere mention or thought of His Name cause a deep love to radiate within you? Do you meditate on it and let it fill you with everything this world can't? Is it sweeter to you than the mention of your spouse, your children or your dearest, longest friend? Does its joy and power rule over all your heart, soul, mind and strength? Does it identify you as the King's beloved?

Jesus' name is holy ground upon which we're called to stand, and, as we receive all He offers us as His children, we're to bless Him. *Blessed be the One who's poured out a measure of Himself that we can't contain: Jesus!* He's the King of Kings, almighty Lord of Lords, Holy One, I AM, Who Was, Who Is, Who Is To Come, Worthy Son of the Living God, Risen Christ and Lamb slain from the foundation of the world. He is Savior, Messiah, bright Morning Star, Wonderful, Counselor, Mighty God, Prince of Peace, Everlasting Father, Root and Offspring of David, perfect Keeper of Covenant and the Way, the Truth and the Life. He's the Faithful and True rider on the white horse in Revelation, whose name is the Word of God, the First and Last, the Living One who is life itself, Alpha and Omega, the Beginning and End. He is Light and Glory, the Creator, Jehovah, the only sovereign God, our Shepherd, Teacher and Holy Guide. He's the Anointed One, the Living Water, the Bread of Life, the Oil of Anointing and the Word made flesh.

God hasn't hidden His Name or intentions from us, but laid them before our feeble hearts and said, "Choose Me. Take My Name as your own." The Word is laced with names for the Almighty and presents them to us as power for life, salvation and strength. It reveals Him as Elohim, the God of Creation; El Elyon, the God Most High; El Roi, the God who sees; El Shaddia, the All Sufficient One, the Pourer Forth; Adonai, the Lord; Jehovah, the Self-Existent One; Jehovah-jireh, the Lord Will Provide; Jehovah-rapha, the Lord Who Heals; Jehovah-nissi, the Lord My Banner; Jehovah-mekoddishkem, the Lord Who Sanctifies; Jehovah-shalom, the Lord is Peace; Jehovah-raah, the Lord My Shepherd; Jehovah-tsidkenu, the Lord Our Righteousness and Jehovah-shammah, the Lord Is There. *Don't pick and choose a name to claim, they're all spread before you. Take all of them.*

No matter how you've judged the Lord according to your circumstances, how angry you've been with Him because of something He's allowed in your life or how long you've ignored or denied Him, *His Name is Truth.* He has revealed the truth of His being, regardless of any opinion your flesh has formed. He's forever demonstrated His passion with His own blood, and has told you who He is and what to call Him. *Call Him by His Name, then. Call Him Mercy, Forgiveness, Grace, Salvation, Justice, Deliverer, Healer and Friend. Call Him New Song, Truth, Redeemer, Lover of your soul, Dearest Treasure, Beloved One and Only, Jesus the Christ, the Son of the living God.*

Establish yourself in the Name of Jesus! Cover and shield your life in His powerful Name! Rest the full weight of your soul on His eternal Name! Let every battle be fought and won beneath the banner and might of His Name! Let His Name fill your heart and fall from your lips. It is beauty, strength and peace; it's salvation, redemption, victory, power for life, rivers poured forth and glory spelled out. JESUS, the highest, fullest, most radiant expression of life abundant, is ready to abundantly be given to you. Hang your fears on His Name and put all your doubts there with them. Let Him soak up your heartaches, disappointments and failures. Lay anger and wrong attitudes there. Allow pride to melt away there. Bank everything on Him.

Take His Name and be completely His! *Don't take a hyphenated name: yours-and His, old creature-new creature, old man-new man, old patterns of thought-new patterns of thought.* That hyphen represents compromise with the world, a lukewarm, fencepost sitter. It's a dangerous line! You've got to take one side or the other. Revelation 3:16 warns, *"So, because you are lukewarm, neither hot or cold, I am about to spit you out of My mouth." TAKE ALL OF HIM. YOUR NAME GONE AND HIS HIGHLIGHTED, SPOTLIGHTED, EXALTED AND LIFTED HIGH.* As I was driving out of a parking lot the other day, I saw a "God is my co-pilot" car tag. Immediately I thought, "That's a hyphen!" I don't want to co-pilot my life, I want it completely surrendered and taken over by the Name above all names, the King of Glory, the Lord Jesus Christ. I have no business co-piloting, because a co-pilot can steer things off course. I don't want to negotiate with the Lord about my direction, I just want to stay beneath His holy wings and faithfully go where He sends me.

Strong's defines "name" as, "a word used to identify a person, animal or thing." In reference to the term "Almighty," the Greek says it "represents the title and dignity of the Lord. It implies authority, rank, majesty, power and excellence, and expresses the attributes of God." The names the Lord uses to identify Himself reveal His heart, nature, character, purpose and passion. He wants us to *know Him.* He intends for us not only to say His Name, but to live in it, be sheltered by it and take it as our own. Over and over in Scripture, we see the Lord take a common, sinful man and change his name: Abram to Abraham, Jacob to Israel, Saul to Paul, Simon to Peter... *Thank God, He changes our very identity as we come to Him. He changes what we're known as, and gives us a name that relates us to Him instead of our sin.*

"A good name is better to be had than great riches," Proverbs 22:1. IT DOESN'T MATTER WHAT YOUR NAME'S BEEN OR WHO'S CALLED YOU BY IT, YOU HAVE A NEW NAME. *And it's a good one, a holy one, given you by Christ Himself that you'll be known by from now on.* No longer will Fearful be your name, but Bold in Christ. No longer will Addicted be your identity, but Delivered. No longer will they call you Downcast, but One Full of Hope—no more Deceived, but Speaker of Truth; no longer Doubter, but Believing One; no longer Forsaken, but Treasure of the King; no longer Prideful, but Humble Worshiper of Christ; no longer Rebellious One, but One Who Walks-Out the Word; no longer Barren Heart, but Heart Full of Glory; no longer Empty and Ill, but Filled and Whole. *Praise the*

King of Kings who's changed your name and inheritance! Worship Him!

The Lord of Hosts is serious about His Name. Many times in the Word of God we see battles fought and victories won for the sake of it. In Joshua 7, when Israel suffers defeat because of sin in their hearts, Joshua pleads to the Lord, *"What then will You do for Your own great Name?"* Joshua knew the Lord would protect His holy Name. Isaiah 63 recounts how the Lord *"guided His people to make for Himself a glorious Name."* He brought them through the sea, shepherded His flock, set His Holy Spirit among them, sent His glorious arm of power to be at Moses' right hand, divided the waters, led them through the depths and gave rest, *"to gain for Himself everlasting renown."* "Renown" is defined in Hebrew as, "a conspicuous position, a mark or memorial of an individual, reputation, memory, fame. It can recall a characteristic, an event, a mood, a statement about the individual. *Indicates continuance..."*

The Lord's renown began even before Genesis 1:1, continues to this day and will carry on from everlasting to everlasting. *It's unspeakable, inexpressible glory to me that the King of Heaven chooses to make Himself known—even famous—through our little lives.* It's a wonder that the One who inhabits all of time and eternity desires to inhabit our tiny hearts, the same ones who've been cold as stone and desperately deceived. Ponder this and celebrate it. Join with Psalm 135:1 and, *"Praise the Lord. Praise the Name of the Lord; praise Him, you servants of the Lord."* Live out verse 3, *"sing praise to His Name, for that is pleasant."* Remind your heart of verse 13, *"Your Name, O Lord, endures forever, Your renown, O Lord, through all generations."* Let this generation praise Him.

From cover to cover, the Word of God tells us to praise the worthy, holy One of Israel. He wants to be conspicuous in your life, made famous in your realm of influence and recognized and praised. *Let worship flow out of you as you draw near Him in Spirit and begin to see the power of His Name.* The Lord inhabits that praise and stamps His Name over you, changes your focus, puts life in perspective and redirects your wayward feet.

As He did with Peter, Jesus asks us, "Who do you say I am?" *Our very life depends on our response.* Our wholeness, peace, rest, purpose, dreams, desires and destiny all depend on how our hearts, *not just our mouths,* answer that question. We can say something all day long and never really believe or mean it. We can merely give a "church answer," or respond religiously. *Instead, we need to reply from the depths of our souls, with full trust and confidence in our hearts that Jesus is absolutely who He says He is and every Word He's spoken is spoken for us, too*—even we Moabites. We need to practice Psalm 103:1,*"all my inmost being, praise His Holy Name."*

I believe the Lord also asks us, "Whose name do you want known, Mine or yours?" When we serve, do we want credit? When we teach, do we want affirmation? When we give, do we want recognition? Do we seek the secret or the public place? *Whose applause matters most to us, heaven's or earth's?* May HIS name and HIS renown be the only desire of our hearts. Genesis 11:4 provides an example of people who boldly declared, *"let us make a name for ourselves..."* and then proudly began building the Tower of Babel. We know how *that one* ended. The result of seeking a name for ourselves (our church, family, etc.), or promoting our own gifts, abilities, talents and desires is *confusion, babbling and scattering.*

While I doubt many of us would make the kind of statement the "Babblers" did, I believe the pride of wanting our name known can sneak in subtly and unconsciously, maybe even wrapped in some spiritual "word." *The Lord is well able to oppose our proud and self-focused name building.*

He's quite capable of confusing all our well-laid plans and bringing us to our knees. He can make the words of our flesh, our flesh-talk, nothing but babble. *And I'm so grateful for that.* I never want to be allowed to continue in error. I want God to correct me and put His Truth in my mouth. I want His words to flow out of me, not my own. I want to speak with wisdom and love, not with Jonah-type criticism that says, "Go get them, Lord." I pray for discernment about any subtle scrap of pride or temptation to put myself out in front, and for humility to MAKE HIS NAME GREAT. *Flesh can never produce things of the Spirit, so don't ever try to exalt it as if it could bring about any move of God.*

In Genesis 17:1, the Lord appeared to Abram and said, "I Am the Lord Almighty..." It wasn't as if Abram didn't already know God, or that this was his first introduction to Him. *As He instructed Abram and established a covenant with him, the Lord was reminding him of who He was.* May He continually remind us of that too, so we'll seek His glory and walk in the power of His Name. Psalm 9:10 says, *"Those who know Your Name will trust in You, for You, Lord, have never forsaken those who seek You."* That's good news. The Name of Christ inspires deep trust and stirs our faith, especially as we call on Him and see Him prove His faithfulness over and over, never, ever forsaking our earnest cry.

In Revelation 3:8, Jesus says, *"I know that you have little strength, yet you have kept My Word and have not denied My name."* In verse12 He promises, *"Him who overcomes*

I will make a pillar in the temple of My God." That's SO beautiful to me. A pillar is a strong, foundational part of the temple, an obvious, strong, majestic, honored *and well-used* position. It doesn't announce, "I'm a pillar!" It just is. It doesn't need to draw attention to itself, it naturally glorifies the builder as it stands in position. *How amazing to think we could be described that way.* Boaz's name was written on a literal pillar of Solomon's temple! It's described in I Kings

7:21: *"He erected the pillars at the portico of the te The pillar to the south he named Jakin, and the one to north Boaz."* Boaz overcame prejudice and discriminatio and welcomed the Moabite foreigner named Ruth, and the Lord established and honored him and his descendants.

The King of all Kings has given us His own Name and equipped us abundantly to stand as pillars in His temple (the body of Christ) with "Holy To The Lord" engraved on our hearts and the seal of the Holy Spirit over our souls. May we go forward in boldness, knowing whose Name covers and directs our feet. Sometimes the only thing I know to do is pray the Lord's name—Jesus, Jesus, Jesus—to let its love and mercy soak my soul and invite its power and strength to cut to my core. I cry out the Name Above All Names, shouting within or speaking it out loud, and wait for Him. I speak His Name over every thought that enters my mind, rejecting those not of Him and cherishing those that are. I speak the Name over…

…every weapon formed against me, some obvious, some not.

…the fears that seek to paralyze me, reducing me to stagnancy.

…the waves of discouragement that threaten to knock me down and freeze my feet.

…stinging rejection, disappointment and relationships in distress.

…all that was, is and is yet to come in my life, knowing that Jesus Christ, Who Was, Is and Is To Come, is well able to mold, transform and glorify Himself through it all.

…every sin that seeks to have me, every stronghold and deceptive pattern of thought that attempts to destroy and every cherished place that may be death in disguise.

n the depths of the pit and know He'll ere's no other name under heaven by l and no other name strong enough f our hearts. So Jesus, Jesus, Jesus, speak Your Name and run to its strong defense. Cut in me all cords of unforgiveness Your Name. Break every binding, crippling chain that threatens. Smash doubt and discouragement to pieces. Then raise up every single thing Your Name represents and be glorified greatly through this little heart.

Questions & Applications

1. **Who do you say that Jesus is? What is stirred in your heart when you hear His holy Name?**
2. **I would challenge you to search through Scriptures for the names the Lord calls Himself and ponder their power and depth. There are many Bible Studies on that topic alone. Go seek His Name- you'll never be the same.**
3. **Bless the One who has not only told you who He is, but has renamed you as His child and a joint heir with Christ. In Him, you are not what the world calls you, but what His own mouth has named you. *Worship Him.***

27

The In-between Time

Ruth the Moabitess said, "He also said to me, 'You shall stay close by my young men until they have finished all my harvest.'" And Naomi said to Ruth her daughter-in-law, "It is good, my daughter, that you go out with his young women, and that people do not meet you in any other field." So she stayed close by the young women of Boaz, to glean until the end of the barley harvest and wheat harvest; and she dwelt with her mother-in-law, **Ruth 2:21-23.**

In essence, Naomi was saying to Ruth, "You're in the right place! STAY THERE! Don't run off to some other field!" And that's what Ruth did. She remained in Boaz's field, gathering, anticipating things to come and waiting on the end of the harvest. Notice the *timing*. There's a season, a perfectly-scheduled, due season of the Lord. There's a time for planting, for getting rid of tares and locusts, for waiting on the fullness of the harvest and for gleaning with others until the harvest is over.

Our lives are like that. The Lord is teaching me to *wait on Him*. To stay right where He's placed me and not let Him catch me in any other field! So many times when I've had a strong desire to move on, the Lord has said, "Wait. Stay here. You're in the right place. Just keep doing what I've put in front of you with faithfulness, obedience and humility. I know when the end of harvest is for this time in your life and will usher you into the next season with joy—and at the right time. *My time.*" I can't even think of one example when His time correlated with mine. But looking back through years, I realize that my time would have left me in a giant heap of trouble, while His has been sweet, satisfying and perfect. His way is always best and brings Him glory.

The book of Ruth has traditionally been read at Pentecost, and because of that I've studied the Feasts of the Lord. In Leviticus 23:14, God says of them, *"...[they] shall be a statute forever throughout your generations in all your dwellings."* We're not meant to overlook or forget the significance and prophetic implications of the feasts of Jehovah! I believe they help spell out God's timing and that, even though they've been fulfilled in Christ, He still loves them and the prophecies to which they pointed. He loves the deep, rich, powerful applications they now, and for all generations, contain. He loves the worship that arises when they're studied—and, yes, still observed. He still loves us to bring Him our best and let Him multiply, bless and build His Kingdom with it. He loves us to present the full, sweet offerings of our heart, soul, mind and strength to the Chief Priest, Christ Jesus Himself.

Passover was celebrated at the time of the barley harvest, Pentecost at wheat harvest. In between was a period of 50 days, sometimes called the Omer. Leviticus 23:16 offers this instruction, *"Count fifty days to the day after the seventh Sabbath; then you shall offer a new grain offering to the Lord."* The passage in Ruth seems to occur during this period. These feasts were celebrated at God's invitation and were His delight, even as they foreshadowed the coming Cross (Passover) and the outpouring of the Holy Spirit

(Pentecost). They were, in Old Testament times, the "joy set before Him."

While Ruth was counting down the days of harvest, Jews were counting up to the days of feasting that involved waving *"two loaves of two-tenths of an ephah. They shall be of fine flour; they shall be baked with leaven,"* (Leviticus 23:17). Ruth would be in Bethlehem at the time of the feast where the two loaves that represented the Jews and the Gentiles were being offered! In many ways she represented the "Gentile-flavored" loaf—the foreigner brought alongside the Jew. *How awesome is the timing of the Lord God!*

I wonder if we're in a similar period today, an in-between time, an "omer" of waiting and preparation? We've tasted some of the feasts—Passover was fulfilled at the Cross and the Holy Spirit was poured out on Pentecost—but are we looking ahead in great anticipation to the next one? Are we preparing our hearts and lives for the final feast, the last harvest of the King?

Look at the disciples in the book of Acts. Christ had been crucified at Passover-time, the ultimate Lamb slain for sin, *then came the 50-day count to the Feast of Pentecost*. What were the disciples doing during that period? Acts 1:12 tells us they returned to Jerusalem and joined together in constant prayer. I wonder what they were praying? How I'd have loved to eavesdrop on those cries to the King! Were they praying the prayer Jesus taught them? Were they earnestly seeking His kingdom to come? Were they asking for those places Christ had said He would send them: Jerusalem, Judea, Samaria and the ends of the earth?

Are we seeking our comfort and blessing, or for His kingdom to come in our lives and everywhere He'd dare send us? What are we doing during our time of waiting on the Lord, our "fifty days"? We've already discussed how scattering, babbling and confusion result from building our own towers. In Acts 2, the believers had none of that, but were all together in *unity*. They were focused, knees bowed, hearts open and eyes fixed on heaven. *Unity is critical as we wait for the King*. Psalm 133:1 says, *"Behold, how good and how pleasant it is for brethren to dwell together in unity! It is like the precious oil upon the head, running down on the beard, the beard of Aaron..."* Oneness releases anointing. It gives the Holy Spirit something upon which to pour Himself, overflow on and run down the face of, like the priests—who are now US. I've heard a few teachers where I've thought, "You can see the anointing oil shining on their face!" Haven't you?

I don't think the disciples had a committee meeting to decide it was time to come together with one heart and mind, but that it took place naturally as they focused on the risen King, who promised them the Holy Spirit. They weren't looking at themselves, because their hearts were captured by the Most High and seeking His presence and glory alone. *How I pray that will become our sole focus also*. WHAT IF NOT JUST ONE GROUP OR ONE CHURCH, BUT THE WHOLE BODY OF CHRIST CAME TOGETHER AS ONE IN FOCUSED PRAYER? WHAT WOULD THE LORD RELEASE IN RESPONSE TO OUR UNIFIED CRIES? HOW WOULD HE ANSWER THAT KIND OF JOYFUL EXPECTATION? I believe He'd reply with Himself, His presence, His power and His delight; with His mighty Spirit breathed out and exhaled for us to inhale, like holy mouth-to-mouth resuscitation. I think we'd see a great move of healing and deliverance, exalting Christ, bringing salvation and establishing His kingdom and will among us.

What happened in Acts in response to the cries of the disciples (and remember, Jesus Christ is the same yesterday, today, and forever)? Acts 2 gives the account: the wind of heaven filled the room, they began to speak in other tongues (Their speech changed! They became bold, full of the Holy Spirit and His Word.), they were ALL filled with the power of the Holy Spirit (I believe one of the Enemy's lies is that power is only for a select few, but here we see 120 praying and 120 filled!) and the crowd outside began asking questions. The door for the spread of the Gospel and the establishment of the body of Christ flung wide open. The disciples used their newfound boldness to preach to the crowd, and the people were cut to the heart, crying out, "What shall we do, then?"

The groundwork for this awesome move of God was prayer. And when the call to repentance was made, 3,000 souls came to Christ! What if 3,000 people we knew saw the power of God in our lives, asked questions, came to repentance and received Christ? What would happen? I don't know 3,000 people, but the Lord certainly can use my mouth to speak to whomever He brings across my path.

That scene in Acts 2 covers one day, but what about the long term? How do we wait on the Lord now? *The same way.* Acts 2:42-47 describes the activities of the Church following this move of the Holy Spirit, and it's basically identical: they devoted themselves to the Word, to meeting together and to prayer. *Sounds like unity again to me*. These first church members weren't just warming a pew, they'd tasted a glimpse of glory, experienced the beauty and power of the Holy Spirit and had seen the effect of prayer for themselves *and wanted nothing less*. I wonder what they'd say if they sat in some of our churches today? I shudder to think what we miss out on with our lack of unity.

What else resulted from the early disciples' unity, study of the Word and prayer? *"Everyone was filled with awe, and many wonders and miraculous signs were done by the apostles,"* (Acts 2:43). Are we awestruck before the Lord and His Word, joining in focused prayer and seeing His wonders and miracles, of which salvation is the greatest? Wouldn't it be miraculous to see a whole church come to its knees, repenting and joining their hearts before the King; to see the prayer altar filled? In verse 47, the body of Christ was *"praising God and enjoying the favor of all the people. And the Lord added to their number daily those who were being saved."* Pure praise filled the hearts of those believers and overflowed into their world. They were selfless and devoted, with eyes fixed on heavenly things and— *"the Lord added to their number daily"*—there was an obvious, outward sign of what was taking place in the Spirit realm.

Jesus said these people would be His witnesses to the ends of the earth. *Their physical feet didn't travel that far, but their spiritual ones did.* God used their faithfulness to send the Gospel not only to the entire world, but down through time to every generation. They were faithful in everything, even to death, and the Lord multiplied His Word and His Church in His time and His way, causing a domino effect. I wonder if those steadfast saints are allowed to peer over heaven's gates and see how far-reaching their impact's been? If so, I'm sure it's such a sweet, overwhelming reward that they fall in fresh worship before Jesus, the King. *How I pray the King of Kings will find us faithful like that, and build His mighty kingdom far beyond what we can see today.* Our feet may never leave town, but our witness can! Our prayers can! The Word made flesh in us can! We don't have to know when or how, all we need to do is press on, trusting His timing and walking in His presence. Our faithfulness can set off some dominoes, too!

The biblical feasts help us see how to prepare for an intimate, powerful encounter with the King of Glory. Preparation was always required. Ours is in our hearts. That's really what He's after; our heart is the desire of His. Most of my study on preparations for the feasts can be summed up like this (something restated over and over throughout the Old and New Testaments): *Repent, be still and know God, ask for eyes to see the contents of your heart and His. Bring your whole self in worship, take back what the Enemy stole and give the King your best.* The Lord has gifted and offered His power to all of us. Let's use everything He's given us to serve Him in unity and with sincere hearts focused above and for His glory alone.

The Lord of Lords is now counting down to the Feast of all Feasts, the Wedding Supper of the Lamb. He's inviting us to joyfully anticipate it with Him as we, the Bride, make ourselves ready and prepare our hearts for the King. We're blessed because, through salvation, we hold the invitation to this great celebration in our hands! *I can't wait for the reception!!!*

Quoting Joel 2, Peter stated in Acts 2:17-18, "*'In the last days, I will pour out My Spirit on all people. Your sons and daughters will prophesy, your young men will see visions, your old men will dream dreams. Even on My servants, both men and women, I will pour out My Spirit in those days, and they will prophesy.'*" THESE ARE THOSE DAYS! Let's anticipate the next great move of God in unity and prayer, and celebrate!

Questions & Applications

1. **Are you impatiently anxious or joyfully content with where the Lord has you today?**
2. **Assuming you've tasted the fullness of the feasts of Passover and Pentecost by accepting the Lord's salvation and being filled with the Holy Spirit, what are you doing with your "omer," the time counting down to the ultimate feast with the King of Glory? Are you merely seeking your own comfort, blessings and fulfillment, or do you seek to build the Body of Christ?**
3. **Ask the Lord to fill you with a fresh fire to be about His business in these days, praying, seeking Him**

in His Word and joining in focused unity with the body of Christ.

28

Lessons from the Threshing Floor

One day Naomi her mother-in-law said to her, "My daughter, should I not try to find a home for you, where you will be well provided for? Is not Boaz, with whose servant girls you have been, a kinsman of ours? Tonight he will be winnowing barley on the threshing floor," **Ruth 3:1-2.**

After the seed had been planted, the field watered and the crop grown to maturity, it was gathered and brought to the threshing floor, where it would be ground out and prepared for use. The process involved a separating, a releasing. The stalk had served its purpose. It had held the grain until it was nourished and matured and was now "freed" by threshing to a new place—its ultimate purpose and call. The harvest wasn't meant to remain on the stalk forever, but to be transformed into something that would nourish others. In the threshing place, grain was shaken from dependence on the stalk and established on its own.

What's your stalk? What has the Lord surrounded you with to nurture and mature you? What has He hidden you in until it's time to stand on your own two feet? Many examples come to my mind—Bible teachers, family members, friends, mentors, groups, counselors or a church family—good things all. But there comes a day in our walk with the King when He will likely need to shake us out of our *dependency* on those things in order to establish us in the irrevocable call He has for our lives. I pray we won't cling to our stalks, with fingernails dug in, when the Lord brings us to the threshing floor to work out His perfect purposes! Co-dependency is not our call. Being rooted, established and perfected in the Lord is. We're called to cling to Him and His Word, depending on Him for life itself.

While the separation the Lord takes you through may involve something outward, more likely it will be from an *inner* reliance on a person or thing. You may remain surrounded by them, but your heart will be taken to a new level of maturity. Mature children no longer depend on their parents to feed, clothe and shelter them. They don't forsake the relationship, they just move into their own place, get their own job and walk out their own call. Threshing usually involves pain; however, it's not meant to create bitterness, hardness of heart, a lack of love and trust or any other poison the Enemy might try to tempt you with during this time. *It's meant to break open the hull that's surrounded you for a season, cleanse you, establish you and plant you firmly in your purpose.*

Otherwise, *the stalk can turn into an idol.* If you cling to something the Lord is calling you to let go of, or grab onto anything or anyone and put all your trust and dependency in it, apart from the Lord Jesus, then you're raising up a false christ, a phony savior, and making it an object of worship. We need to examine our hearts and loyalties, repent of unhealthy and unholy dependencies and press on in Christ. If grain refuses to be released, it may well rot on the stalk. It certainly forsakes its ability to be formed into something nourishing to others. It misses the whole point of its existence.

Once again, it's related to the Lord's divine timing. He's ordained seasons of sowing, watering, fertilizing, gathering, threshing and forming into bread. We need to praise the God Who Was, Is and Is To Come in every blessed season, and be willing to let Him usher us from one to the next without screaming, sulking, looking back or refusing to move. Recalling times the Lord has brought me to the threshing floor, I have to say that none was simple, easy and comfortable. *But He's held me close every single time, and it's been good. Perfect.* Once we arrive at the new point to which He's taking us, we won't regret the process or find ourselves longing for what used to be, we'll rejoice over where He's brought us.

Don't be afraid of the threshing floor. From cover to cover, the Word tells us not to fear. If you're being threshed, it's evidence that the Lord's hand is pushing you into a new, more effective arena with Him. It's good. He's good. His seasons are good. He's good when He plants and good when He threshes. Rejoice in Him, no matter where you are. If you're in the midst of a threshing, be assured the Lord Jesus is right beside you. He won't leave you alone there; He will absolutely *not* forsake you. As He sets in motion the necessary process to pull you out and set you apart, maturing you, establishing you in your purpose, using you as He's planned all along, He'll not depart your side for a second. He may be separating you from old habits and dependencies, but you'll NEVER be separated from His heart.

Consider Romans 8:35, *"Who shall separate us from the love of Christ? Shall trouble or hardship or persecution or famine or nakedness or danger or sword?"* I would add "threshing" to the list. While being threshed you might feel anxious, troubled, fearful, persecuted, stripped naked or endangered, in spite of which you can rest in the same assurance Paul had. *"For I am convinced that neither death nor life, nor angels, nor demons, neither the present nor the future, nor any powers, neither height nor depth, nor anything else in all creation,* [not even threshing] *will be able to separate us from the love of God that is in Christ Jesus our Lord,"* (v. 38-39).

If a kernel of grain could think, I wonder if it would realize why it was being pulled out of the stalk and thrown around on the floor? Would it have a vision of the bread it was soon going to become? Of course a seed can't think, but we can. And I pray we'll be a harvest in the Lord's hands that's full of vision—not despising the day of separating and hardship, but looking ahead to what's to come, trusting the Lord's process and anticipating with joy the feast He's preparing us for. Isaiah 28:28 contains some good news about the season of threshing: *"Grain must be ground to make bread, so one does not go on threshing forever."* Thank God! Sometimes, I feel like I've been threshed for ages. Guess I'm a slow learner, or that I've had a lot of "stalk" in my life. But God is good, *and I can smell the bread baking*. God's threshing floor may not be the place of our choosing, but it's worth it. Don't resist Him. Trust Him. Rest in the beauty of sweet, powerful surrender. He's drawing you near and establishing you in His great mercy.

You can't determine your own times of threshing. It's the Lord's doing. Let it be marvelous in your eyes. Put your heart in the hands of Almighty God, and let the Thresher thresh! Worship Him in the process. Don't tell Him, "If you get me out of this, I'll worship You," or, "When this hard part is over, then I'll get in Your Word." *Praise Him now, even in a place of stripping, where you don't yet see or understand.*

There's a flip side to this. *When the grain is released from the stalk, it's not to glory in the fact that it's feeding others. It's not to walk in pride that it's now on its own and being used by God.* Remember, the King of Kings and Lord of Lords is well able to humble. We need to glory in Him alone, and bless the holy Hand that lifts us out, sets us apart and uses our lives for His purposes. Besides, it takes the whole Body, threshed, baked and working together, to make a loaf of bread worthy of the Lord. Just rejoice that *you* are a kernel in His hands, take your place and give Him the honor due His Name.

The Bible offers many examples of individuals the Lord raised up and separated out for his service, who then stumbled in pride. Gideon, the "least of the least," was used mightily by God to help his people. Yet, following his victories he took gold earrings from the plunder of battle and formed what became an idol. The Word tells us that, *"Gideon made the gold into an ephod, which he placed in Ophrah, his town. All Israel prostituted themselves by worshiping it there, and it became a snare to Gideon and his family,"* (Judges 8:27). Later, we observe stumbling pride as Saul (who hid behind the baggage when it was time to be presented to the people as king of Israel) sets up a monument to himself (1 Samuel 15:12). As the Lord chooses to use us, may we never draw a hint of attention to our names, our reputations or anything else about ourselves, but give all glory to the King of Kings and Lord of Lords, the eternal, immortal, invisible, only wise God, the Almighty, Holy One of Israel and Risen Christ. He alone is worthy. To Him be the glory, honor and power forever!

There's another aspect of this to consider. Imagine an immature kernel screaming out to the harvester, "Okay, I'm ready. *Get me out of this stalk!* I'm tired of this place. You called me to be formed into bread, but have left me here too long! I'm tired of being closed in and waiting. I want to move on. I've got things to do and business to be about that can't be done here." Only the Lord knows the right timing for the seasons in our lives. His eyes alone see to the core of our heart and know if it's mature enough to move on. What good is grain if it's removed too soon from the stalk? Can immature souls deal wisely with mature things, or is that what Scripture describes as *"zeal without knowledge"?*

In the immature stage, it's all about you—what you're doing and what your call is. In the ripened stage, it's all about Christ, bringing Him glory and exalting His Name and purposes. You may be more mature than last week or last year, but it still may not be time to fly on your own. *Wait on the Lord. Trust His vision, timing and seasons, and He will be glorified as you do.* In Hebrew, "thresh" means, "to tread out, break." I think of treading on something as walking on it. We need to let holy feet walk across our hearts and make them like His! Isaiah 60:13 says, *"I will make the place of My feet glorious."* Tread on, King Jesus. Here's some soft ground to step on.

What do you need the King of Kings to tread on in your heart? Maybe it's not separation from a growing season, but fear, doubt, pride, stubbornness, bitterness, unforgiveness, strongholds, addictions, self-reliance, a need to control—or any number of crippling, "ingrained," mountainous things. I love what Isaiah 41:15-16 says in relation to this: *"Behold, I will make you into a new threshing sledge with sharp teeth; you shall thresh the mountains and beat them small, and make the hills like chaff. You shall winnow them, the wind shall carry them away, and the whirlwind shall scatter them; you shall rejoice in the Lord, and glory in the Holy One of Israel."*

As the King of Kings threshes your heart into something new, He'll equip you with powerful weapons that can tear down and break apart those huge, looming mountains in your soul! You'll tread on them with the Word and prayer. They won't trample you!

It's noteworthy that following two accounts of David's sin, the Lord told him to buy a threshing floor, build an altar and sacrifice on it there (2 Samuel 24:18-25; 1 Chronicles

21). Here's the awesome part of this: *2 Chronicles 3 informs us that the threshing floor where David poured out his heart before the Lord became the very spot God told Solomon to build His temple!* The Lord used that place of threshing and repentance to set up His holy sanctuary of beauty and holiness, where He would meet and tabernacle with His people. *We also need to take our sin to the threshing floor of Christ's blood, shed on the Cross, and allow Him to build His holy temple in our threshed hearts.*

The Lord will not waste our time on the threshing floor! I believe those occasions will become like a memorial ground in our hearts, a marking point, a place that won't only bless us, but others as well. *How amazing to think they might even become a springboard in our children's hearts to cause them to want to be a temple of Christ, to build His Kingdom and to carry His Spirit.* We need to realize that threshing is not in vain! Harvest will spill out of it and victory will come through it. It will overflow your life! You're meant to participate in the harvest, not just be a spectator merely hearing of others being used. In Leviticus 26, threshing is listed as part of the blessing of obedience and as a sign of harvest. Verse 5 says, *"Your threshing will continue until grape harvest, and your grape harvest will continue until planting, and you will eat all the food you want..."* It promises season after season of abundant blessing.

We need to be on guard, because the Enemy will try to keep us off the threshing floor and rob us of the power it releases in our lives. If he can't steal our souls, he'll surely try to paralyze us on the stalk and keep us from fulfilling our call in Christ. 1 Samuel 23:1 says, *"the Philistines are fighting against Keilah, and…robbing the threshing floors."* The Enemy will do all he can, blatantly and/or cunningly, to *rob your threshing floor!*—to keep you off your knees and in self-pity, fear and confusion. *We have to stand, firmly covered in all the armor and defense Christ died to give us!*

Jesus told His disciples when He sent them out, *"Behold, I give you authority to trample on snakes and scorpions, and over all the power of the enemy, and nothing shall by any means harm you. Nevertheless, do not rejoice in this, that the spirits are subject to you, but rather rejoice because your names are written in heaven,"* (Luke 10:19-20). Be on guard. Let the Lord do the threshing. Don't resist Him, and as you walk on in Him and His strength, you'll tread on the Enemy's schemes against you. Remember, the true source of our rejoicing—the ultimate threshing floor of heaven—is the Cross that bought you and inscribed your name in red in the eternal Book of Life.

Questions & Applications

1. **Look back over your life and thank the Lord for the seasons of threshing through which He has already brought you.**
2. **Is there anything—any "stalk"—in your life today upon which you're depending (and perhaps clinging to) apart from the Lord Jesus and His will for your life?**
3. **If you're currently in a place of threshing, of being shaken and poured out, stay face down in the Word, worship and prayer, and ask the Lord to enable you to wait with joyful anticipation for the new thing He's seeking to do in your life. Be assured that He'll bring you out—and will bless others with the overflow.**

29

Changing Clothes

"Therefore wash yourself and anoint yourself, put on your best garment and go down to the threshing floor; but do not make yourself known to the man until he has finished eating and drinking. Then it shall be, when he lies down, that you shall notice the place where he lies; and you shall go in, uncover his feet, and lie down; and he will tell you what you should do," ***Ruth 3:3-4.***

I've heard Ruth criticized for being just a bit too forward here, as if she were doing something dishonorable. But to me, this is one of the story's most precious passages. I don't believe Naomi was encouraging Ruth to be pushy or tacky, but giving her blessing for Ruth to go to the feet of her (Naomi's) kinsman-redeemer and welcome a new chapter in her life. I think of Naomi's message like this: "You've honored and blessed me by mourning my son, you've followed me to a foreign land out of faithfulness and love and have shown me your pure heart. You've watered the ground from Moab to Bethlehem with your tears, and every step has been a reminder of shattered dreams. *Now, precious daughter of my heart, I bless you to go where I know you can find favor and redemption, to my kinsman who is able to lift you from the pit of despair and establish you in a house of bread."*

Ruth was being encouraged to *change clothes,* to take off the garments of grief and mourning for those of rejoicing, go humbly to the feet of the redeemer and quietly position herself there with great expectation. In other words, by her presence and dress Ruth was declaring she was no longer emotionally frozen in another place and time, but had exchanged a spirit of heaviness for one of hope. *I've been there*. Have you ever worn something other than a spirit of praise? Have you shed tears and put on something other than your "best garment"? Has sorrow of heart ever threatened to freeze it stone cold where it was hurt? Have you been bold enough to lay those dark clothes down and go to the threshing floor of the Redeemer—to step out and ask for His favor and redeeming grace?

Was the past unkind to you? Have you walked through some hard things? Are you in a difficult place right now? Will you be bold enough to "re-dress" the part of you that hurts so deeply? Can you see that place from the perspective of Light and Truth, instead of darkness? As the Lord took me way back to such a place in my life, I whispered, "It hurts, Lord. But do it. I want to be whole." I felt the Holy Spirit whisper back, "Change clothes. You're in My house now! You don't have to wear tattered, tear-stained garments ever again! Those rags will glorify My holy name as I use them for good, but you're not to carry them or wear them around anymore. *Put your dancing clothes on."*

Ruth had lost and sorrowed much. *What have you lost?* Perhaps it wasn't a deep, personal tragedy like Ruth's, but a loss of peace in your home, of innocence, of security, of trust, of someone's love, of faith, of dreams, of health, of vision for the future, of financial success, of ministry, of reputation, of honor, of humility or perhaps it was everything that child you once were longed for. *Take it all to the feet of the Redeemer.* He alone is able to transform your heart with all its deep-rooted veins of pain, its strongholds of sin and every seed of deception subtly planted. Only He can free your soul, put a new song in it and turn what threatened to undo you into something of strength and beauty.

Only Christ has the power to do it! Go to His feet wearing the bright colors of hope and expectation, and cry out to Him to move on your behalf. It won't only affect you, but your family line after you. For so long, my plan for success was simple: do the opposite of whatever hurt you and you'll do well. *Not even close to Truth when the opposite is still flesh.* Pain has to be dealt with in Spirit and Truth. Our fleshly nature will lie to us every time! Thank God, He's willing to meet us where we are to cleanse and heal us, so we can rise up whole and walk with Him. *Take off whatever your mess or grief looks like and accept His glorious robe. Joy is coming. It's woven into the very fiber of all the King offers.*

I wonder how long Ruth wore the dark colors of grief and blindness? *How long have you?* It doesn't matter and it doesn't define you. It's time to be washed afresh by the blood of the Lamb and the perfect, powerful Word of God. It's time to be anointed with the perfume of sacred, priestly oil. It's time to put on the best of the best, the heart of King Jesus. *How do you do it?* The flesh can't. It's a sacred work of God. *It begins with Truth, Christ Himself,* and recognizing Him as the only Redeemer, then searching His Word for His heart and seeing who you are in Him: a new creature, for whom the old has passed away. *It continues in Spirit,* going to the feet of the King on the threshing floor of prayer and renewal, entering deeply into the Holy of Holies and pouring your heart out like a river before Him. There, Living Water rushes over your heart's cries and all those years of collected tears, and you're *washed indeed.* That's where your "ground" gets well watered.

Jesus put on the grave clothes so you could take off yours! He was resurrected so you can be, too! He took on darkness so you can wear light! *He took every dark fiber so your clothes could be "fine linen, bright and clean"* (Revelation 19:8)*, and fit for the Feast!*

As we choose to go in faith to the feet of the Redeemer, I believe we're speaking a clear message that says, "I'm taking off my mourning clothes and my heavy, worldly garments, and I'm going to allow the King to cover me in His best. I'll let Him strip me of shame, sin and all the residue that disappointment, pain, pride and guilt have left behind in my heart. I'll let Him take the fear away as He establishes me in Truth and allow Mercy's streams to cleanse the guilt. I'll let His blood forever wash away the death sentence that sin stamped on my soul. I'll boldly wear His attire and plant myself quietly at His feet, where I'll stay. I'll place my whole being and entire future in His mighty hands and welcome His every move with anticipation. I'll listen for His every whisper and accept His holy invitation of love. HE'S THE KING OF GLORY, and I'll wait for Him." He won't turn you away or deny you either. Hold on to Isaiah 60:20, "*... for the Lord will be your everlasting light, and the days of your mourning shall be ended.*" Thank God, threshing isn't forever—and neither is mourning.

One thing about changing clothes is that you don't do it all at once. You take shoes off, then socks, shirt, pants, etc. *It's been the very same with my heart.* The Lord has slowly peeled it back and let me deal with things one by one in His perfect timing for His beautiful glory and my complete healing. He's so good.

Psalm 37:4 says, *"Delight yourself in the Lord, and He will give you the desires of your heart."* So, I've begun to ask the Lord to let me desire His best for me, to wish for change where change is needed and not grow too comfortable in old, nasty clothes. Old, ripped jeans may be comfortable, but they're not the best thing to wear to a king's feast. Likewise, we can grow at ease with our familiar clothes and refuse to allow the Lord to change them. We may even avoid removing them for fear of being exposed. *But the Lord Jesus won't expose and condemn you; He'll instantly cover you in grace and mercy, in deep, satisfying love and in His Name and the power of His blood. He'll hide you in HIMSELF.* Oh, that we'd all go there!

There's something else about this passage that strikes me. Here, Naomi took on the role of *encourager.* I wonder if Ruth would ever have gone to Boaz's feet if Naomi hadn't sent her there—if, in other words, Naomi hadn't urged Ruth "to stop being identified with and paralyzed by circumstance. It's time to put on faith and hope, and walk those things out."

Your situation may *naturally* tempt you to find a hole of self-pity to crawl in; *however, with eyes of faith, it can be viewed as a great opportunity for the Lord to move in your life.* What's discouraging and weighing you down—personal sin, corporate sin in the body of Christ, a broken relationship, battle scars, fear, doubt, the state of our nation, disappointment, pride? You need to wash off your thinking on the matter and put on the perfumed and beautiful garment of Truth. We realize, as Jeremiah tells us, that our hearts are deceitful. We're also aware that only God fully knows our hearts. We need to go to the Word, bow in prayer and ask the Lord to renew them and our minds. I'm always shocked and grieved by how quickly I can slip into the slime of carnal thinking. *It's ugly. I want it washed away.*

Ruth had Naomi to urge her to press on, but what if you have no "Naomi" in your life? Then encourage *yourself* in the Lord. King David talked to himself, saying, *"Why so downcast, O my soul?...Put your hope in God,"* (Psalm 42 & 43). Drink in the Word yourself, and pray it right back to the Lord of Lords. Put your hope and trust in Him, even if there's not a single soul speaking a word of encouragement or blessing over you. *It's not pride, it's faith.*

1 Samuel 30 presents a dark time for King David, as his family and those of his followers were captured by enemies. In their sorrow and grief, David's men threatened to stone him. (Have we ever threatened to destroy one another out of grief, anger or disappointment?) David couldn't find encouragement from his family; they were captives (how many of us have family members held captive by the Enemy, who are simply *unable* to encourage us?), nor could he find it among his friends, who were wrapped up in their own pain. So, he did what we should all do, *he encouraged himself in the Lord his God.*

The Hebrew for "encourage" means, "to fasten upon, to seize, to take hold of, to be strong and courageous, to recover, repair, fortify, prevail, confirm, be constant, stout, urgent, valiant." How much victory would we experience if we all grabbed onto that definition and took it to heart? I love the "confirm" part. As we grab hold of the Word of God, it's such a joy to see Him confirm it in our lives! The Lord often affirms specific instruction to me by letting me hear it in several places, like a friend's prayers or conversation, or coming upon the same Scripture in more than one place. After starting my study of *Ruth*, I bought a book on the Feasts of Israel in which the author stated, "We are between feasts." What an awesome confirmation of the perspective God was giving me!

In Deuteronomy 31:6, as He directed the Israelites to take the Promised Land, the Lord said, *"Be strong and of good courage..."* Years later, He offered the same encouragement to the returning captives as they began to rebuild the temple: *"Do not fear...let your hands be strong..."* What a testimony of His grace. After Israel got knocked down in battle, the Bible says, *"the men of Israel encouraged one another and again took up their positions where they had stationed themselves the first day,"* (Judges 20:22-23). As members of the body of Christ, *we're called to encourage one another* to stand firm in serving the Lord with our whole hearts. When we get knocked around in battle or stray from where we started, we need to do what the Israelites did: gather around, uphold each other and GO BACK to the place the Lord called us in His service. The account in Judges 20 ends well. Encouragement was followed by humility before the Lord and an earnest seeking of Him, which led to *victory!*

In 2 Chronicles 35:2, King Josiah *"set the priests in their duties and encouraged them for the service of the house of the Lord."* This one man in a position of leadership brought order, helped people walk out their calling and admonished them to serve in the House of the Lord. *That's my prayer for our homes, the place the Lord sets us in leadership.*

We need to take care, though, not to encourage anyone in a direction we haven't prayed over, or with merely what makes common sense, instead of a heart of wisdom and words that echo Scripture. We have to avoid helping others walk in "selective obedience." If we're following fleshly, carnal thinking, we can easily lead people into deeper pits. We can sympathize with and excuse sin and unholy desires, keeping folks we're supposed to bring to the King's feet wandering in a barren wilderness. It's so easy to do: "Yeah, they hurt you. Walk away from that relationship!" But, did you ask the Lord if that's His direction? Or people start talking negatively about someone, and we chime right in with our gossip and condemnation. Psalm 64:5 says, *"They encourage each other with evil plans..."* That puts a holy fear in me. I want to encourage through truth and wisdom, which only comes from the Lord.

We need to seek a pure heart. We can hardly begin to imagine what words from a clean, godly heart can accomplish! Naomi's encouragement positioned Ruth at the feet of her kinsman-redeemer, where her life's fulfillment awaited her. *What about ours, and what does that of others do for us?*

I pray the Lord will give us strength to be encouragers, even to those who've hurt or disappointed us or whom our flesh would just as soon see fail. Naomi knew the depth of Ruth's pain and urged her in the right direction. She didn't just say, "Get over it. Move on." And neither should we. While never discounting the depth of someone's pain, we should always do what Naomi did—point them to the One who can help them. He alone can heal and produce change. He alone can heal and change *us*. Naomi offered Ruth some timeless, godly advice:

1 "Wash yourself"—with the blood of Christ and the Word of God. Let Him give you a new heart and renew your mind.
2 "Perfume yourself"—bitterness and despair STINK. Put on hope's fragrance and faith's perfume, and pour out the incense of your prayers.
3 "Put on your best clothes"—you don't have to wear pain or disappointment like a banner of self-pity. When you're hurting, it's tempting to put on "sick" clothes, all wrinkled, spotted and blemished. Wear the righteousness of Christ, instead. Put on the whole armor of God.
4 "Lie at the feet of the Redeemer"—position yourself in humility, Spirit and Truth. Surrender all you are to the King of Kings and expect Him to move. Expect favor to come in the morning.

Questions & Applications

1. **Ask the Lord to search your heart and see if there are any places where you need to "change clothes." Is there bitterness that needs to be redressed with**

forgiveness, despair that needs to be redressed with hope or unbelief that needs to be redressed with faith? As He brings them to mind, repent, and ask Him to dress you in His best. Whatever it is, the King of Kings wants to exchange it for His robe of strength and beauty.

2. **Ask for eyes to see the places the Lord has called you to be an encourager, and pray for feet to follow through.**

Ephesians 2:2
"Prince of Air"

30

Watching and Praying

So she went down to the threshing floor and did according to all that her mother-in-law instructed her. And after Boaz had eaten and drunk, and his heart was cheerful, he went to lie down at the end of the heap of grain; and she came softly, uncovered his feet, and lay down, **Ruth 3:6.**

Notice that Boaz, the owner of the field, positioned himself WITH THE HARVEST! The grain had been gathered and threshed, and he wasn't about to leave it for some thief to sneak in and steal! He was willing to forsake the comforts of home and his own sweet bed in order to *not* forsake his grain. It was dear to him, and bringing it in had cost him something. Now that it was threshed and heaped up, he had reason to celebrate—and to be on guard. Boaz was tending and guarding what he'd planted and gathered. He was protecting that crop with his own powerful presence. Who'd dare try to rob him before his eyes? If anyone tried, he wouldn't stand a chance when Boaz stood against him. *Thank God that Jesus, the mighty Warrior for our souls, called our "Shepherd and Overseer" in 1 Peter 2:25, has planted and gathered in our hearts and has positioned*

Himself there forever, promising never to leave or forsake. The presence of the King in our hearts should cause them to tremble with gratitude and passion, and the Thief to shiver with panic and fear.

It's absolutely the permanent will of Almighty God for the Lord Jesus to abide in you, fill your heart and stand guard over it. In John 15:7 He says, *"If you abide in Me, and My Words abide in you, you will ask what you will, and it shall be done for you."* There's a lot at stake. It's critical that we stay in the Word and on our faces, asking the King of Glory to continually pour out His Living Water, renew our minds, create in us clean hearts and right spirits and go to battle for us.

The cry of my heart is to never become slack or weary in seeking Him, but to grow stronger and more urgent every day. I ask Him to keep me in the abiding place—right in the center of His precious heart—and to shield all He's planted in me and in my family. I entreat Him to put out unholy fires and fan His own holy flame in me, and to keep spiritual disease and rot away from my soul so bread can be formed from its grain. I implore Him to let no enemy steal, kill or destroy what I'm intended to taste, to keep the harvest in HIS barn and on His threshing floor, not in mine, and then to post His blood over the door. I plead for His Holy Spirit to guard my heart, fly high over me the banner of His Name and to continually remind my heart that, "Greater is He that is in you than he that is in the world."

The word "guard" in Hebrew means, "an attendant, a ruler of an army, an audience, part of the royal court, a watch." It's also sometimes translated as "lifeguardsman," *which I love.* The King of Kings, the One, True, Holy God, the Almighty Captain of the Host, Lord Sabaoth, the Sovereign, Supreme Lord who eternally reigns, is your lifeguardsman. He who spoke all things into being is speaking over your life. The One who stretched out the heavens and made the earth His footstool gives audience to you. The Most High is diligently attending *your* life. The eyes of I AM, the One Who Was, Who Is and Who Is To Come, watch you well. They see thieves in the shadows, flaming arrows aimed against you and pitfalls and traps laid for your feet. They search before and behind you and delegate holy troops on your behalf.

The Master has blessed you with Himself and His harvest and claimed your heart as holy ground, and He's well able to keep what His hands have established. We need to rest and shield ourselves with deep, abiding faith in that fact. Because I've been in some battles myself, I know the Enemy will whisper otherwise in your ear. The father of lies will do all he can to lure you into doubt and chase you out of the resting place and straight into fear. He wants to devour all the Lord is doing in you. 1 Peter 5:8 says, *"Be self-controlled and alert. Your enemy the devil prowls around like a roaring lion, looking for someone to devour."* 1 Thessalonians 5:6 urges, *"Therefore let us not sleep, as others do, but let us watch and be sober..."*—sober here meaning free of anything that would cloud our judgment, not just a bottle of wine! Many things can intoxicate us: wealth, honor, relationships, careers, religion, etc.

Our wicked Enemy loves nothing more than to catch us off-guard and intoxicated with things of the world, when he can attempt to devour our harvest. I've felt the devourer breathing down my neck, but *I also know the strength of Christ, who will always gain the victory.* Concerning the devil, 1 Peter 5: 9 continues admonishing us to *"resist him, standing firm in the faith."* Faith is the mighty shield that the Thief can't penetrate. Let's ask the Lord Jesus to give us a double portion of it, and to *"gird up the loins of our mind"* (1 Peter 1:13). We need to saturate our thoughts with the powerful Word of the living God, and ask the Holy Spirit to bring it to remembrance at just the right time. It's our double-edged Sword, and we're foolish to forsake it. *I pray we discern the urgency of the times and pick up our weapon quickly*—and that we'll be truly alert and never found off-guard, eyes closed, lulled to sleep by the world and sitting as prime targets for the Enemy.

2 Corinthians 10:4 informs us that the weapons of our warfare aren't carnal. They're not of this world and can't be manufactured or overcome, but are "mighty in God" and able to pull down all the Enemy tries to raise up against us. They're more than strong enough to stand guard over the harvest of righteousness the Lord Jesus has reaped in us. Christ is the Word made flesh, and the Word is our sure Sword. *Christ Himself, the King of Kings and Lord of Lords, has formed Himself into our defense and weapon. He faced evil head-on and swallowed up its power in the victory of the Cross, so we're not left alone, helpless and defenseless.* He tells us in Isaiah 54:17 that *"no weapon formed against you will prosper..."* He didn't say we'd never face opposition (quite the contrary), but promises victory in battle to His own. This is a good place to praise His Name!

The father of lies is a ruthless, brutal enemy. He doesn't play fair and doesn't sit back. His dark kingdom is at stake, and he wants all who oppose it and serve the Lord he despises robbed and silenced. *It's critical that we stay at the feet of the only One able to guard our hearts, tear down every veil of deception and open our eyes to Truth*. There's grave danger in thinking, "We've been working a long time and our crops look pretty good. Some battles have been won. We can sit down and relax, put down our weapons and have some entertainment now."

I find no instruction in Scripture to lay down our weapons, close our eyes and take it easy! Where does the Bible say, "If you're tired of the battle, take off those shoes of the gospel of peace, put down your Sword, let your shield of faith fall to the ground and put away your breastplate of righteousness." YOU WON'T FIND IT. Instead, you'll find words like resist, stand firm, be on guard, don't grow weary, put on the armor and hide yourself in Christ. We're urged to pick up our divine weapons, put on our holy armor, be alert and positioned for battle and stand ready to defend all the Lord Jesus has placed in us. Sounds like marching orders to me, not summer camp.

Even as God blessed them, the Israelites were warned to be on guard. The Lord knew that despite seeing His mighty miracles and provision, they were completely capable of growing complacent and saying in their hearts, *"My power and the might of my hand have gained me this wealth,"* (Deuteronomy 8:17).

We'd be wise to apply this to ourselves, lest we think this could never happen to us. There's a very real danger of growing fat, dropping our guard and subtly shifting our worship. Ponder also what happened in the Garden of Gethsemane. Peter, James and John were in the very presence of the Lord of Glory, who'd asked them specifically to, *"stay here and watch with Me,"* (Matthew 26:38). But, three times the Lord found them sleeping, saying, *"What! Could you not watch with Me one hour? Watch and pray, lest you enter into temptation. The spirit indeed is willing, but the flesh is weak."*

When I bow before My King in glory, I don't want to hear Him say, "I positioned you specifically in that generation to watch and pray, but you went to sleep. Couldn't you watch one hour?" God, help us. As I look at our nation, and even at our churches, I wonder if this isn't exactly our condition—fat and sleepy (or lazy?). The Lord's led me to pray Daniel 9 for our nation ("O, Lord...we have sinned and done wrong..."), and I'd urge you to as well. We need to humbly remember that we're mere flesh and blood, and that, as Jesus told us, our flesh is weak. There's no way to defeat in the natural realm what the Word tells us we battle: principalities, powers, rulers of darkness and spiritual wickedness in high places (Ephesians 6:12)—the very things coming after our harvest. If we're counting on our abilities for victory, we might as well count on defeat. WE ABSOLUTELY MUST POSITION OURSELVES AT THE FEET OF JESUS AND THE FOOT OF THE CROSS AND LET HIS BLOOD BATTLE FOR US. We must all be alert and dressed in the armor of Christ.

The battle is over the very souls of men, and against those who wear salvation's helmet. The Thief is after you, your relationships, strength, effective witness and call on your life. Hell is hungry, and so is Despair. May that knowledge serve to wake us up and become better soldiers of the Cross! Let it send us running to the throne room with repentance for our pride and programs! May it not cripple us with doubt or paralyze us with fear, but serve to sharpen and quicken us instead! We're NOT given a spirit of fear, but of power, love and a sound mind. Let's walk in it, in Jesus' mighty Name!

Victory is found nowhere but at the foot of the Cross. On that holy ground, there's a powerful humbling, a deep crying out, a pouring out of compassion and forgiveness and a divine touch from the King of Glory. In that sweet place, you're equipped, strengthened, established and given wisdom, direction and revelation of His Word. There, the King delights in you, sings over you and unveils His plans for you. Deep worship will pour from the depths of your soul there, *and the Enemy will have no choice but to flee*. May we daily resist the Thief with all the power of Calvary!

Our laziness, rebellion and blatant disobedience serve as an engraved invitation for the Thief to come and take what he pleases. Repentance and alertness, on the other hand, slam the door in his face. What are we choosing? If we choose greed and pride, we open the door to the devourer. If we choose unforgiveness, we open the door for stone-cold hearts. If we choose criticism, we open the door for judgment on our own heads. If we choose to sleep, we make it easy for the Thief to steal. If we choose pleasure, we become foolish idolaters. But, if we choose to make Christ our first love, we receive protected wholeness. If we choose to take the power of the Cross, we gain the victory. If we choose to stand firm, even if we stand alone, we get heaven's stored-up treasures. If we choose to forgive, we're forgiven. If we choose holy Bread, we're satisfied indeed. *"Choose you this day whom you will serve...as for me and my house, we will serve the Lord."*

I've searched Christ's letters to the churches of Revelation 2-3 to see what they were choosing, how they were letting their guard down and what the warning and result was. Here's what I found:

1st church, Ephesus: did good things, BUT they left their First Love and received a serious warning, *"Remember and repent, or your lampstand will be removed."* If the lampstand is what makes us as "a city on a hill," a light that testifies of Christ, then it appears if we choose to love something more than Jesus, it darkens our witness. *I pray we'll choose to make Christ Jesus, the Lover of our souls, our first love, and that nothing would steal our blazing devotion to Him.*

2nd church, Smyrna: a persecuted but faithful church. They weren't rebuked at all, but encouraged to press on, choose good and not to fear or lose faith. May we be so faithful.

I pray we will allow nothing to be stolen through fear or unbelief!

3rd church, Pergamos: did some good, BUT tolerated false doctrine. It had *"those there that hold the doctrine of Balaam and the Nicolatians" (see Rev.2:14-15).* Were they afraid of offending the popular culture? Did they tolerate blatant blasphemy and mind-tickling because they didn't want to sound harsh? DO WE? *I pray we'll love and walk according to the whole counsel of God, and not be among those who pick and choose what they'll obey or who twist the Word to suit their needs.*

4th church, Thyatira: did some good, BUT allowed the spirit of Jezebel—false prophecy leading to sin, or teaching lies as if true and seducing through what the flesh likes to hear—to infiltrate as if it wouldn't be a stumbling block. Jesus warned them to repent, or God Himself would fight against them. "IT IS A FEARFUL THING TO FALL INTO THE HANDS OF THE LIVING GOD." I don't want to fight against Him, but for Him. *I pray for wisdom and discernment and that we would close the door to false doctrine that would give the Thief some ground.*

5th church, Sardis: Those in this church have "a reputation for being alive, but are dead," (Rev.3:1). God calls them to wake up and strengthen what remains, because their deeds are not complete in God's sight. Their works might have looked good on the outside, appearing quite sufficient in the sight of men, but apparently stemmed from flesh instead of Spirit. *I pray we would give the Thief no ground through works of pride rather than Truth.*

6th church, Philadelphia: The Lord commended this Body for keeping His Word and not denying His Name, even though they had little strength. They endured patiently, and received great and awesome promises from the mouth of the Lord Most High. Due to their perseverance, He told them He would *"keep them from the hour of trial which shall come upon the whole world,"* urged them to *"hold fast to what you have, that no one may take your crown"* and said He would cause the overcomer to be *"a pillar in the temple of God,"* (Rev.3: 10-12). *I pray that we, too, will persevere even in our weaknesses and hold fast to the King's Word and Name, refusing to let the Thief steal what He has given us by grace.*

7th church, Laodicea: This church was lukewarm in the eyes of God, neither hot nor cold. Sounds to me like a body of believers with one foot in the church and one foot in the world, effective in neither place. This church claims to be rich, wealthy, having need of nothing, yet the Lord tells them they are in reality, *"wretched, miserable, poor, blind, and naked,"* and warns that *"I am about to spit you out of My mouth,"* (Rev. 3:16-17, NIV) Yet, verse18 is so beautiful to me as the Lord does not leave them in that state without hope, but says to their lukewarm hearts, *"I counsel you..."* He did not rebuke them without a solution to their miserable, deceived state. *I pray the Lord would open our eyes to any place the Thief has stolen our fire for Jesus, and that through the counsel of the Word of Truth and the great mercy of the Lord we would have all things restored for His glory and become passionate, fiery servants of the King of Kings.*

Over and over in these two chapters of Revelation, the Lord says to all our hearts, "He who has an ear, let him hear what the Spirit says to the churches." *I pray that we will absolutely hear with our hearts the warnings and great promises given. I pray we will be an eyes-wide-open, Swords-in-hand and always-on-guard generation of faith that falls for no voice and no plan but the Master's and that stands before God with nothing stolen by the Thief.*

Boaz was resting by and guarding a harvest that would feed more than his own mouth. SO DO WE. Our fervent intercession, watchfulness, alertness, readiness to use the weapons issued by Christ, discernment, faithfulness and willingness to let the Holy Spirit bear holy fruit in us WILL FEED MORE THAN OURSELVES. There's a generation coming up around us that will be deeply affected by the yield of our hearts. There are family members, friends, co-workers, neighbors, people in the body of Christ—even those who despise us—whose lives can be touched because we refuse to be put to sleep by the Enemy's deceptive lullaby, but instead plant our hearts firmly at the feet of the Lord Jesus, because we choose to forgive when wounded, to bless when persecuted, to let go of an offense, to let God purify our hearts, to press on when we want to settle in, to let judgment be the

Lord's and not ours and to let repentance and mercy cover hardness of heart. In short, because we opt to agree with the Word of God, instead of the Enemy's deceptions.

May we, as the body of Christ, corporately and personally disagree *strongly* with anything that opposes the Word of God. We would never allow a thief to take physical things we've worked long and hard for. *May we not in the Spirit, either.* The Enemy is constantly trying to get us to us agree with him. Pride says we deserve some recognition, and we agree. Greed wants to be satisfied, and we agree. Bitterness wants revenge, and we agree. The battle seems too hard, and we agree. Self-pity wants to be stroked, and we agree. Tolerance says be quiet and blend in, and we agree. Let's renounce every unholy decision and reverse every scheme set in motion by them in Jesus' name. Let's never reinforce the Enemy's weapons against our harvest, but be ONES WHO WATCH.

There's glory when we watch. 2 Corinthians 3:18 says, *"We all, with unveiled face, beholding as in a mirror the glory of the Lord..."* Unveiled faces can see the King and His glory. Sleepers miss out, as well as those off-guard. May we press on into the deep place of Spirit and Truth in prayer and the Word, with eyes to see and ears to hear, trusting the Overseer of the freshly-threshed grain. Bread will come. Boaz celebrated his harvest, and stretched out on the floor with it. Ruth came softly and humbly to his feet, and there she was covered. At the feet of Jesus, so will we.

Questions & Applications

1. **Which of the seven churches of Revelation most closely resembles you, and what, if any, changes do you need to make in your life as a result?**
2. **You are placed, planted and positioned specifically in this generation to be one through whom**

Christ Jesus can produce a harvest. Stop now and pray over that harvest the King has planted in you.

3. **Scripture tells us that our King, the King of Kings and Lord of Lords, is our rock, our fortress, our deliverer, our shield of favor, our victory, the horn of our salvation, our stronghold, our refuge, our Savior, our strength, our help and our defense. This is the One who guards your life. This is the Most High God who never closes His eyes to you, who never slumbers or sleeps, leaves or forsakes. You can rest in perfect confidence that He is for you. You may know that with your head- celebrate it now with your heart.**

31

Knowing Who and Whose You Are

Now it happened that at midnight the man was startled, and turned himself; and there, a woman was lying at his feet. And he said, "Who are you?" So she answered, "I am Ruth, your maidservant. Take your maidservant under your wing, for you are a close relative," **Ruth 3:8-9**.

Midnight closed in and found Ruth lying humbly, but boldly, at her redeemer's feet. SHE KNEW WHO SHE WAS IN RELATION TO HIM AND THAT HIS FEET WERE THE ONLY PLACE TO GO. Likewise, we need to position our hearts at the mighty feet of Jesus and know who we are there, whether at midnight or noon! When questioned about our identity, is our answer the same in the dark as in the light of day? Do we respond out of our relationship to the Redeemer, whether we like our circumstances or not? When situations drive us in desperation to the King's feet, are we sure of who we are then?

Because of our privileged place at the foot of the Cross, we need to be ready to stand up and boldly state who we are and what our relationship to the Redeemer has made us. *Our circumstances don't define us as His, the Cross does.* If we base our identity in Christ on the brightness of our outward situation, we're mistaken and will be sadly disappointed. We need to know that we know Him *at all times*, whether it's a cold midnight or a sweet summer afternoon.

I've heard a lot of prosperity preaching in the body of Christ and believe it's dangerous, shaky ground. How do you preach that at midnight? How does that stand in the face of severe suffering or persecution? Would that teaching stand if the Lord chose to melt His Body down to pure gold? What do you say to believers in Muslim nations whose lives are threatened daily? I've heard it reported that there is more persecution against lovers of Christ in these days than ever before. If you count your worth in God's eyes only by obvious, tangible favor—like health, wealth and happiness—then what happens when you hit a hard time? Aren't there numerous examples from God's precious Word of people the Lord led into hard, trying, testing places: Israel in the wilderness, Job in trials, David pursued by Saul, Joseph in prison for years, Paul persecuted, etc.? What then? *Who are you then?* A Sunday morning, feel-good, "bless me" Christian, or a faithful, fiery, confident, bold, blood-bought child of the King of Kings?

While I believe the King absolutely desires to bless us, I also believe He allows seasons and times that test and sift our souls. Sometimes He allows the sun to go down, and in the dim light we can only throw ourselves on His mercy. For the time being, we live in a groaning, fallen, sinful world that's not always bright and pleasant. You only have to watch the nightly news or sign up for a prayer chain to see that. At times, it's the consequences of sin that push us into a low spot, at others it's the nature of this fallen world that does the trick. But sometimes the Lord leads us into dark valleys with His own hand, not because He's cruel but because He is working out holy, unseen and eternal purposes. We need to know *in every hour* the answer to the question, "Who are you?" We must also ask God to help us trust who He is. Who knows what far-reaching and long-term effects will be set in motion by your response, how your family line will be affected by your faith or what the Lord may do through a life that cries out in every season, "Praise God. I'm the King's!"

2 Timothy 4:2 says to *"Preach the Word! Be ready in season and out of season..."* Seems to me that midnight definitely qualifies as an "out of season" hour. No matter what the time of day or night, how clear or unclear our vision or what the situation, we should be fully prepared to depend on and testify to the Lord Jesus. Stating your relationship to Christ in your darkest hour may be merely a whisper, *but it's enough*. He can work with that; He can reinforce it in Spirit and Truth and echo it in your heart. And He can fill your soul with confidence through it. You won't give a legalistic, Sunday School answer at midnight—at that hour you'll cry out what you know is *Truth*.

At one particularly dark hour in my life, a literal midnight, the Lord led me to Psalm 138:3, *"When I called, You answered me; You made me bold and stouthearted,"* (NIV). The New King James states it this way: *"In the day when I cried out, You answered me, and made me bold with strength in my soul."* For a long time I kept the Bible by my bed open to that verse. During another hard night, I implored the Lord to strengthen me, and to put me on someone's heart to stand with me in prayer. The very next morning, a friend called and said, "I woke up at 4 am with a burden to pray for you. As I did, the Holy Spirit impressed two Scriptures on my heart for you."

What a precious, faithful God we serve! And you better believe those two verses are well marked and read over and over. *I believe our blackest hours can become some of our greatest times of blessing, because in them we begin to cry out to the King with fresh urgency.* And His response to us at His feet in the dark of night will be a sweet treasure to our soul. It will build solid, secure strength and impart a boldness in us we never had before.

No hour spent at the Lord's feet is wasted. Every second will be woven together in strength and bring glory to the name of Christ Jesus. Hear Isaiah 45:3, and believe it with all you are: *"This is what the Lord says...'I will give you the treasures of darkness, and hidden riches of secret places, so that you may know that I am the Lord, the God of Israel, who calls you by name.'"* I believe there are unknown blessings in our nights with the King that we probably won't recognize until morning, but they'll be riches we'd never trade, even for the whole world. They'll be true treasures, which the world can neither produce nor touch, that will make us rich indeed, as gold refined by fire. *We'll be different because of them.* What the Lord of Glory gives in the dark will empower and strengthen us for the day. Praise Him! (bad times)

If it feels like midnight, there's only one place to go: the Redeemer's feet. Go, expecting some treasure. I pray we'll also use "corporate midnights" in the body of Christ to seek corporate riches. I am on the Pulpit Committee for our church, as we seek a humble but passionate man of God to step into pastoral leadership. I can tell you, operating without leadership can definitely seem like a church-wide midnight! Yet, as we cry out to Him, the Lord has shown Himself faithful over and over and is leading us beyond what any of us imagined. In the end, I expect to see great treasure come out of what He's teaching us in these times.

One of the most precious rewards of darkness can be a keen awareness of God's presence. I've heard that the blind have heightened hearing and other senses, and wonder: is it possible that when our understanding is darkened and desperation deepens, we become more acutely aware of the

Lord's every whisper, touch, intervention and heartbeat? Wouldn't encountering the King in the dark like that change us in the morning? Would that meeting at His feet not plant a bold, stout heart in us? When the sun hits our face again, might it reflect a different countenance?

Several people have told me, "I know you; you're not bold. It has to be from God." I can tell you, I'm definitely NOT bold. But I can also tell you that I've been at the King of King's feet in a lot of darkness and have learned to hear His whispers, soak up His every Word and appreciate the treasures revealed there. AND I CAN NEVER BE THE SAME. How can you *not* become gallant for Christ when you've watched Him fill your midnights? The Lord Jesus told us what to do with those precious utterances—boldly proclaim them! In Matthew 10:27, He instructs, *"Whatever I tell you in the dark, speak in the daylight; what is whispered in your ear, proclaim from the roof."* Those sweet, quiet moments in the dark are meant to fill your soul and mouth with praise and Truth to share with others. A rooftop is a pretty daring, conspicuous place. If you're going to shout from the roof in broad daylight, you might be ridiculed, persecuted or misunderstood. You may have to get over what people think of you. *I believe what happens at midnight at the King's feet will do that for you.* His opinion, not those of men, will become your priority.

2 Corinthians 1:3-4 states, *"Praise be to the God and Father of our Lord Jesus Christ, the Father of compassion and the God of all comfort, who comforts us in all our troubles, so that we can comfort those in any trouble with the comfort we ourselves have received from God."* Comfort received, comfort expressed—whispers in your darkness to share with others in theirs. Personally, I hear better in the dark. Not just the darkness of trial, but the literal darkness of the morning before the sun rises. That's when I seem to discern and worship the deepest. It's not a legalistic stan-

dard, just a matter of fact. I love to get up very early, pour coffee, sit at my dining room table with the Word open before me and bow in prayer before the King of Kings. I wrap an afghan around my shoulders to remind me of Him in Whom I am wrapped, covered and shielded, and I wait at His feet in Spirit and Truth. He faithfully meets me there, and has provided comfort the world can't touch that He's slowly opened doors for me to share with others.

Isaiah 50:4 says, *"The Lord God has given me the tongue of the learned* (an *"instructed tongue,"* NIV*), that I should know how to speak a word in season to him who is weary."* As the Lord leads you through the night, He teaches, instructs and gives you His Word to give to those in their own darknesses—words that aren't birthed of pride or shared as an earthly display of knowledge, but come from pure, true wisdom gained in midnight hours spent with the King. *What you receive in your dark times is the real thing. Self-reliance, self-sufficiency and hypocrisy can't survive the midnight hours. They'll either turn to bitterness, or surrender and turn to faith.* It's a precious thing to allow the Lord to capture and replace natural thoughts that arise in those times with nuggets of Truth that glorify Him and will eventually bless others.

I pray my answer to the question, "Who are you?" will always and forever reflect the words found in the Song of Solomon: *"I am my Beloved's, and He is mine;"* that I'll not react to midnight by saying, "The Lord has forsaken me," but, "The Lord is preparing me for the morning's work. He's sifting self out of the picture, molding my heart into His image and dressing me for Himself. I'm His beloved here at His feet in the dark, and I'm His beloved when the sun fills the morning sky and everything seems clear."

Ruth went to Boaz's feet in the darkness of desperation. *How desperate are we for a touch from Christ?* Do we seek Him at all hours of the day and night? Are we willing to lose some sleep to seek His presence, to be ridiculed for appearing bold or forward, to press into Him no matter what people say and to break out of tradition, away from a religious spirit, and position ourselves at His mercy with a life-hanging-in-the-balance, desperate heart? Are we truly urgent for Him, or do we merely desire our own comfort? Are we really after His perfect will, or just seeking idyllic happiness and ease?

If we are desperate for Him, are we yet *stingy*, desiring Him to loose rivers of wisdom and anointing in our lives with no urgency for other souls—no real burden for their salvation? Are we seeking revival for our own hearts, while unconcerned about other's dried up faith? I pray we'll have a sense of desperation for God's Word and in praying, *"Thy Kingdom come, Thy will be done,"* at every stage of our lives, for ourselves and everyone the Holy Spirit presses on our hearts, no matter what the time of day.

We also need to be on guard for other voices in the darkness. We're wise to remember that God may not be the only one asking, "Who are you?" in those midnight hours. When we're weak and it's dark, the Deceiver loves to whisper all kinds of things in our ears to get us to question our identity in Christ, like doubt, fear, distress, condemnation, abandonment or despair. Something catches you off guard, and the Enemy murmurs, "You know, if you were *really* walking with God, He wouldn't have allowed that. You're getting what you deserve." Or you set out to do something the Lord's asked of you, and here come the lies, "Who are *you* to do that for God (to speak for Him, to counsel, to be an instrument of grace and honor, etc.)? I know you...You know you, too. Just stop right here." Sound familiar?

We need to learn to walk out James 4:7, *"Resist the devil, and he will flee from you;"* to resist with prayer and the Word and obey Jesus' words, *"Come to Me...and I will give you rest."* Not resist and sit down; resist and go to the King's feet. To possess ears and hearts that are deaf to deception and condemnation, especially in the dark, it's critical for us to allow the Lord to establish our identity firmly in Him.

Midnight has certainly been the setting for some of the fiercest battles in my mind. However, both Hebrew and Greek words for "midnight" can mean, "between, in the middle or midst of." That's SUCH GOOD NEWS! To me it says the dark, lightless hours are not the end! They're something we pass through, merely brief periods when it's hard to see. That knowledge, along with the promise of nighttime treasures and what Job 35:10 calls, *"songs in the night,"* should cause worship to well up in our hearts.

In Luke 12:38, Jesus states, *"It will be good for those servants whose master finds them ready, even if he comes in the second or third watch of the night."* What happens on our knees in the dark will bring about *good things* in the day. Because of our righteous position in Christ Jesus, there's absolute power in our prayers—no matter what watch we're in. *Do we pray like we believe that?* I know I always haven't. After witnessing answers to supplications for the international arena uttered at my women's Bible study, the Holy Spirit has whispered in my heart, "Do you think the group's prayers had anything to do with that?" which brings my heart to its knees as I realize my sin of unbelief. Somehow, I've felt that others' prayers could shake the heavens and affect nations, but not OUR LITTLE PLEADINGS.

I once shared with the group that the Lord had impressed me to pray for Muslims, especially leaders, to have visions and dreams of Christ, and to accept Him as Savior. Not long after, and even to this day, I began to see headlines and hear reports of that *very thing* taking place. The world calls that mere coincidence, but what does the Lord call it? That's challenged my prayer life like nothing else, and has caused me to ask God to burden me with what He wants to accomplish in these dark days. I've been led to specifically pray for New York City, California, universities (I had that burden

BEFORE the Virginia Tech tragedy), the body of Christ, government, Jews, Israel and for my lineage and seed. I pray for faith to believe and for eyes to see.

WE NEED TO STAY ON OUR KNEES, EVEN IN THE DARK, EXPECTING MORE THAN WE EVEN KNOW TO EXPECT, and to trust the Holy Spirit to lead us in praying Scripture and to intercede through us. *God's Word commands us to pray without ceasing, and it can certainly show us how.* I pray we'll have the faith to anticipate the "divine unexpected," that we'll come before the Lord in Spirit and Truth, be available to hear His voice and then echo Isaiah's response to His call: *"HERE AM I, SEND ME."* He'll send us to our knees, fill our mouths with His Truth and use us to speak His comfort when we least expect it. May we always remember that *"the joy of the Lord,"* not the joy of our situation, *"is [our] strength,"* and that the King will use that fruit of His Spirit expressed through us to build and bless His kingdom in every hour. I implore God that we'll know that we know that we know the answer to the question, "Who are you?"

From time to time, as if to test me, I hear God whisper in the depths of my spirit, "DO YOU KNOW WHO YOU ARE?" My response is, "Tell me again, Lord. Pour out such delight in what You've named me through Christ that my heart will feel like bursting wide open. Tell me again what my soul knows well: of Your pleasure in me, my faith and my prayers because of the blood of Jesus, that nothing is impossible and of the power of Your Name enveloping mine. Tell me again and again and again, my King, who I am in You. May it not just be my head that echoes Your Word, but every fiber of my being. May my heart, soul, mind and strength be fingerprinted and consumed by the mark and seal of the Holy Spirit. Tell me who I am, Lord, and help me believe it. Let me pray like I know who I am, love like it, speak like it, sing like it and do every task set before me like it. It's the thrill of my soul and the joy and strength of my heart forever just to know I'm Yours, because the Cross says so. Thank You, King Jesus. Let me wear Your Name *well,* even at midnight.

Questions & Applications

1. **If you find yourself in a "midnight watch," cry out to the Lord with all you are. Don't stop or give up there, keep pressing into Him and His Word. Expect to come to know the King of Kings like never before, and ask Him to reveal His treasures to you.**
2. **Thank the Lord for the privilege of midnight hours at His precious feet. Praise Him for all He's taught you there, and get ready to "shout from the rooftop" in the morning light. There's a word He wants to speak to others through your night-time experience.**
3. **As you learn to trust the Faithful One, ask Him to burden you with what burdens Him, far beyond your own personal needs. He desires to build His Kingdom through your prayers.**

32

Young Things and Impossibilities

Then he said, "Blessed are you of the Lord, my daughter! For you have shown more kindness at the end than at the beginning, in that you did not go after young men, whether poor or rich. And now, my daughter, do not fear. I will do all that you request, for all the people of my town know you are a virtuous woman. Now it is true that I am a close relative; however, there is a relative closer than I. Stay this night, and in the morning it shall be that if he will perform the duty of a close relative for you—good, let him do it. But if he does not want to perform the duty for you, then I will perform the duty for you, as the Lord lives! Lie down until morning," **Ruth 3:10-13.**

Bethlehem was home to Boaz and another close relative, and, I daresay, Boaz knew the other guy well. He was undoubtedly familiar with the fellow's family situation, reputation and character—or lack of it. It seems to me that as Boaz told Ruth to *"stay this night...lie down until morning...,"* he already knew what the other man's answer would be. Personally, even as he spoke the words, *"...if he will perform the duty of a close relative for you—good, let him do it,"* I believe he knew he probably wouldn't.

The Lord Jesus says the same thing to us: "If he (anybody or anything else) doesn't want to perform the duty (redeeming you, rescuing you, providing for you), *then I will.* If those other relationships, that humanism and cultural deception, your bank account, home, career, shopping sprees, pursuit of fame and fortune, pleasure and peace or *even that ministry,* isn't doing it for you, *then I will."* He gives us a choice, knowing all along that *He alone* is the Redeemer, the Author of faith and salvation and the only One who can set you free and establish you in everything for which you were created. *The King of Kings isn't intimidated in the least by anything else you may seek after. He knows they'll fall short and fail you, and stands waiting through the night of your searching to fully redeem, heal and settle your heart in the morning light.* He is, after all, the Bright and Morning Star.

The Lord Almighty offers this challenge: *"Choose you this day whom you will serve."* There are "young things," which naturally attract us and that we're given free will to go after and pursue. The King knows they'll never satisfy our souls or bear good, lasting fruit in our lives, but allows us to pick them, if we wish. He understands how close and "in-your-face" some of the things are that compete for our hearts, and how their voices can sometimes drown out His. He's aware of how tempting it is at times to pursue our own ambitions, solutions, plans, purposes, will and glory, and to seek things that tickle our flesh or offer false security.

Jesus became flesh, walked this fallen ground and can absolutely sympathize with us in our weaknesses, temptations and attractions to other things, including those packaged in religious wrapping. *But He also knows that when we opt to wait for Him, positioning our hearts at His holy feet and waiting for His direction and instruction above all else, we're choosing blessings this world can't touch.* When we do that, we're joining our hearts with His in a sweet, holy union through which His kingdom can be established upon the earth. *What greater blessing is there than to be joined to the King of Glory, planted in Truth and settled in His call?* What could be more thrilling or burn brighter in your soul than to be transformed, renamed and established in authority and blessing as the beloved of the Lord?

What's distracting your heart today? What "young thing" have you fallen for? Are there any deceptions you've lived with so long you don't even recognize them? Whatever they're offering you, they can't cut it. Don't expect them to. Money can't redeem you from poverty of heart. Over-achievement can't redeem you from insecurity. Blocking out memories can't redeem your hurt. Relationships can't redeem your desire for true love. Pleasure can't redeem your need for the thrill of knowing God and the joy of the Lord. Even trying to build some kind of ministry can't redeem your need to sit at the Savior's feet. Anchor all your hopes and expectations for redemption on the Lord of Lords, Jesus Christ. Forget those young things attracting your attention and seeking to steal your affections, all the short-lived loves of this world, full of shallow promises. They can't redeem you or calm your heart, and won't come through for you when midnight closes in. Rest in the Ancient of Days, the Matchless, Changeless, Eternal, Magnificent, Holy One of Israel, the Lord Jesus Christ, who desires you.

Boaz's words to Ruth must have poured over her heart like warm, soothing oil. They were wrapped in comfort, promise, hope, dignity and honor, and they addressed and calmed her fears. They called her what she wasn't, a virtuous woman. She wasn't, after all, a woman of God. She was still a Moabite—yes, one who had a reputation for doing good, yet still a Moabite—a Gentile, a heathen. But this Moabite's heart and life would be changed forever by a few simple sentences spoken on the threshing floor at midnight, just as

God does for us. He calls us what we're not because of the blood of Christ, addresses our fears and calms them with His Word. He holds our shaking hands and urges us not to be afraid, but to ask, seek and knock so we may receive, find and have the door opened. *The Lord comes to the threshing floor of our hearts and says: "Rest here with Me a while and get used to My presence, because I WILL NEVER leave or forsake you. Ask Me for the Kingdom here and get ready to be astounded in the morning light."*

Have you heard the King's healing whispers in your heart as you've stretched out boldly and humbly at His feet? *You're supposed to*. His sheep are meant to listen to and know His voice. He doesn't speak only to one or two people, but to *all* who dare ask for ears to hear. So ask! The meeting between Boaz and Ruth that night was intensely personal, just as our relationship with the King of Glory is designed to be. He invites you there.

In Ruth's seeking favor from Boaz, I hear God asking us, "Are you seeking Me for the impossible? Do you only seek what is safe, or what is solely available by My absolute doing?" Ruth was looking for redemption in that midnight hour, and so am I. There are still pockets in my heart I've held back out of fear or doubt that need to be redeemed, and *many* things, absolutely not possible in the flesh, that I yearn for through the Spirit. As I pondered those things, I felt led to write down my "Impossible List," which could also be called, "It'd Take A Miracle List," and then lay it on the threshing floor of prayer. I also sensed the Lord's challenge to "believe Me for it." *That's a test of faith for sure*. But as the weeks went by, I found myself adding bolder and bolder impossibilities.

Why don't you do that, too? Take the Lord up on His offer. *It's okay; He can take it!* Make your own Impossible List, lay it all on the table before Him in prayer and then rest. Wait. *See what the King will do*. I believe He's just waiting for the invitation to *blow our little minds*. HE'S DONE JUST THAT IN MY LIFE MANY TIMES.

The fact that this page is in your hands is a major example of that. The call to homeschool my precious children in the midst of a chronic illness, through His strength, is another. The times He's called me to take a microphone when I really just wanted to find a seat on the back row; times He's brought the right person with just the right word of encouragement into my path; times He's confirmed His Word over and over and times I have witnessed miraculous healings and provision. *He is a big God, and He invites us to ask and believe Him for BIG THINGS. Impossible things.*

After laying many impossibilities before the Lord, I asked Him to show me if there was any deception in me that could hinder their coming to pass. He answered by continually bringing to mind a scene from my life *over 20 years ago*. All the emotions of those days were suddenly fresh—fear, insecurity, loneliness, no vision...It's amazing how that stuff can creep in, hang on and create a deceptive stronghold. Realizing how those kinds of things were still silently affecting my life certainly amazed me.

The Lord then led me back to the great truth, *"'I am the Alpha and Omega, the Beginning and the End,' says the Lord God, Who is, and Who was, and Who is to come, the Almighty,'"* (Revelation 1:8). He also reminded me of John 1:1, *"In the beginning was the Word, and the Word was with God, and the Word was God,"* and finally whispered in my heart, "The Word *was* 20 years ago, whether you were walking in it or not. You were trapped in some strongholds and emotions, but I STILL WAS. I did not put those things in you, BUT I CAN TAKE THEM OUT!!!" Then He sweetly implored, "Will you go back to that scene, that memory, one more time, but this time take Me with you? Take the Word Who Was back to that 'was' place, and let it speak?" I can tell you my flesh was screaming, "No, thank You. That would hurt too much. I don't want to go back, even in memories. It's off limits." However, my spirit was saying, "Yes, but only if You go with me. I won't go alone."

Thankfully my spirit won, and I went. The Faithful One went with me, exposed the lie and recalled His Word in Deuteronomy 2:2, *"You have made your way around this hill country long enough..."* He then gave me a deeply personal word for that intensely personal place. I tell you, Truth will finally and thoroughly set you free. It's a precious matter of incredible honor and beauty. It's intimacy beyond words, full of enough love to make you blush and rich enough to make you believe your Impossible List just might be possible after all. The Way, The Truth and the Life can rewrite the way your past affects your today. *When you allow Him to, it's a blessed, holy, set-you-free experience*. Painful as it may undoubtedly be to revisit those things, I HIGHLY RECOMMEND IT. How good is the Lord and greatly to be praised!

As Boaz gazed on Ruth's lovely face cast on his mercy, he may well have thought, "Oh, beautiful one, you've wandered around the hill country long enough. You've journeyed through pain, rough roads and dusty fields as a servant long enough. *I'm going to do all I can to make you my bride, the object of my delight and honor, the keeper of the fields instead of the hired help."*

God also speaks this way to our needy hearts through His wonderful Word: "You are My Beauty, My Beloved. You're meant to be a vessel of honor, one in whom the King of Glory abides. I love to dwell in your heart. It's My joy to unfurl my splendor there, and it will be your joy to display it. It's not pride; it's beauty that glorifies My name. I AM your Wonderful Counselor, the Mighty God unbound by time. I can redeem not just your heart, but every second you've breathed on this earth. You're My absolute delight. Your beauty enthralls me. Honor Me, for I am your God." How

He loves us. How sweet are His Words and how precious is His favor and delight. Scripture tells us the Lord of Lords rejoices over us with singing. How humbling and amazing to think of the Most High God performing a sweet song that has *our name in it!* How personal our Savior is and full of amazing love, grace and freedom. *I can't find words enough to praise Him.*

Questions & Applications

1. **Take the time to ask the Lord, as I did, to reveal anything in your heart that's hindering His full work in you.**
2. **I challenge you to sit before the Lord and make an "Impossible" or "It'd Take A Miracle" list. Knowing how deeply He loves you, be bold. Then get ready for Him to astound you. Ask for eyes to see, ears to hear and faith to believe your list will come to pass, according to the Faithful One's perfect ways and season. *"Now to Him who is able to do exceedingly abundantly above all that we ask or think, according to the power that works in us,... to Him be glory,"* Ephesians 3:20-21.**

33

Pondering and Prospering

So she lay at his feet until morning, and she arose before one could recognize another.

Then he said, "Do not let it be known that the woman came to the threshing floor." Also he said, "Bring the shawl that is on you and hold it." And when she held it, he measured six ephahs of barley, and laid it on her. Then she went into the city, **Ruth 3:14-15.**

That intensely personal time on the threshing floor was just that, personal. It was sacred, precious ground out of which something beautiful grew. I believe Boaz treasured his exchange with Ruth, yet he also knew how fast the wheels of gossip would spin if what happened there became public. His heart was tender and merciful toward Ruth, and he sought to protect her name, reputation and heart. He honored her, shielded her and then blessed her with all her shawl could hold. But OBVIOUSLY, what happened there eventually did get out. It is, after all, included in the eternal Word of God for every generation to read and study. So much more than an account of one night, it's a God-breathed record woven into our great weapon, the Sword of the Spirit, meant to instruct, equip and train.

I believe this passage is another sweet example of the Lord's perfect timing, protection and shielding of our hearts. The King of Kings, the Holy One who whispers in your heart, isn't out to embarrass or shame you. He's not bent on making you the stuff of gossip. He's the Lover of your soul who meets you on the threshing floor of prayer with His Word in precious, sacred encounters. *And sometimes, those special moments are meant to be pondered a while, laid up in your heart to fill it with hope and joy and treasured in that deeply personal place until He opens the door for them to be shared.* Our Christ is personal, and He'll whisper some very personal things in your ear— whispers you should spend some real time ruminating on.

Luke 2:19 provides just such an example. Here we find Mary having given birth to the Messiah, treasuring up and pondering in her heart all the Lord was doing. The excited shepherds were running around Bethlehem, *"making widely known the saying which was told them concerning this Child"* (Luke 2:17), but Mary was sitting by the Holy One, contemplating the profound drama in which the Lord had called her to participate. She didn't rush into the streets with a loudspeaker, write a book or schedule a speaking tour. *She sat with the King and worshiped, treasuring God's Word and promise to her and mankind. She considered everything that had taken place, and was filled with deep worship as she looked ahead to the day of salvation.* I believe songs must have naturally sprung from that pondering place as she held and rocked the King of Glory, much as when Elizabeth greeted the pregnant Mary with, *"My soul magnifies the Lord, and my spirit has rejoiced in God my Savior."* No doubt Ruth seriously pondered what was happening to her too, and praise-songs may very well have escaped her lips as she replayed Boaz's gracious words in her mind.

What about you? When was the last time you sat with the King and so deeply treasured His Word to you that a song of praise spontaneously sprang from your spirit? When was the last time you pondered the Lord's goodness and merciful actions in your life, until you just *broke into worship*? Consider with your heart, not just your "Sunday School head," a few things about the Lord of Glory who sits with you as you pray and soak in His Word:

> The Most High God, who's given His Holy Spirit to abide in you and the Lord Jesus, who made the way for everything heavenly to happen in your life, *is the SAME GOD* who spoke creation into existence. This is the God who established the nations, parted the Red Sea before His people, poured out the Law from the mountaintop, walked on water, brought deliverance and healed the oppressed.
>
> This God, who dealt with man's sin "face to face," taking it on and defeating it once for all on the Cross, expresses His profound love in indescribable abundance and *is no smaller because He's sitting with you.*

God doesn't reduce His strength because it's *only you* asking, seeking, knocking and searching for the impossible. He's not disappointed that you're not Billy Graham and doesn't reserve His mighty, awesome power for those "more worthy" than you. Maybe that's never been an issue in your heart, but for one who's battled fierce and crippling insecurity, it's *HUGE*—and more than enough to set these lips to praise. Whether your voice is beautiful to men or not, it's a precious thing to the King's ears. Psalm 47:6-7 urges us to, *"Sing praises to God, sing praises; sing praises to our King, sing praises. For God is the King of all the earth; sing to Him a psalm of praise."* Maybe it's time to do some pondering...

While doing just that, I heard the Lord's whisper in my heart: "I ponder things, too. I ponder your prayers, your cries, your tears, your love—all that dwells in your heart and all that it desires. I'm not deaf or mute. I consider with delight your cries to Me and move in power in due season. I contemplate My deep, pure wells of love for you and My holy and beautiful plans to build My kingdom through your heart. I'm the King of Kings, who gives you plenty to consider in Spirit and Truth. And, even as you delight in My Word to you, I treasure your words to Me and observe your praises with *joy*." As the Psalmist said, *"What is man that You are mindful of him...?"* How amazing to be on the mind of the Most High God.

Boaz protected Ruth's heart, gave her some things to ponder then asked her to bring her shawl so he could fill it full and bless her. Notice that when she did, he gave her *six ephahs* of barley. If you remember from Ruth 2:17, the *one* ephah she'd been given before was enough to cause Naomi to say, "Blessed be the man who took notice of you!" I bet Naomi was *really* excited when Ruth came home this time!

Ruth's shawl was a *physical* one. However, there's a *spiritual shawl* over each of us, the covering of prayer. The King of Kings urges us in Scripture to open up that shawl, so He can move in power and fill it to overflowing. He counts your life as worth filling, because of the blood of Christ. He looks at you as one He longs to bless with every spiritual blessing. He has gifts, answers and power waiting for you—impossibilities waiting to become realities. He just asks you to entrust your heart to Him, and ask, seek, knock. I believe the six ephahs of barley represent an invitation to ask for and expect more than one or two impossibles from Him. As the prophet put it in Jeremiah 32:1, *"Ah, Sovereign Lord, You have made the heavens and the earth by Your great power and outstretched arm. Nothing is too hard for You,"* to which the Lord replied, "*I am the Lord, the God of all mankind. Is anything too hard for Me?"* (v. 27). He's big enough to take on more than one impossible thing at a time. And He certainly has more than one "ephah" of provision available for you.

Along with personal needs and impossibilities to spread the prayer shawl over, there are also unfeasible corporate, national and international issues for which to intercede. I picture intercession as a "prayer web" with our hearts at the center, because we have to deal with our own impurities and eye-logs first at the feet of Christ. *"Create in me a clean heart, O God, and renew a right spirit within me,"(*Psalm 51:10). I love the word "clean" here, because to me it doesn't indicate innocence, but cleansed, washed, purified and made what we're absolutely *not.*

The next circle in the web is family, praying they'll love the Lord with all their hearts, walk in Truth, be hidden in Christ with their souls guarded and that He'll bring to pass all He's planned for them. Then comes the corporate body of Christ, locally and worldwide, invoking Jeremiah 32:38-39, *"They will be My people, and I will be their God. I will give them singleness of heart and action, so that they will always fear Me for their own good and the good of their children after them."* I ask for the members of the Body to begin to walk in unity, bowing at the Lord's feet as one and free of prejudice, building each other up in Him, fighting darkness and exalting Christ together, standing firm and seeing His work accomplished.

Then in the web there's the "spoke" of the municipality in which we live, asking for it to become "a city on a hill," shining forth the Truth of God. Jeremiah 33:9 says, *"Then this city will bring Me renown, joy, praise, and honor before all the nations on earth that hear of all the good things I do for it; and they will be in awe and will tremble at the abundant prosperity and peace I will provide for it."* Wouldn't you love to live in a place like that?

There's also intercession for government and church leaders, and for the hearts of the people to turn to Christ at the state level. After that comes the nation, asking God to bless and guide our president and national leadership and to lift the Sword on our country's behalf, and that we would humble ourselves, seek His face, turn from our sin and compromise and see our land healed—for revival to begin. Last but not least is the international arena, imploring God's protection for His servants suffering persecution, for the Word to penetrate even closed nations, for the leaders of false religions to have visions and revelations of Christ and lead their followers to Truth instead of lies, for a worldwide harvest of souls to begin and that we would be privileged to have some part in it. Knowing that all authority in heaven and earth has been given to Christ and that the cries of our hearts to Him can even affect *nations*, I see it as Great Commission intercession, preparing the way of the Lord to make disciples.

We're not on a picnic. WE ARE AT WAR! Deceptive strongholds must be torn down. We have to take charge over Enemy ground in our souls with the Sword of the Word, crying out for the Holy Spirit to burn in our hearts the Scriptures we should pray over every area. And He'll do it! We also need to go to prayer with our Ephesians 6 armor fully in place. *We can't afford to neglect our protective covering, drop our Sword or cease our cries to the King*. We're held accountable for prayerlessness. It's sinful. And if we, the people of God, become discouraged, distracted or lazy and stop fighting for the Kingdom, *who will do it?* The Commission is *to us*. What are we doing about it?

As I've prayed over my Impossible List, the Lord has challenged my heart with questions like these: "How do the items on your list relate to Kingdom purposes? How would answering them further those purposes? How would they glorify and exalt the King of Kings?" What would you say?

Who or what is the focus of your requests? Next, the Lord has queried, "What are you anticipating as you hold out your prayer shawl? Are you expecting answers and looking for mighty Kingdom moves?" We should! *"Blessed is she who has believed, for there will be a fulfillment of those things which were told her from the Lord,"* (Luke 1:45). Lord, I believe. Help my unbelief! With faith, our entreaties will be answered beyond even our greatest expectations.

Boaz filled Ruth's shawl with all it could hold—and probably far more than she expected—abundance she again took back to share with Naomi. Likewise, we can expect the Lord to fill our hearts with His Word and Spirit, until they're as strong in us as Jeremiah describes, *"a fire in our bones... that we indeed cannot hold in."* We can then take that harvest to our homes and beyond to build Christ's kingdom, ask God's will to be done in confidence and expect the great unexpected that will bless many.

Questions & Applications

1. **When was the last time you really spent pondering something God said to you in His Word? What was it and what was the outcome?**
2. **How do the items on your Impossible List relate to God's kingdom purposes?**
3. **Get in the habit and pleasure of seeking the Lord's personal, precious Word to you on a daily basis. Sit with Him in prayer and ponder the depths and riches of His living, active, sharp Sword. He bound it in black and white to equip and thrill you beyond anything you ever expected.**

<u>34</u>

The Life-changing Power of Hope

When she came to her mother-in-law, she said, "Is that you, my daughter?" Then she told her all that the man had done for her. And she said, "These six measures of barley he gave me; for he said to me, "Do not go empty-handed to your mother-in-law." Then she said, "Sit still, my daughter, until you know how the matter will turn out; for the man will not rest until he has concluded the matter this day," **Ruth 3:16-18.**

Ruth had been with her kinsman-redeemer. She'd been touched, spoken to tenderly, guarded and given great provision in her current need. I believe that abundant measure was a type of down payment, a hint of things to come. *Ruth had cause to be excited. She had a deep-rooted reason for hope—of which her arms were full of evidence! She was holding a portion that said to her heart, "You can trust the man,"* and she carried that confidence home. When Ruth walked through Naomi's door, I don't think Naomi asked, "Is that you?" because she wasn't sure who was entering her home, but because *Ruth looked different*. She'd met her hope face to face, trust had been established and expectation must have swelled in her heart and spilled over to her smile, her weary face shining with a beautiful radiance.

HOPE CHANGES YOUR VERY COUNTENANCE. The knowledge of God's promise being worked out in your life alters even your physical appearance. Burdens lifted looks *good* on you! Freedom from anxiety and fear does wonders for those wrinkles trying to etch themselves into your forehead. There's a lightness of heart that comes from time with the Redeemer, and trust birthed there will transform your outlook—and even the *way you look. "Those who look to Him are radiant; their faces are never covered with shame,"* (Psalm 34:5).

Knowing the Holy Spirit is set in our hearts as a guarantee and deposit of what's to come, that we're the beloved of the Lord, that He's given us salvation and anointed us as His own and that the King of Glory is guiding our way no matter where we've been before, should cause hope to rise up and show itself in our lives and faces! Even if your circumstances haven't changed yet, you still can't see what you're looking for and your Impossible List remains impossible, *hopefulness will change you.*

What stirs in your heart when you hear the word "hope"? What rises to the surface? For me, it's the promises of God's Word coming to pass *even* in *my* life, empowered by the Faithful One. It raises the anticipation of answered prayer, of godly desires becoming realities and impossible things being lived out in joy. It energizes the fact that my current trial doesn't define my life but will be woven into good, and that because of the Lord's great love and mercy I'll *"see the goodness of the Lord in the land of the living." (Psalm 27:13)* It shouts that every deception I've been ensnared by will fall before Truth, the Lord's great purposes will be worked out and that, even in me, the King of Kings can be exalted.

Hebrew and Greek define "hope" as, "favorable expectation, a thing longed for, something waited for, confidence, security, *a forward look with assurance, trust.*" Hope is full, rich and beautiful—a precious, holy thing that serves to keep us forward-focused. Hope looks ahead. It's wrapped in faith and trust that whatever the Lord says, He'll certainly do. It can be patient, because it's grounded in the faithfulness of the Living God. It can endure the "right now," knowing there's great promise for the "yet to be." I believe our hopes also reveal what's rooted in our hearts. What are you hoping for? *Even our hopes need to be grounded in Spirit and Truth, or they can quickly become fleshly and misguided*. On whom or what are your hopes based? Whom would they serve and glorify? How would they build the kingdom of the Risen Christ?

DO YOU TRUST HIM? Do you truly believe He'll do all He's shown you, that He's really working on your behalf, can absolutely be trusted and that it's His good pleasure to give you the Kingdom? Do you believe He has a plan of action for your life that's for your good and have faith for what you've yet to see? Are you confident that "this," too, will end well? WHERE THERE'S NO TRUST, THERE'S NO HOPE.

As Ruth had to believe that Boaz *really was* searching out the other kinsman and making a way for her redemption, we have to trust that our Lord is out to redeem our lives, working powerfully in the unseen and weaving our circumstances together for good. There are days (or weeks!) when nothing looks like it's working out well, when my natural eyes see only difficulty and I honestly want to give up in many ways. If anyone's flesh is weak, it's mine. *That's why we can't trust our natural inclinations, emotions and reactions—much less our hormones—but must base our hope and trust in Spirit and Truth. It's a matter of life and death.*

Nor can we rely on our own good deeds or righteousness to pull us together. In Isaiah 64:6, our righteousness is compared to "filthy rags." In that day it referred to the menstrual cloth (another graphic example). I wondered why the Lord chose that comparison, so I asked Him. The answer in my heart was that just as that physical rag signifies *there will not be a birth* in nine months, spiritually what we try to accomplish in our own righteousness *will produce no real fruit. Your righteousness births nothing. DO NOT TRUST IT. DON'T BANK YOUR HOPE ON THE GOOD THINGS YOU'VE DONE FOR THE LORD, LIKE HE OWES YOU.* No harvest will come to fruition from your own virtue. That's definitely a misplaced hope.

As I've prayed about the matter of trust, God has confronted a stronghold of unbelief in my heart that routinely rears its ugly head and spews its venom into my thoughts. As I've dealt with reoccurring physical symptoms that I've asked the Lord to remove, I've battled fierce thoughts like, "You're still sick because you deserve it. You're not worthy or faithful enough for healing. Nothing will change. You're a drag on your family. The sooner you get to heaven, the better off they'll be." Those kinds of arrows can take you down quick. *Words like that are not from Jesus, but are straight from the Pit and part of the scheme to shut you up.* They're Despair's words, not the Redeemer's. Which will you believe in the day of darkness or weakness? What do you trust in then? How I pray that every deception or misplaced area of faith will be dug out of my heart and replaced with Truth.

The Lord tells us that our Foe is out to steal, kill and destroy. And don't think he hasn't noticed you. While God's Word speaks hope and deliverance, the Enemy's got words for you and me, too—defeat and death. *BUT I refuse to believe him, and will not trust in his lies.* I will put my faith in the Word of the Most High, as David expressed in 2 Samuel 22:2-4: *"I will call upon the Lord, who is worthy to be praised; so shall I be saved from my enemies."* I'll cry out to God. I'll praise Him, and I'll see victory and the goodness of the Lord in the land of the living. *"They confronted me in the day of my calamity, but the Lord was my support,"* (v. 19). The Lord is your strong support. Trust in Him alone.

Another thing you can't believe in is a Sunday morning smile. If you passed by me at church, you'd have no clue about the battles raging around me, just as I wouldn't know what you needed prayer for. *You can't tell what's ravaging a person by their church face. It's so important that we really get to know what's going on inside each other, so we can specifically minister to, pray for and encourage each other to keep our hope centered in the Word of God and avoid the pits of misplaced faith.*

A clear example of this is found in 2 Kings 18:1-5. Hezekiah was a righteous king who *"removed the high places and broke the sacred pillars, cut down the wooden image and broke in pieces the bronze serpent that Moses had made; for until those days the children of Israel had burned incense to it, and called it Nehushtan."* God's chosen people were actually burning incense to a bronze serpent that Moses had made. *Why?*

Tracing the history, we find in Numbers 21:4-8 the Israelites in the wilderness growing impatient and grumbling. The Lord made it very clear how he felt about that display of unbelief by sending venomous snakes among them. (Unbelief lets the serpent in. It'll kill you.) When the people began to cry out and repent, the Lord instructed Moses to *"Make a snake and put it on a pole, and anyone who is bitten can look at it and live."* It was a foreshadowing of Christ, as John 3:14-15 informs us, *"Just as Moses lifted up the snake in the desert, so the Son of Man must be lifted up, that everyone who believes in Him may have eternal life."* Any of us bitten by sin and unbelief (that would be ALL of us) can look to the cross of Christ and find the power of the Enemy *nullified.*

Here's the danger. The Lord had delivered the people, but they began to worship the *symbol* of their deliverance instead of the Deliverer Himself! Don't think you're too sophisticated to fall for the same scheme! Has the Lord given you something to help you trust Him that you've begun to put your faith in—a teacher, a book, an experience, a pastor, a conference, a friend, a movement, a study, a miracle...? It could be something good; something in the church—*but it's not meant to become an object of your worship!* The Israelites were told to look at the serpent, but they took it a step further and started burning incense to it. *Be sure that when the Lord gives you your Impossible List, and I'm believing He will, He alone is worshiped, glorified and exalted. It won't be your doing, but solely His. When you see it, be glad but be careful to give all the praise to the King of Kings. GUARD YOUR TRUST WELL.*

Hezekiah's was a life of rightly placed faith. In 2 Kings 19:10-37, he's confronted by Israel's enemies. The foreign ruler of an overwhelming army sent taunts, threats and mockery written in black and white and put in Hezekiah's hand. He faced a dilemma: trust in men and try to fight, or lay your heart before the Lord God Almighty and believe Him. *He made the right choice*. Verse 14 tells us, *"Hezekiah received the letter from the messengers and read it. Then he went up to the temple of the Lord and spread it out before the Lord."* I love the phrase, *"spread it out before the Lord."* Hezekiah just laid it all on the table and cried out to the King. He praised the awesome God, asked for His mighty ear, presented the problem and prayed for deliverance, not just on his behalf but *"so that all kingdoms on earth may know that you alone, O Lord, are God."*

That's where we find our answers, too. Taking whatever it is to the Lord and trusting Him to work out His glory in the situation—not devising our own plans and asking God to bless them, but spreading them out and waiting on Him first. Whatever unsettles, threatens or taunts; whenever fears, circumstances, relationships or persecutions threaten; whichever battles you face, deliverance you need or impossibilities you desire, *lay them on the table before the King*.

In fact, in addition to our impossibilities, I believe the Lord also wants us to bring before Him the things we don't trust Him with. It's a little hard to look at where you're not believing the Almighty King of Glory, the One who redeemed your life from the Pit, called you from darkness to light, speaks His Word in Spirit and Truth and has never proven unfaithful. Yet He doesn't ask us to spread even unbelief before Him so He can condemn us, but so that He can free us.

When I first sensed the Lord's invitation to do this, despite knowing He was trying to release me into Truth, I didn't go there. SO HE WENT THERE! As I showered that morning, I heard His voice say strongly in my spirit, "YOU AVOIDED THE LIST! You're afraid I'm going to leave you in sickness forever; you don't trust Me for your physical body." He then proceeded to nail my heart with five more huge examples of my lack of faith. I cried out, "Forgive me, Lord. *'When I am afraid, I will trust in You. In God, whose Word I praise, in God I trust,'* (Psalm 56:3-4). *'You have tested my heart,'* and I've found that Your mercy overrules and grace abounds. I will trust You in this hard place and will expect joy and blessing. I'm going to believe this will turn out WELL, no matter what it looks like today. I choose to trust. Help me to *actually do it.*" IT'S A PRIVILEGE TO TRUST OUR LORD, BECAUSE IN THE END WE'LL SEE MORE OF HIM THAN BEFORE WE ENTERED THE HARD PLACE.

Hezekiah ran to the Lord's table, laid his heart out in prayer and received an answer. Here's how he described his situation in 2 Kings19:3, *"This is a day of trouble, and rebuke, and blasphemy; for the children have come to birth, but there is no strength to bring them forth."* Verses 21-37 record the Lord's response to his enemy's destructive threats, including verse 22: *"Whom have you reproached and blasphemed? Against whom have you raised your voice, and lifted up your eyes on high? Against the Holy One of Israel!"* I translate it as, "YOU MESS WITH MY OWN, YOU MESS WITH ME!" The Lord doesn't take lightly the stuff coming against us. He goes on to say, *"Therefore I will put My hook in your nose and My bridle in your lips, and I will turn you back by the way which you came."* I love it. He expects us to shield our hearts with faith and cry out to Him, and HE takes the Enemy captive and sends him packing. *"Not by might nor by power, but by My Spirit, says the Lord Almighty,"* (Zechariah 4:6). In the meantime, we fall deeper in love with our Redeemer as we trust Him and watch Him move.

The things opposing us aren't meant for our defeat alone. The Enemy wants to hinder the Kingdom building assigned to you. He can NEVER defeat the Lord God, so he's out to defeat the Lord's purposes in your life. He wants to steal the breath out of everything God intends to birth in and through you, just as Hezekiah described. It's CRITICAL that we allow the Lord to continually breathe His Spirit and Word in us. Then we can absolutely trust that, *"Faithful is He who called you, and He also will bring it to pass,"* (I Thessalonians 5:24). Bring it on, Lord. I'll wait in expectant, confident belief!

In 2 Kings 19:29, the Lord says, *"This shall be a sign to you..."* I believe the Lord *loves* to encourage us, give us glimpses of what He's doing and show us evidences of His Word coming to pass, so that our faith increases in the small things as we wait on Him for the big. He celebrates our victories in taking baby steps, while preparing us for the marathon. He teaches us to trust Him and builds our faith as we go. The Lord was saying, "As you see these small things happen, you will know your huge deliverance is on the way." HE'S ALWAYS GOOD—AND WORTHY OF OUR TRUST. I believe Hezekiah's zeal for the Lord was greater after his crisis than before. The problem became merely another way for the Lord to display His mighty power, build the faith of his people and cause them to worship and trust *HIM alone,* not some symbol on a pole.

I don't know why God heals some and not others. I don't understand why He allows some things, or why some prayers are immediately answered while others take years or may never be seen on this side of glory. Here's what I do know: *my Redeemer lives and He is good. He's working His glory out in our hearts and pouring out splendor for us to display. He laid down everything for me on the Cross and loves me deeply, SO I WILL TRUST HIM. He has a plan. He's spoken His Word, assigned glory for our lives and is working it all out. I'll humbly bow before the King of Kings, take Him at His Word and bank my life and very breath on it.*

Here's what I call my **TRUST LIST:**

1 Psalm 7:1: *O Lord my God, in You I put my trust; save me from all those who persecute me; and deliver me.* TRUST HIM FOR SALVATION AND DELIVERANCE.

2 Psalm 9:10: *And those who know Your Name will put their trust in You...*TRUST CHRIST TO REVEAL HIMSELF AND THE POWER OF HIS MIGHTY NAME MORE AND MORE...*for You, O Lord, have not forsaken those who seek You.* HE WON'T DISAPPOINT, FAIL OR LEAVE YOU! TRUST HIM AND SEEK HIS PRESENCE AND WORD.

3 2 Corinthians 9:8: *God is able to make all grace abound toward you, that you, always having all sufficiency in all things, have an abundance for every good work.* TRUST GOD'S GRACE, HIS SUFFICIENCY,

HIS STRENGTH AND HIS ABUNDANCE. TRUST HIM FOR ALL YOU NEED TO PERFORM EVERYTHING HE'S CALLED YOU TO DO.

4 Deuteronomy 33:12: *Let the Beloved of the Lord rest secure in Him, for He shields him all day long, and the one the Lord loves rests between His shoulders*. TRUST THAT YOU'RE JESUS' BELOVED, PRECIOUS, FAVORED ONE. YOU'RE SECURE, SHIELDED AND COVERED, RESTING ON AND IN HIS MIGHTY HEART.

5 Isaiah 26:3-4: *You will keep in perfect peace him whose mind is steadfast, because he trusts in You. Trust in the Lord forever, for in YAH, the Lord, is everlasting strength*. TRUST FOR A STEADFAST, STEADY MIND OF PEACE. TRUST FOR THE ENDURING KIND OF STRENGTH THAT'S IN NO WAY DEPENDENT ON YOURS.

6 Deuteronomy 33:27: *The eternal God is your refuge, and underneath are the everlasting arms. He will drive out your enemy before you, saying, "Destroy him!"* TRUST THAT GOD IS TIMELESS AND ABLE TO HANDLE YOUR WAS, IS AND IS TO COME. TRUST THAT HE'S YOUR SHELTER AND DEFENSE. TRUST THAT HE'LL UPHOLD YOU AND KEEP YOU FROM STUMBLING AND FALLING APART AS YOU REST IN HIS MIGHTY ARMS. TRUST HIM TO DESTROY WITH HIS WORD WHAT SEEKS TO DESTROY YOU.

7 Joshua 1:6,7,9: *Be strong and courageous...very courageous...Do not be terrified, do not be discouraged, for the Lord your God will be with you wherever you go*. TRUST THAT THE LORD DOESN'T WANT YOU TO FEAR OR FALL BEFORE DESPAIR OR

DISCOURAGEMENT. TRUST THAT HE'S WITH YOU TO LEAD AND ESTABLISH YOU.

8 Psalm 16:11: *You will show me the path of life; in Your presence is fullness of joy; at Your right hand are pleasures forevermore.* TRUST THAT THE ALMIGHTY WILL REVEAL HIS PATH TO YOU, AND THAT YOU WILL WALK WITH HIM ON IT WITH INEXPRESSIBLE JOY AND PLEASURE IN HIS COMPANY.

Questions & Applications

1. **What are some of the areas in your life with which you have difficulty trusting the Lord? Spread them out before Him, as Hezekiah.**
2. **Keep on going through the Word of God, turning Scripture into a prayer and declaration of trust. The Lord is with you, mighty warrior. He is your hope and defense.**

35

Doing Business in the Meantime

Meanwhile Boaz went up to the town gate and sat there... **Ruth 4:1a.**

I love the word the NIV begins with here, "meanwhile." It indicates that while Ruth was doing one thing, Boaz was busy, too. We left Ruth believing that Boaz was going to do what he said he would—work for her redemption—even though unseen by her. She trusted him to perform his word to her and settle the matter, as Naomi said, "this day." Ruth was hoping, resting and being sustained and encouraged by the harvest already given her. And, *meanwhile,* Boaz was doing business. He knew what must be done, had a plan of action and was committed to doing it. He "went up to the town gate and sat there," ready to do everything necessary for the joy set before him named Ruth, just as our Redeemer does with us.

You can rest assured that even *this day,* though unseen to your natural eyes, your Redeemer is taking care of business on behalf of your heart. He's paying the ransom for your soul with His own holy blood and taking back the rights your sin gave our Foe. He's planning a future and a hope for you and your seed, exposing the Enemy's plans and setting His own in motion. He's interceding for every aspect of your life and performing His living, active Word. He's doing business on your behalf, so you can join Him and be about HIS—not as a charity case BUT AS HIS BRIDE, His covenant partner and His pure joy and delight. *You know it in your head, now celebrate it in your heart.*

Scripture gives us an amazing, backstage glimpse into our Redeemer's actions on our behalf. Let these passages on God's intercessions for us fill your soul with faith, confidence, trust and expectation of glory to come:

1 Romans 8:26-27, *In the same way, the Spirit helps us in our weakness. We do not know what we ought to pray for, but the Spirit Himself intercedes for us with groans that words cannot express. And He who searches our hearts knows the mind of the Spirit, because the Spirit intercedes for the saints in accordance with God's will.* The Holy Spirit is praying God's will over you, which is always His Word, even when you don't have a clue.
2 Hebrews 7:25, *Therefore, He is able to save completely those who come to God through Him, because He always lives to intercede for them.* Key words: always and completely. The King of Glory never ceases acting on behalf of His own, and His work is forever thorough and complete, lacking nothing—more than you dreamed. Who am I that Jesus should even *notice* me, let alone cry out for me?

In John 17:6-26, the Lord Jesus intercedes for His disciples and for all believers, bragging on their faith and asking out loud for their protection and unity, *"that they may have the full measure of my joy within."* His Word brings joy and sanctifies us. The pure pleasure of His attention and sheer thrill of His voice whispered through it should stir everything in us. Just think, the same Voice that instructed Noah, spoke to Moses in the burning bush, led Joshua into the Promised Land, filled David's soul with psalms, confronted Paul on the way to Damascus and spoke the earth-shattering words, *"It is finished,"* is the *same Voice* speaking to you today. Shouldn't we *tremble* before the God of all time who has something to say to us? Do you open the Word thinking, "Oh, what will the King say to my heart today? What wonders will He reveal in His Word and in prayer? What is the risen Christ interceding for me about today?"

This is no "dry toast" of tradition. *This is interacting with Glory itself, the Most High God and Holy One. This is hearing the voice of the One before whom all of heaven worships, before whom every knee in heaven and earth will bow, the God of Genesis and Revelation.* It's no small, casual or ordinary thing to speak to and hear the King. *And the fact that He cries out for my life is nothing short of miraculous to me!* The truth that there's something going on in the heavenlies with *my name and yours* stamped on it is, as the psalmist said, *"knowledge far too wonderful for me."* Jesus asks for unity among his followers twice in the John 17 passage (how important must *it* be?), and for His own to SEE HIS GLORY. That's a prayer I can hardly wait to see the fullness of, and one I've prayed for years.

Jesus goes on to state that He'll continue to make God known to us, so that His love may dwell in us and that CHRIST HIMSELF MAY BE IN US. *Christ in me, the hope of glory*, is something I NEVER WANT TO GET OVER OR USED TO. May this CONTINUALLY amaze and humble us. I heard a car alarm go off in a parking lot one day and watched as, of course, no one responded. I've never seen anyone take action at those blarings, because we're so used to hearing them. Too many people set them off accidentally, or, like me, to find their car when they can't remember where they parked. As I thought about that, my cry to the Father was, *"LORD, DON'T LET ME EVER GET USED TO YOUR GLORY, YOUR WONDERS, YOUR WHISPERS, YOUR WORD OR THE FACT THAT YOU'RE INTERCEDING FOR MY LIFE. LET IT ALWAYS AND FOREVER ASTOUND ME AND SET MY FEET TO ACTION."*

In addition to our Lord's intercessions for us, here's a few Scriptures on God's planning actions on our behalf:

1 Jeremiah 29:11, *"'For I know the plans I have for you,' declares the Lord, 'plans to prosper you and not to harm you, plans to give you hope and a future.'"* A familiar verse, but one the Lord has used to challenge my heart as He whispers, "You trust that I'll allow hard things and suffering because you've tasted some of them, but do you trust that I'll bring about blessings you haven't earned, a prospering you haven't imagined and a future better than you could plan? Can you believe all this ends well?" Nailed again. May our answer always be on the side of faith—YES, LORD, I BELIEVE.

2 1 Peter 5:10, *May the God of all grace, who called us to His eternal glory by Christ Jesus, after you have suffered a while, perfect, establish, strengthen, and settle you.* One of my favorite verses, it tells me there's a purpose in suffering that, once served, will be used by the Lord Jesus to establish and settle us in His perfect, glorious plans. Settle us, mighty King, in Your perfect plan.

3 Ephesians 2:10, *For we are His workmanship, created in Christ Jesus for good works, which God prepared beforehand that we should walk in them.* What comfort this verse holds! It assures me there's a plan already prepared, formed by Christ Jesus Himself, just waiting for me to walk in. It sets us free

> from thinking we have to make something happen. You can't manipulate His work for you; manipulation is of the flesh.

Ruth didn't say, "I trust Boaz," and then start manipulating her situation and trying to work it out on her own. She didn't beg, plead, steal or turn on her feminine charm. She didn't talk about it in town and try to rally sympathy and support. *Help from other people is good, but don't count on it. Our battle is not with flesh and blood, and our assurance, confidence and hope aren't to be either! The task laid before you and the anointing on your life isn't based on what others think of you.* Ruth didn't promote herself, defend herself or highlight her good qualities. She didn't cry and stomp her feet, or rush out to see what the other guy had to offer. She rested in the right thing, faith. She trusted and anticipated the good to come and a future of hope. She set herself apart and waited for God's timing.

Are we waiting for the Lord to unleash His perfect plans for our lives with hopeful anticipation, like Ruth? Do we trust? Do we set ourselves apart for Him alone? Do we do what God commanded Joshua, *"Consecrate yourselves, for tomorrow the Lord will do amazing things among you."* The Hebrew for "consecrate" is so powerful! Along with "a setting aside for special use," it can also indicate, "to be full to overflowing, not just filling to the limits of something, but filling so as to go beyond its limits." In a military context, it means, "preparing your hands for war." *Let's be consecrated as we wait, then!* Not checking off a legalistic list, but filled to overflowing, equipped, commissioned and prepared by and for the King of Kings.

How great and amazing is the Lord, who has plans for our lives! *"Many, O Lord my God, are the wonders You have done. The things You planned for us no one can recount to You; were I to speak and tell of them, they would be too many to declare,"* (Psalm 40:5). Do everything you do as unto the Lord. Worship Him with all you are, and trust Him to carry out what He's already planned. As you do, He's moving, establishing, opening doors, working out His holy purposes and getting ready to exalt Himself even in your everyday life. He's making a way for you to *walk His plan out,* not just wish, dream or think "maybe someday...," but putting one foot in front of the other and *living it. Doing it.*

The Word of God is full of the Lord's activity on our behalf! It's given to us so that we may know, see, believe and glorify the Lord Jesus. From cover to cover love spills out of it in black and white, the battle plan is laid out, assurance is spoken, purpose is determined, deep satisfaction is given and victory is secured. It doesn't contain enough pages to tell of all the Lord has done, is doing and will do, *but what a thrill to discover it little by little and day by day.* In addition to the Scripture, when you stop and look at what God's already done in your life, how can you not fall down in worship and rise up in faith? Deal with the trust issue and any misplaced hopes, and you'll drink a cup of pure joy as you see the One you're trusting *move.*

When I dealt with these issues, I felt a flood of joy like never before. I prayed, "Lord, I almost feel guilty having this much joy!" He whispered back, "It's a product of trust- a fruit of the Spirit- a gift. Enjoy it." NO WONDER THE ENEMY OF OUR SOULS WORKS SO HARD TO MAKE US FALL INTO DOUBT AND UNBELIEF! No wonder he continually questions, as did Hezekiah's enemy in 2 Kings18:19, *"On what are you basing this confidence of yours?"* to which we must be ready with a faith-filled response: THE BLOOD OF CHRIST! We need to know the Word of God, raise it as our defense and refuse to be tossed about by Enemy taunts!

James 1:6 admonishes, *"But let him ask in faith, with no doubting, for he who doubts is like a wave of the sea driven and tossed by the wind."* I've experienced that kind of tossing, driven by the hot, stinking breath of the Enemy's lies. I've looked at my flesh, at weakness and at circumstances, and watched my emotions bounce around like a ship in a hurricane. Can you relate? Physical weakness-toss. Hormones make themselves known-toss. Old wounds tap you on the shoulder-toss. Insults and rejection, especially from those you expected to support you-*major toss*. Nothing's going according to your plans-toss. Unfulfilled dreams-toss. Someone announces they're living out the very desire of *your* heart-toss. The problem: every one of those tosses comes from LOOKING AT MYSELF. WRONG FOCUS. My issue hasn't been so much doubting God, but that He'd dare to love and use someone like me. (I wonder if Ruth had the same feelings about receiving attention from Boaz?)

If Ruth had focused on her circumstances, she may have drowned in doubt and despair—and never even approached Boaz. It's critical for us to look up to God instead of down at flesh, and to gaze ahead instead of just at what we see today. We need to go to our knees and the Word, and dig out the memorial stones of the Lord's past faithfulness, remember His promises and ANCHOR OUR HOPE in faith, absolutely refusing to be tossed about. The kids and I were talking about roller coasters one day, because we heard a report of a child dying on one. I said, "You know, God didn't make our bodies to be slung around like that," to which I felt the Holy Spirit say, "I didn't make your emotions, faith, dreams or vision to be either." God, help us.

It's not about us, but building the kingdom of the Living God. HE'S COMING SOON, and we need to be about His business. YOU CAN'T DO IT IN A TOSSED-AROUND, UNSTABLE VESSEL. It makes you easy prey, and gives the Enemy easy access. You'll pitch yourself right onto one of his arrows. ANCHOR YOURSELF IN THE LORD!

Proverbs 3:26 says, *"The Lord will be your confidence, and will keep your foot from being caught."* OR TOSSED! I want to walk on top of the water, not be knocked under by it. I want to gaze straight at Christ, not at my flesh or circumstances. Have you ever been tumbled about in some storm until you cry out, "Lord, don't You care that I'm drowning here?" like the disciples in Mark 4:38-40. HE IS LORD. He could say the Word and calm everything in a millisecond, but MAYBE He's inviting you to exercise some faith. Haven't you seen Him move and work before? Why fear now?

Jesus asked his disciples, *"Why are you so afraid?"* DOUBT opened the door to FEAR. They're partners in crime and killers. GET RID OF THEM through the Word of God. Not only does doubt toss you around, but it would appear from Mark 6:5-6 that it also *limits the miraculous* in our lives, the very thing we need and long for. Over and over in the gospels, Jesus performed miracles as people believed. Their "impossibles" unfolded. *That's what I want to see in my life*—to be off the wave-tops, and seated with the King in faith and tasting the impossible, with nothing stolen, killed or destroyed by Enemy schemes, but with a full plate of the Lord's good plans.

We once had a lady helping to clean our house, who began to steal from us. Nothing huge, yet I still felt so violated. But I refuse to be violated in spirit, because we're given the authority of Christ and the power of His Name. *Faith will shield us well.* In Mark 11:23-24, Jesus states that if we tell a mountain to jump into the sea believing, it will. That's faith released, and how we're to speak our "mountains." Doubt is rooted in the heart. We need to examine ours, and then ask for a "full-filling" of the Holy Spirit that leaves no room for it. We must go to the throne room in prayer, be bold enough to *ask* and then wait in joyful expectation for it to come to pass. Jesus said in Luke 17, *"If you have faith as small as a mustard seed, you can say to this mulberry tree, 'Be uprooted*

and planted in the sea,' and it will obey you." That's a little bit of faith doing a lot of the miraculous! Mulberry trees DON'T NATURALLY GROW IN THE SEA! I take this as a holy invitation to rise up, speak in confidence and watch the supernatural happen before my natural eyes—to see the impossible made possible and witness what doesn't normally occur accomplished anyway!

I repent of doubt and renounce that boat I was being tossed around in! I'M GETTING OUT OF IT STARTING TODAY! I want, ask and believe for *aggressive, bold faith* that takes God at His Word and refuses to be hindered or stolen from. I WILL NOT LET DOUBT STEAL WHAT THE LORD HAS SPOKEN FROM THE HOLY OF HOLIES. Don't you, either.

As I've considered the situation in Israel, I've heard the Lord whisper in my spirit, "I AM COMING SOON. DO WHAT YOU CAN," which I take very seriously. We can't do anything if we don't trust Him—if we don't believe He's busy on our behalf, interceding, arranging, smoothing, straightening, paving the way, guarding, protecting, establishing and strengthening. I want to fall before His throne knowing I DID ALL HE PLANNED FOR ME TO DO TO BUILD HIS KINGDOM AND EXALT HIS NAME.

Questions & Applications

1. **Are you waiting confidently for the Lord to unleash His perfect plans for your life, or are you seeking to manipulate your circumstances for your own wellbeing?**
2. **Thank the Lord Jesus for His divine intervention on your behalf, in the seen and unseen. Thank Him for the good plan He has to build His Kingdom through your life.**

3. **Deal with the doubt issue. It is dangerous, unstable ground. Cry out to the Lord as the man did in Mark 9:24, *"I do believe; help me overcome my unbelief!"***

36

Seeking and Keeping Covenant

...and behold, the close relative of whom Boaz had spoken came by. So Boaz said, "Come aside friend, sit down here." So he came aside and sat down, **Ruth 4:1b.**

Ruth was waiting with great anticipation. Boaz was in town taking care of business and *some amazing things were about to take place*. Boaz was out doing everything necessary to make and keep covenant with Ruth. I believe love for Ruth was already pulsing through his veins as he spoke to that close relative, and that he had every intention of securing Ruth's heart for himself. He was smitten. Ruth was his desire, and he was on a mission—*a mission of covenant*.

In Hebrew, "covenant" means, "a political agreement, an agreement between men, a mutual agreement confirmed by oath in the name of the Lord." It involved words, law, precepts and testimony, and was a serious, binding matter. Boaz probably had plenty of other business to which he *could* have been tending. After all, it was harvest season. Yet, he pushed everything aside to pursue and secure his bride through a legal contract. His purpose and intent were amazingly clear. His word to Ruth and duty to perform it was his ultimate focus. He'd do everything necessary to enter into relationship with the desire of his heart, foreigner though she was. He wanted more than anything to make his home hers and be joined in fullness of relationship.

Our precious Redeemer is also bent on pursuing our hearts and securing them for Himself, for our good and His great delight. He's on a mission of covenant too, an assignment of grace that joins us to Him, giving us His Name, the fullness of His kingdom and the authority and power of His Word. *Strong's* defines God's covenant purpose as, "that man be joined to Him in loving service and know eternal fellowship with Him through the redemption that is in Christ Jesus." It further states that, "God's grace always goes before and produces man's response." The King is after our hearts, and redemption-establishing covenant is the heartbeat of His. *He's doing business with everything else that's attempting to steal your affections or become an inadequate redeemer. He knows He's the only way, the only Truth and the only source of Life, and He wants you to know and experience it, too.*

According to Psalm 121:3-4, *"He who keeps you will not slumber. Behold, He who keeps Israel shall neither slumber nor sleep."* The King of Kings never sleeps in His pursuit of you. He never closes His eyes to your heart, but is always and forever wide-eyed over you, watching over and performing His Word (promise) as you go to Him and wait in faith. The covenant He's provided for you is an eternal one. Ruth was about to see some wonderful things happen, because Boaz was faithfully carrying out his word. *We, too, will witness wonders because Christ is speaking and actively performing His Word to us; He's actively keeping covenant. It's called GLORY—His glory. We see it in the Word made flesh. Christ IS the Word, and the more you abide there, the more you see of Him.* THE DEEPER YOU DIG INTO IT, THE GREATER YOUR VISION OF GLORY.

Boaz publicly demonstrated his faithfulness and passion, just as Jesus did for us. Boaz "went to the gate and sat down," which may indicate that he was *just outside* of town. He went to the appropriate location for business contracts, the place where deals were made and secured before witnesses. In the Old Testament, sacrifice also was often made *outside the town gates.* Serious transactions took place there. Covenant was walked out and demonstrated there. Christ also went outside the city gates to establish His agreement with us, to a place called Golgotha. Jesus transacted the ultimate business there on that hill called Calvary, which was located on Jerusalem's outskirts, sealing the "deal" for our souls forever.

Psalm 111:5 says of God, *"He remembers His covenant forever,"* and Psalm 37:5 instructs us to, *"Commit your way to the Lord, trust also in Him, and He shall bring it to pass."* If you're Christ's through the gift of salvation, then you're in covenant with the Almighty. Business has been transacted for your soul. A holy, eternally-binding contract has been made, securing divine promises for you, matters the Lord Himself is going to bring to pass. It's made the Word of the Living God living and active in you through the power of the Holy Spirit. It also causes a stir about you, sparking amazing discussions about your life in heavenly places.

Go there with me. Christ has fixed His eyes on you and is speaking to the Father about your heart. His holy finger is pointing your way, and He says, "I *love* that one, Father. Give her what she asks in My Name! She's My beloved, precious to My heart and beautiful in My sight. Let's work on those plans prescribed for her. Let's set her free from all bondage and captivity. Let's release her soul to proclaim the praises of the One who's called her out of darkness into marvelous light. Let's open her eyes and let her behold Truth. Let's fill her with wisdom and revelation that she may know Us better. Let's take her to the deep waters of the Word and bathe her in them. Let's show her the wellsprings of My mercy and grace and baptize her with them. Let's amaze and astound her. Let's release healing, the miraculous and the impossible, as she releases faith. Let's convict her of sin, so she can walk away from its deadly chains. Let's give her holy bread daily and then use her to lead others to the table. Let's write a song of delight and sing it over her, and put a new song in her mouth. Let's bear fruit in her heart and heap it up to overflowing. Let's take her to the fields and let her participate in the joy and glory of the harvest. Let's bring her face-to-face in Spirit and Truth and fill her heart with pure vision.

"Let her arise and shine, for her Light has surely come. Let wisdom and revelation dwell in her heart. Let grace be on her tongue. Let her confidence be Christ. Let faith shield her, and let the mountains be moved. Let's protect her walls and be her rear guard. Let's restore her soul as she's led by quiet, deep waters. Let's guide her in the path of righteousness for My Name's sake. Let's comfort her with Our rod and staff. Let's prepare a table of beauty and abundance before her, even as her enemies look on. Let's anoint her with holy oil and keep her lamp blazing with sheer, holy brilliance. Let's set goodness and love on her trail and allow her to dwell in Our house forever. Let's instruct, teach, counsel, guide, prepare, establish, strengthen and settle her. Let's be the stronghold of her life. Let's give her amazing glimpses of glory. Let's hide her in the shelter of the tabernacle and help her make music in her heart to the Lord. Let's listen to her cries and receive her as she seeks Our face. Let's show her the goodness of the Lord in the land of the living and set eternity's worship deep in her soul. Let's turn her wailing to dancing, remove her sackcloth and clothe her with joy. Let's keep her feet from stumbling and set them in a wide place as we enlarge her steps and territory. Let's fill this one to overflowing for My Name and glory, and let's surround her with unfailing, never-forsaking love. *She's walking in faith, let's blow her mind."*

You're the subject matter of that conversation. *You're* the one the King is passionately pursuing and with whom He desires to work-out and walk-out covenant. I'd say rejoicing is in order: *"For He spoke, and it came to be; He commanded, and it stood firm,"* Psalm 33:9. If it's in His Word, His Covenant, then wait for it in faith. The business has been transacted. It's coming. Keep watching. The King is going to bring you face to face with the holy plans of Almighty God. Patiently trust the Lord. He's faithful.

The Lord has shown me two places, two "zones," where we wait for Him: one of comfort and blessing, the other of trial and testing. We can stumble over the flesh in either one! It's crucial for the eyes of our hearts to be open, watching for the King in Spirit and Truth, in prayer and in the Word.

Psalm 106 is an account of Israel waiting on God's promise to be made manifest in their lives, and their reaction to that window of trial and testing. The Lord had just led them out of captivity with a great display of miraculous power, a supernatural deliverance of the grandest sort. Verse 12 tells us that following their release from slavery and bondage, *"they believed His promises and sang His praise."* YET, and here's the scary part—the dire warning in the very next verse—it says that they *"soon forgot what He had done and did not wait for His counsel. In the desert they gave in to their craving; in the wasteland they put God to the test."* Verse 15 sadly concludes, *"He gave them their request but sent leanness into their soul."*

They'd walked in deliverance, yet wouldn't wait on the Lord for the next step in their zone of testing. They wanted the Promised Land *yesterday*. The fruit of patience and the power of faith weren't growing in them. They were consumed by self, and began to resent God for not giving them what THEY DID NOT PLANT. They reaped what they sowed, but wanted the results of a different seed. They forgot the wonders of Jehovah and stopped looking at their spiritual markers. Crippling emotions like unbelief and jealousy were tolerated, allowing their destructive work to begin. They progressively went from bad to worse, eventually engaging in outright idol worship. They caved in to the culture of the day, because their eyes were out of focus and their ears were dull, exchanging "their Glory for an image" (v.20).

They'd been freed from slavery, but didn't expect the wilderness. That was a waiting zone they neither asked for nor wanted. It was unfamiliar and uncomfortable, and they quickly grew weary of it. As Moses climbed the mountain of God, they wrestled with unbelief. They got sick of that manna—who cared if it was the bread of angels?—and wanted onions and meat. *Nothing was working out as their flesh had planned.* It's human nature to look at today's difficulty and forget the miracles and deliverance of yesterday; to ignore the past fulfillment Christ has given us the minute we run into unexpected obstacles. *That's why we have to "crucify our flesh."* That's why we're told to live in Spirit and Truth. Your flesh will lie to you and lead you astray. It'll do to you what the Philistines did to Samson, blind you and cause you to walk in circles, serving it instead of fulfilling your call.

Don't think you aren't capable of falling for the same scheme. You've seen the hand of God move in your life, you've been delivered and seen wonders and miracles, yet how do you react to a time of trial and testing? What are you tolerating in your heart that's about to sow destruction and make you stagnant and blind? Is anything tempting you to exchange your Glory for it? Is any image or false redeemer—a cultural, or even religious one—urging you to bow? Are you angry with God because He hasn't blessed you the way you wanted Him to? Do you sow grumbling, jealousy, envy and fleshly cravings, but expect to reap a harvest YOU DIDN'T PLANT?

We can start out with the pure purpose and vision of following the Lord all the way, but can so easily get off track when that cloud of glory and pillar of fire stop in a place we don't like, didn't expect and don't want. *That's where sin can creep in in the form of anger, envy, grumbling, slander and unbelief. Instead of confessing and dealing with it, it becomes easily rationalized.* In that waiting zone, whatever lurks in our hearts comes rushing to the surface and out of our mouths. It's a place of searching and trying, of revealing and, hopefully, unlike the Israelites, *of repenting,* so we can walk on in freedom.

We want a cushy ride into the fullness of the Lord's plans for us, our Promised Land. But the Lord wants well-trained, thoroughly prepared and pure hearts. We have something holy to carry, the plans of Almighty God, and we MUST carry them—even through our waiting zones of testing—with purity and faith. If you're counting on some promises the Lord has revealed to your heart and, in the meantime, find yourself in a hard, dry place, be on guard! Watch your thoughts. Take them captive to Christ. Pay attention to your words and the emotions you're tolerating. Be careful about what you're sowing. Get out the Word of God. Remember what the Lord's done. Remind yourself of His faithfulness, love and mercy. Help and encourage one another there. Take seriously the warnings given in the Word. Coming through that window of time with victory will be a thing of great celebration. Don't give in to temptation. It won't last forever. Wait on the Lord and watch for His goodness in the land of the living.

The other waiting zone is one of blessing and comfort. The danger there is to allow ease to lull you to sleep, to pursue pleasure and comfort and spend your blessings on yourself, to become self-reliant and independent, trusting your clout and checkbook to make things happen instead of the King. It's growing so comfortable with milk and honey that you don't seek the meaty, deep places of the Lord, and expecting to be served rather than pouring your life out in service. Blessing can blind us as easily as testing. Revelation 3:17-18 describes just such a church. (These aren't heathens, but the body of Christ. Now, THAT'S SCARY!) The Lord says to them, *"You say, 'I am rich; I have acquired wealth and do not need a thing.' But you do not realize that you are wretched, pitiful, poor, blind, and naked* (pretty serious list). *I counsel you* (better listen to His counsel!) *to buy from Me gold refined in the fire, so you can become rich; and white clothes to wear, so you can cover your shameful nakedness; and salve to put on your eyes, so you can see."* These can only be acquired at Calvary, through the covenant and business transacted for your heart *just outside the gates.*

I want the King of Kings to have the freedom in my heart to continually interrupt my business WITH HIS. Whatever zone I'm in waiting for those impossibles, I want to be about SEEKING HIS COUNTENANCE—not His blessings, not His intervention and not the fulfillment of my desires, but *His Face.* If we seek Jesus first and foremost, then pray, ask and wait for His rest, *we won't be disappointed.*

Questions & Applications

1. **Was your last waiting zone one of testing or of blessing—and did you sow to the flesh or to the Spirit during that time?**
2. **If you've accepted Christ as Lord, then you're in covenant with Almighty God. Expect His plans to come to pass, and wait in faith as He works them out. Keep your Ephesians 6 armor on tightly, guarding your heart whether in blessing or testing.**

3. **Your name is on the heart of the King of Kings, the Most High God, and He has given Christ's blood to forever seal the deal for your soul. Rejoice, bow down, bless His Name and thank Him for the sheer privilege and joy of salvation.**

37

The Obligation of Confirmation

And he took ten men of the elders of the city, and said, "Sit down here." So they sat down. Then he said to the close relative, "Naomi, who has come back from the country of Moab, sold the piece of land which belonged to our brother Elimelech. And I thought to inform you saying, 'Buy it back in the presence of the inhabitants and the elders of my people. If you will redeem it, redeem it; but if you will not redeem it, then tell me, that I may know; for there is no one but you to redeem it, and I am next after you.'" And he said, "I will redeem it." Then Boaz said, "On the day you buy the field from the hand of Naomi, you must also buy it from Ruth the Moabitess, the wife of the dead, to perpetuate the name of the dead through his inheritance." And the close relative said, "I cannot redeem it for myself, lest I ruin my own inheritance. You redeem my right of redemption for yourself, for I cannot redeem it." Now this was the custom in former times in Israel concerning redeeming and exchanging, to confirm anything: one man took off his sandal and gave it to the other, and this was a confirmation in Israel, **Ruth 4:2-7.**

In these verses we're allowed to eavesdrop on a very serious, legal transaction being worked out between Boaz and the other relative. Witnesses were assembled and the results of what happened that hour would be forever binding. Ruth's destiny was hanging in the balance, held in the hands of those two men. The results of that meeting were going to be confirmed according to the law of the day by publicly removing a sandal and passing it to the other party. Shoes were hard to come by in those days; they weren't manufactured in mass quantity. If you were willing to part with one, you were serious. And when it came off, it was a "done deal." What once belonged to one person, or potentially belonged to them, now belonged to another.

Boaz was a faithful Jew, so Numbers 30:1-2 was probably very familiar to him: *"This is what the Lord commands, 'When a man makes a vow to the Lord or takes an oath to obligate himself by a pledge, he must not break his word but must do everything he said'"* (NIV). Boaz was well aware of the implications of the agreement he was pursuing and was fully prepared to keep them. Even before the hour of redemption came, I believe he was ready, willing and able to legally affirm what was a settled matter in his heart—his love and desire for Ruth. *No doubt, his heart was pounding with eagerness to redeem the one who was already the bride of his heart, just as Ruth's was as she awaited the outcome. Imagine the joy that must have filled Boaz's soul as the relative's sandal was slipped off and placed in his hand.*

Put yourself in that heart-thumping scene. You're the one desperate for redemption, and Christ is the One working out the deal. He's gathered a great cloud of witnesses and is paying the price for your soul. The "sandal" has been exchanged, and He's declaring the transaction on your behalf legal, binding and eternal—in fact, He pursued your redemption even before you knew you needed redeeming. In essence, He's walked to the gate and said to every false redeemer, "Come over here. I want to have a word with you."

Christ Jesus is the One who, *"Having disarmed principalities and powers, made a public spectacle of them, triumphing over them by the Cross,"* (Colossians 2:15). Boaz disarmed the other guy through reasoning; Christ disarmed by His death. He took, at the cost of His own blood, the claiming rights of anyone or anything else to your heart. He purchased the legal right to your soul, and when you accepted Him as your Redeemer it became a done deal. It is finished. The sandal is off, and it's absolutely confirmed in the heavenlies. You're officially not only His, but the Bride who carries His Name and is established in His household.

The word "confirmation" is a powerful one. It's Hebrew root indicates, "to surely perform, to establish, to accomplish, to make good, to cause to succeed, to strengthen, to bind, to repair, to recover, to fasten, to mend, to take hold of, to harden, to make provision for, to ordain." It refers to something solidly established, firmly anchored, unchangeable, fixed, certain, trustworthy and true. In one case the same word is used for "confirm" and "consecrate," meaning, as you may recall, to be filled to overflowing, set apart or prepared. The Greek for "confirm" also has clear implications for Ruth: "the settlement of a dispute by an oath to produce confidence." That's an *awesome* thing. God's Word states that the great dispute over our souls is *settled forever through Christ*—that His precious, holy feet walked Calvary's hill to *legally and permanently seal the deal*. That's a good word, and definitely one you want actively operating in your life through the Spirit's power. Let the richness of its meaning fill your soul.

Thank God, you don't have to wait on *people* to confirm His Word and plans to you. *The Lord, Himself, through the Holy Spirit, will absolutely do that for all who ask.* Other Christians can certainly testify and encourage and the Lord uses their mouths to teach us, but *we're not to depend on them.* If God has sworn with His mouth, it will certainly be performed. He's convicted me sharply for blindly wishing at times for someone to come along and affirm His Word and call to me. Ever been there? "What do *you* think I should do? What do *you* think God's will for me is?" The Lord exposed my thinking for what it was: a lack of faith in Him, and an insecurity in me that needed other hands to prop me up. *I had to lay that down in repentance.* And I pray I never pick it up again.

Have you experienced the sheer thrill and wonder of bowing before the Throne of Grace in prayer, taking the Word with you and having the Holy Spirit confirm it to you? Have you seen God's promises come to pass? Have you witnessed some impossibles become realities? Have you experienced the living, active Word do a living, active work in your heart? Have you allowed the Lord Jesus Himself to plant a deep-rooted assurance and confidence that all He's spoken will surely take place—*will be confirmed*—in your life? Do you believe in your heart that He'll bring you out of your "Moabs" into what Psalm 66:12 calls "rich fulfillment"? Do you believe with all your soul it's time for you to *"arise and shine, for your light has come, and the glory of the Lord rises upon you"* (Isaiah 60:1), not just for that super-saint, who looks like they've got it made, but *you?*

The Word confirmed in your heart is like the glory of the Lord rising upon you. It cries out, "Arise and shine." There are things to do in building up the Kingdom before Christ breaks open the skies; there's business to be about and darkness all around desperate to see the light of heaven through you. We need to grab hold of Scripture, ask the Holy Spirit to confirm it, fill our hearts with its power and beauty and then rise up out of all that's held us back with hearts *ablaze*. We need lay aside the murkiness and blindness of sin, and put away all hints of self-pity, greed, slander, judgmentalism, shame, pride, fleshly cravings, bondage, the need for affirmation, the desire for a seat of honor, foolishness, self-focus, deadly emotions, idle words, cutting memories, insecurity, fear, unbelief—everything that doesn't originate in the heart of Almighty God.

Jesus Christ rose from the grave so we could rise up out of all our "stuff" and shine with the brilliant radiance of heaven's glory, the light of the King of Kings. We're meant to exude the reality of the Lord's presence, allowing the floodlight of His face to shine through ours. We need the living Word of God affirmed in our lives, actively at work, lighting the path beneath our feet and spilling over to others. We're to allow God's fire to ignite our souls and then fling sparks even to the nations. We serve a brilliant, glorious, radiant King. In Revelation 1:14-16, He appears with *"eyes blazing like fire, His feet like bronze glowing in a furnace, His face like the sun shining in all its brilliance."* If He's abiding in us, shouldn't every fiber of our being radiate like that? Our Light has surely come, and it should be blazing throughout the world through the bride of Christ. The earth is full of His glory; the heavens declare His wonders. And so should we.

Daniel 9:27 details the part of Daniel's vision that was explained while he *"was speaking and praying, confessing my sin and the sin of my people and making my request to God..."* Confirmation came while he was seeking God's face. If we want the same experience with God's Word, *we have to be in it! We can't exist on and be empowered by what we don't know!* I believe enlightenment comes while we, like Daniel, speak and pray, confess sin and repeat Scripture back to the Lord, absorbing it into our very being and walking it out. God will surely perform His holy Word as we grab onto it by faith.

However, there's a *very serious warning* that goes along with this. We all want God's Word to abide in us, fill and prosper us and lead and guide us, and that should be the desire of our hearts. *But we're accountable for it—we're responsible for what we know and for everything the Lord shows us!* That puts a holy fear in me for the day I stand alone before my King and He asks, "So, My love, what did you do with the Word I burned in your heart?" Here's what the Lord says in Ezekiel 33:7-8, *"Son of man, I have made you a watchman for the house of Israel; so hear the word I speak and give them warning from Me. When I say to the wicked, 'O wicked man, you will surely die,' and you do not speak out to dissuade him from his ways, that wicked man will die for his sin, and I will hold you accountable for his blood."* That's a heavy responsibility to carry. We who know the Lord of Glory and His Word are watchmen, and are absolutely accountable before God to speak, teach, sound the alarm and warn the lost of the dread to come if they don't accept Christ Jesus. If we refuse out of fear, laziness, selfishness, distractions, pride or other excuses we come up with, we'll be held responsible for our silence. As the Lord has whispered in my heart, "It's not pride to share what I give you, but sin to hold it in."

I don't hear much preaching about hell today, as in, *"O wicked man, you will surely die."* It's not politically correct, socially acceptable or easily included in sermons focused on prosperity and purpose. Yet, it's a truth we're called to proclaim. Skipping that part diminishes the beauty of salvation and degrades the work of Christ. If we don't know what we're saved from, we can't possibly worship with honest praise. Like it or not, there are two parts to eternity, heaven *and* hell. We're to tell the whole truth with hearts full of worship's fire, continually thanking the King for performing the work of redemption for us, confirming His Word in us and calling us to "arise and shine."

Consider Luke 19, where Jesus tells a parable about ten servants being given ten minas (about three month's wages) by a king with the command to "Put this money to work until

I come back," (v.12). When the king returned the servants were held responsible for the way they handled their share. The faithful ones were rewarded, but the one who "kept it laid away in a piece of cloth," hidden, unused and unshared, lost even what he had. The Lord used that to reconfirm the message of Ezekiel 33 in my heart: that we're accountable for what He's given us and for what we know. Our harvest isn't intended to fluff us up, but to be invested in the kingdom of the Risen Christ. We're meant to share God's Word with others. The gifts placed in our hands, those ephahs of grain, have little to do with us, and the fire of the Holy Spirit in our souls isn't meant to warm our souls alone.

We have the eternal Word of God! There's a wellspring of life flowing through our souls. We've been gifted and blessed by the Most High God Himself. Holy Scripture is planted, confirmed and established in our hearts. *What are we doing with it?* We need to invest it in the hearts of others. Their response isn't our responsibility or burden, but the call to share it is. You may not be welcomed or reacted to positively—you may instead be chased out of town! You might be rejected and mocked, brazenly told to shut up or thrown in jail, like Paul in the book of Acts. *It doesn't matter.* Keep moving and sharing. Keep the wells within you flowing.

Jesus said in Matthew 10:14, *"If anyone will not welcome you or listen to your words, shake the dust off your feet when you leave that home or town."* I take that to mean, "You're to walk in faithfulness and peace. Don't let rejection's dirt stick to your feet. I walked in that kind of filth on My way to seal the deal on Calvary, and I've confirmed, and will continue to confirm, My Word in your heart. You walk on in peace and purity *and keep telling what you know."* May we be Your faithful witnesses, mighty King of Kings who redeemed us for Glory!

Questions & Applications

1. **What do you tend to rely on or look to for confirmation regarding God's Word and will in your life?**
2. **Ask the Lord to put a burden in you to share the joy of salvation with the lost. He "loves the world so much that He gave His only Son, that whoever believes in Him should not perish but have eternal life," (John 3:16)—abundant life, life as a chosen treasure, life that is fully and completely satisfied by Christ Himself, matchless life that no other "relative" can touch.**
3. **Calvary confirmed Christ's passion for your redemption. He was determined to purchase your soul for himself, and He did so with His own blood. Bless the One who has transacted business and paid the purchase price for your heart—Jesus Christ the Messiah.**

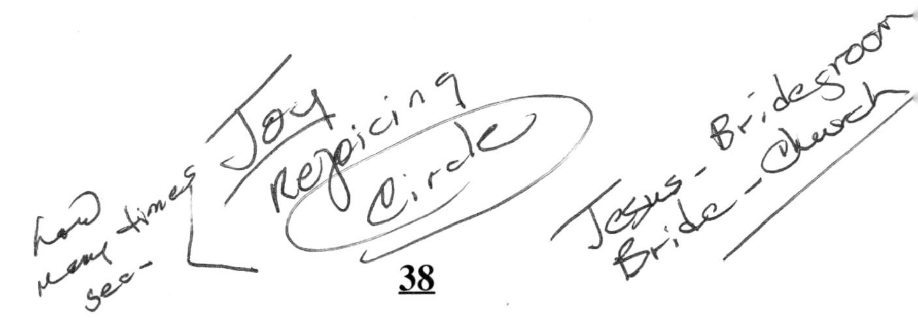

38

Mere Business or Beloved Bride?

Therefore the close relative said to Boaz, "Buy it for yourself." So he took off his sandal.

And Boaz said to the elders and all the people, "You are witnesses this day that I have bought all that was Elimelech's, and all that was Chilion's and Mahlon's, from the hand of Naomi. Moreover, Ruth the Moabitess, the widow of Mahlon, I have acquired as my wife, to perpetuate the name of the dead through his inheritance, that the name of the dead may not be cut off from among his brethren and from his position at the gate. You are witnesses this day," **Ruth 4:8-10.**

This whole scene seems a little cold and business-like when you first read it. It appears to be more about perpetuating Mahlon's name than declaring desire and passion for Ruth. Who wants a marriage proposal that isn't laced with love? What woman doesn't long for sweet romance? Who wants her potential groom to say, "Okay, I'm going to rescue you. I'm going to acquire you as my wife. I'm going to take care of some legalities and make sure you're provided for. I'm going to do the right and proper thing and make an honest woman of you." Some marriages have probably started on that note (I personally know of a few), but I'd bet that wasn't the desire of the bride's heart.

Doesn't every little girl dream of a marriage proposal more along these lines: "You're the most beautiful woman in the world to me and have absolutely captured my heart. When you walk in the room, my heart leaps for joy within me. I *have* to marry you. You're my passion. I desire you alone. You're the only one with whom I want to share all my days, grow old and enter into covenant before the Most High God. I want to minister to you and with you, and together walk-out the Lord's purposes and raise godly children. I want to hold your hand and love you until the Lord calls us home." Maybe those kinds of proposals are few and far between, but isn't that still a deep-rooted desire?

Perhaps Boaz spoke those kinds of words to Ruth in private, or whispered "sweet nothings" like that to her in the night. We aren't told. Their intimate conversations aren't recorded, only the formal part of things. Still, we're shown enough to know that the kinsman-redeemer *redeemed.* He took care of the first order of business, the most pressing issue at hand, and bought Ruth back so he could then marry her.

If you're single, in a troubled marriage or just disappointed with the declarations of love from your spouse or a friend, *look up.* Release that person from your expectations. Lay down everything you hoped they'd do for you, and find your satisfaction in the only One who can truly offer it, *your Redeemer.* Unmet relational desires can become a perfect set-up for the Enemy to establish a critical, sarcastic spirit, self-pity, anger, bitterness or depression. The Lord has convicted me of my own need for people to meet certain expectations. "If you're my spouse, you should ___________________. If you're my boss, you should _______________. If you're my pastor, you should _____________________. If you're my parent, you should _______________. If you're my child, you should ____________. If, if, if...Fill in your own blanks.

This is the only "if" we should live by: If the King of Kings is your Lord and God, then He's the place to plant your expectations. He's the One who works in you both to will and to do His good pleasure. He's your ultimate Groom who perfectly desires you, your Hope and Redeemer and the Satisfier of your soul. Seek Him face-to-face. Imagine what He can grow with your hopes and dreams firmly sown in Him. Ask the Lord to reveal any misplaced desires you may have, and then let all those "close relatives" off the hook. They're incapable of meeting your heart-needs, no matter how able or appealing they appear. They weren't meant to.

The deepest longings of our hearts are meant to belong first to the Lord Jesus, our incredible Redeemer. *"God, who has called you into fellowship with His Son Jesus Christ our Lord, is faithful,"* (1 Corinthians 1:9). The faithful King calls you to intimate relationship. Go there. Pour out your heart there. Enjoy Him richly there. Find every fiber of your soul satisfied there. Let His whispers thrill you there. *There are no words like those ushering from His holy, precious mouth, and no relationship like the one you can have with Him.* The more I seek His face, the more I desire Him and the less I expect of others. *There's a sweet freedom in that* for me—and for you, too.

Of course, we realize the transaction Boaz engaged in was about much more than business. It was destiny. I envision destiny as that special plan formed for each of us in God's heart, the place for which He's been specifically shaping us. It's something I believe every breathing person longs for, whether they know the Lord or not. Those who love the Lord Jesus and those who don't both desire to fulfill the purpose of their lives. How many books exist on this subject? Whole shelves are filled with publications on how to be all you can be, overcome your circumstances, rise to your potential and discover your purpose. Some are based on the Word, others on human philosophy. Either way, it reflects how much all of us want to have a sense of fateful providence in our lives. In ancient times, there was literally a god named Destiny. Even among the pagan, heathen lost, there's a *desperate desire* for what can be found in Christ alone.

Jesus Christ, the King of Kings, our Kinsman-Redeemer, took care of business at the Cross, so He could place us in destiny's seat of honor: at His royal table as His beloved Bride. *That's a source of overwhelming joy to me. When I think of the unspeakable privilege of being part of the bride of Christ, not just begging for crumbs as a Gentile but the very desire of His mighty heart, I'm astounded and filled afresh with the new wine of His joy.* In light of that, how can we ever let life steal away the joy of our salvation?

Perhaps Boaz's intentions were essentially romantic, after all. For if the business meeting hadn't happened, neither would the marriage. I've never viewed Christ carrying that heavy Cross, the business part of buying us back from hell's claim on our sinful hearts, as a picture of Him wooing and romancing our hearts. But it can easily be regarded as the most romantic thing ever done by anyone in all of history. Look at the scene with fresh eyes, especially you who've heard and read it a million times. Boaz and Ruth's intimate whispers aren't recorded, but the romantic thoughts behind every drop of the Lord Jesus' holy blood have been. Here's how I imagine some of them would sound if strung together in a love letter:

Oh, Beloved of My heart,

I've come to proclaim freedom, comfort and provision to you, give you a crown of beauty, pour out the oil of gladness and dress you in a garment of praise. I've planted you in My heart to display My splendor (Isaiah 61:1-3). I will give you a new name, you will be a royal diadem in the hand of your God (Isaiah 62:2-3) and I will rejoice over you as a bridegroom rejoices over his bride (Isaiah 62:5).

Arise, My darling, beautiful one, and come with Me (Song of Solomon 2:10). My desire is to be your first, most precious love (Revelation 2:4). Many waters cannot quench My love for you; rivers cannot wash it away (Song 8:7). My love is pure, patient and kind. It always rejoices with the truth, always protects, always trusts, always hopes and always perseveres. It will never fail or forsake you (1 Corinthians 13). Enjoy it. Relish it. Walk in it (2 John 6).

I am the I Am—the Way, the Truth and the Life—and I am preparing a place for you (John 14:2). I will bring you with great joy into the King's chambers (Song 1:4), and there I will delight in you and rejoice over you with singing. You are forever, eternally, without fail, My Beloved and Betrothed. I desire your pure heart, which I Myself purify. Every time you enter My presence, My heart pounds for you, My holy Bride, My royal priestess (Song 5:4).

I love you. Come down the aisle. Come to the altar. You will never, ever be a forsaken, neglected or rejected Bride. My love for you endures forever.

Hallelujah, for the Lord God Almighty reigns! Rejoice and be glad and give Him glory! For the wedding of the Lamb has come (Revelation19:7). How can we not rejoice in such a Savior with such a deep love that surpasses even our most romantic dreams? And that was just a tiny portion of His loving words to us.

Hosea 2:14-23 offers another heart-pounding passage of God's loving betrothal to His people—*it's beautiful and powerful, a precious word from the mouth of the King.*

Verses 14-15 are much like our place in Ruth, though they are addressed to Israel. The NIV study notes here bring me to my knees, stating that the Lord was going to "lead her into the desert, *for a second betrothal.* It refers back to the days of Israel's desert wandering, before she was tempted by the Baals in Canaan." The punch in the heart for me is the "second betrothal," the redemption of what was stolen, lost or given away the first time. It's another chance. In His faithfulness, the Most High God promises to return and *"allure, to lead her into the desert, to speak tenderly to her, to give her back her vineyards, to make the Valley of Achor a door of hope, to cause her to sing as in the days of her youth."*

The bride ran away from the Groom, but the groom didn't give up. He pursued her again. How many times have we done that, fellow bride? How many times has the Groom pursued us in the desert places? How many times have we rejected His first proposal, but been brought to our knees by His second? Ruth was experiencing the joy of her second betrothal. The first had occurred in a foreign, pagan land, this one on holy, righteous ground.

For most, our "first proposal" also comes to us in a pagan place—the world. The Enemy wants to seduce us straight into a place of captivity and strongholds. Thank God, even if we fall for the devil's wooing for a time, there's a second chance, a second betrothal, one offered and proclaimed in holiness that's pure and eternal and positions us in destiny. Here's another thought. In the history of God with men, is it possible that His first betrothal to mankind was *the Law,* and that the second is *the Cross?* In any case, thank God for second chances!

The Valley of Achor in the Hosea passage, the place God said He would make into a door of hope, is worthy of our consideration. Take this powerful, little rabbit trail with me...Achor derives from a man named Achan. Joshua 7 gives an account of this man's sin. In fact, the whole chapter in my Bible is titled, "Achan's Sin." It must've been a significant thing Mr. Achan did against the Lord to have a whole chapter devoted to it! (Imagine a chapter of the Bible, or the newspaper or the church newsletter being titled, "your name here's Sin"?)

Here's the story: Israel had experienced an unexpected defeat on their way to the Promised Land. When Joshua fell on his face and cried out to God, He revealed that, *"Israel has sinned; they have violated My covenant, they have taken some of the devoted things, they have stolen, they have lied, they have put them with their own possessions. That is why the Israelites cannot stand against their enemies. They turn their backs and run because they have been made liable to destruction*" (v. 6-12). The Lord's instruction was clear, *"That which is devoted is among you, O Israel. You cannot stand against your enemies until you remove it,"* (v. 13).

The next morning was a day of judgment. And you guessed it, Mr. Achan was the man who'd stolen some of the devoted things, hidden them and lied about it. His sin had made all of Israel "liable for destruction," and his sentence was exactly what we deserve, death. He was taken to the valley that would infamously bear his name, along with his family and possessions, and killed. All of them. Stoned. Burned. Dead. *How do you think those things that had been so tempting appeared to him then?*

If it weren't for Christ's second betrothal, our plight would be the very same! It's easy to look at Achan and judge his sin. Yet, if we look closely, I believe we'll realize that a whole chapter is devoted to it because it's so incredibly common. What did he do that brought defeat and death to himself and his loved ones? *The same thing we all do*. The temptations he fell for are the same ones freshly packaged for us by the same Enemy. We don't hide precious, little golden idols in our tents, but we do cling to precious, little invisible sins in our hearts. Like Achan, we've all sinned and fallen short of God's standard (Romans 3:23). Were it not for Jesus, we could all easily trade our souls for a tiny bit of the world.

What did Achan trade his life for—some silver, a wedge of gold, a few lovely jewels, a silken garment (v.20)? Seems so foolish, but look at your own heart. Have you ever wanted what the world is "wearing"? Do its robes look beautiful, rich, plush and comfortable? Ever been tempted to stay in the Lord's house, while trying on the world for size? Ever tried to hang out in the sanctuary with the people of God, but keep something hidden in the closet? Have you ever filled your own pockets with the tithe of God, the "devoted thing," that really belongs to Him? Have you ever been careless with the riches of your storehouse? You don't have to divert church offerings into your account to sin, you can just keep yours there.

We need to let the Valley of Achor teach us! It should cause us to rejoice even more in our Redeemer, the One who seeks a second betrothal with us instead of the stoning in sin's valley we all deserve. It should cause us to drink in the Lord's mercy with fresh thirst and gratitude. The warning here applies to every one of us, and we need to heed it. This is the root of Achan' sin: "I saw...I coveted...I took...I hid it." Isn't that just like us? We see something desirable...dwell on it until we think we can't live without it...take part in or partake of it...and then we hide. The "thing" can be anything, even something good. But it can be our absolute downfall, and can only be redeemed through Christ. *It will hold us captive until we let the King of Kings set us free.*

One way or another, you're going to be held captive by something. Why not let your thoughts be held captive to Christ? Seems to me that our minds are the birthplace of sin. The battles waged there are fierce and relentless, which must be why we're told to align our every notion with God's Word. What if Achan had taken *his thoughts* captive, instead of letting *his desires* capture him? Maybe the heading of Joshua 7, rather than "Achan's Sin," would be "Achan's Victory." (May that kind of title characterize our lives!)

Don't let your thoughts run wild. Like a runaway train, they'll carry you straight to destruction. They'll take you headlong into pride, envy, lust, resentment, bitterness, anger, jealousy, judgment…You won't be able to stand in victory against temptation if your thoughts aren't captured and captivated by—betrothed—to Jesus. *ACHAN SOLD OUT TO THE FIRST SUITOR, THE LUSTS OF THIS WORLD. May that never be said of us.* How sweet is the Lord's promise that put us on this rabbit trail to begin with to *"make the Valley of Achor a door of hope,"* (Hosea 2:15). The Lord continues with even better news in verse 16, *"In that day," declares the Lord, "you will call me 'my husband.'"*

You may have stepped into the Valley of Achor, a place where you gave in to loose, wild thoughts and temptations, big or small. Perhaps, like Ruth, you've lived in Moab all your life. Still, Achan's judgment doesn't have to be yours. *Hope's door is wide open, and that door's name is Jesus.* And not only do you get to be rescued, redeemed and pulled out of sin, *YOU GET TO BE BETROTHED*. You're given the proposal of your dreams, the best, purest, most faithful and romantic one ever offered anyone! You receive an impossible, eternal, heart-pounding offer meant to sweep you off your feet and forever capture you. *I'm captured, and that's my prayer for you.*

Questions & Applications

1. **Look at your closest relationships. Is there anyone you need to release from your expectations?**
2. **Does something other than Christ hold you captive today? Confess it, repent of it and ask the Lord to captivate you.**

3. **If you're in a valley that some temptation has led you to, get up and thank the Lord Jesus for the Door of Hope He's swung open before you through the Cross! Bless the Lord, the Lover of your soul. Accept His betrothal.**

39

Blessing or Cursing?

And all the people who were at the gate, and the elders, said, "We are witnesses. The Lord make the woman who is coming into your house like Rachel and Leah, the two who built the house of Israel; and may you prosper in Ephrathah and be famous in Bethlehem.

May your house be like the house of Perez, whom Tamar bore to Judah, because of the offspring the Lord will give you from this young woman," **Ruth 4:11-12.**

The elders at the gate, as well as ordinary folks who'd gathered to watch, poured blessings on Boaz. All questions and criticisms were cast aside and swallowed up in a pure, heartfelt prayer. There's no record of the witnesses discussing Ruth's painful past, arguing about her worthiness or rejecting her because she didn't meet some legalistic standard. *There are just powerful words of blessing, prosperity and fruitfulness.*

Do we do that? Do we let words of blessing pour from our hearts and mouths, even on those we could easily judge—those who are different from us, or who don't live up to our standards? What flows out of us toward the hard to love, or those who've sinned against us or haven't met our expectations, who rub us wrong or appear way too "foreign"? What are we speaking about *them?*

It's easy to love those who love you. It's no trouble encouraging those who encourage you. How hard is it to bless those who bless you? Where's the challenge in speaking blessing over those your flesh deems worthy? It's not difficult to say a good word about people who are *just like you*—those who think like you, order their homes like you, are from the same background as you, socialize with you, are in similar economic standing with you, educate their children like you, have identical goals as you, agree with you and are pleasant to be around. I don't know about you, but *I'm nailed again.*

Jesus knew we'd struggle with that, so He included Matthew 5:43-47 in His Holy Word: *"You have heard that it was said, 'You shall love your neighbor and hate your enemy. But I say to you, love your enemies, bless those who curse you, do good to those who hate you, and pray for those who spitefully use you and persecute you, that you may be sons of your Father in heaven; for He makes His sun rise on the evil and on the good, and sends rain on the just and the unjust. For if you love those who love you, what reward have you? Do not even the tax collectors do the same? And if you greet your brethren only, what do you do more than others? Do not even the tax collectors do so?"*

The responsibility to love and speak blessing over everyone falls on us all. I can tell you, your flesh won't like it. But like it or not, and easy or not, as children of God we're called to *love as He loves.* He doesn't give His sunrise, His rain, His provision and His beauty only to those who seek Him. The One true King pours out goodness on the earth, and we all get to drink it in and benefit from it, whether we choose to worship Him or not. *He is good. May we be truly like our Father and extend kind words to everyone, whether they choose to accept us or not.* That's not easy, and definitely unattainable in the flesh. It's vital that we put on the armor of God, let Him dress us in righteousness and allow the Holy Spirit the freedom to bear good fruit in our lives, especially the fruit of love.

We need to notice who was blessing Boaz at the gate. It wasn't just the elders, the leaders and those in authority that were expected to say a word or two, but "all the people who were in the gate." We know Jesus is the Gate, the Door of Hope, the Arch of Glory, the Way, the Truth and the Life. *If you're in Christ, you're "in the gate," and you have a responsibility to speak the truth in love and let blessing be on your tongue.* You're called as a witness to stand and say prayers of grace for others. *"You are My witnesses,"* says the Lord in Isaiah 43:10.

I'm not talking about condoning sin, but learning to live-out and walk in Matthew 5: to look beyond another's past and bless them where they are, to open the door of our hearts just as Jesus opened His to us, to look for the good potential in people instead of the potential they've wasted and to pray that the Lord's best will be manifested in their lives and down through their family lines. Let's learn not to "greet your brethren only," but to seek the well-being of those our flesh doesn't naturally or easily love and to practice 1 Corinthians 10:24, *"Let no one seek his own, but each one the other's well-being."* The "others" aren't listed here—guess it includes every "other" the Lord plants in our path. *There are no loopholes, no place where bitterness and hatred are given ground. No allowance is made for those you just can't stand to be around, who've stabbed your heart or have bitterly let you down.*

The people at the gate could have rejected Ruth because of her days in Moab. They could have reminded Boaz of her foreign lineage and sent her packing in shame. *Do we do that? Do we resist certain types of people? Would we rather not deal with the drug addict? Would we prefer to send someone with a troubled, dysfunctional past (and maybe present) to a counselor, instead of loving on them ourselves? Do we judge the broken, the overly needy or those enslaved to some habitual sin? How about the person who's hard-hearted toward us, has spoken harshly about or to us or has sinned against us—do we forgive and love them or avoid them?*

Take a minute and search your heart here. Is the Holy Spirit bringing to your mind some "others" who've been a thorn in your side? Is there someone you find very hard to love and very easy to avoid, or anyone in your life who's extremely easy to bad-mouth? Has your response to hurt been gossip, instead of blessing? For me, the answer is yes, yes and yes. And because we all walk on fallen ground, I daresay you have a yes somewhere in there, too. What, then, do we do with our mouths? Let Proverbs 8:34 sink in: *"Blessed is the man who listens to Me, watching daily at My gates, watching at the posts of My doors."*

We go DAILY to the King's gate, to His door, to the Holy of Holies, and we listen. We watch. We take our fill of Him, find our strength in Him, see our own sin in the presence of His holiness and let Him cleanse us. It's much more difficult to step into the sin of judgment and criticism when we've laid ourselves bare before the King of Glory, the Most High God, the Lord of Hosts, the Lamb slain for our sin. When we lay our hearts there and allow Him to make them His vessels, *His* grace overflows our mouths instead of the outpourings of our hurts, opinions and judgments.

If I refuse to acknowledge resentment in my heart and lay it before the Cross, it will inevitably find its way to my tongue. If I hold onto hardness and hatred toward someone, it will eventually find words to express itself. If bitterness has a root in me, it will grow and grow until it's strong enough to "rise up and defile many." *The inability to speak*

blessing over someone is a HEART ISSUE, revealing some deep-rooted matter you haven't dealt with. It clearly identifies where your love has grown cold, or was never warm to begin with. (All I can say is, "LORD, have mercy on me!")

Isaiah 62:10 says, *"Go through, go through the gates! Prepare the way for the people; build up, build up the highway. Take out the stones, lift a banner for the people."* We're called to stand "in the gate"—in Christ—and proceed to the fullness of Spirit and Truth. However, we need to realize that we're not there merely to seek our own blessing, but to pave a pathway for others. As we move deeper into Jesus, our words, blessings, prayers, love, conversations, interactions and speaking the Word are to be tools the Holy Spirit can use to stir a hunger in the hearts of others for God—to "prepare the way of the Lord." We're to build up the King's Highway so others can run on it, to remove the "stones" of bitterness, resentment, hard-heartedness, negative thoughts and attitudes, unconfessed sin, generational strongholds, fear, unbelief—jagged, cutting things that cause people to stumble—and raise the banner of love and victory of the Risen Christ. *Criticism will do none of that. We need to watch our careless words.*

Like us, Ruth had some "stones" in her path. She had a pagan lineage, was a foreigner and a widow, was impoverished and had plenty to be depressed about. We all have our "issues." We all have an ample supply of material to nurture bitterness, all have spent some time in Moab, all have inherited something we've had to overcome, all have sinned and fallen short and all stand at the complete mercy of the King. *Thank God, He was willing to give us Christ to remove our hearts of stone and give us hearts of flesh.*

Some of the hard things in our lives are "generational stones" that raise their ugly heads over and over. Accounts of Abraham, Isaac and Jacob in Genesis reveal similar stumbling blocks rolling into their paths from generation to generation. In their case, it seems to boil down to a pattern of *fear and unbelief, and how they were expressed.* Abraham, fearful of being killed in Egypt because of his wife's beauty, claimed she was his sister. Then Isaac tripped on the *same stone*, declaring that his wife was his sister before a Philistine king. Isaac wasn't even *born* when Abraham lied about his wife, and somehow I doubt it was a family story told around the campfire at night. ("Remember the time I lied about you being my wife, Sarah? Oh, tell Isaac! That's a great story!") Yet, the very same sin was repeated. *Children don't have to personally witness a sin to repeat it.*

Look closely at what was happening. Faulty, fleshly, *natural* reasoning was tolerated, not taken captive. Uncaptured thoughts then led to fear. Fear made room for deception and manipulation, and those things took root and repeated themselves. Jacob, whose very name implied deception, came after Isaac and became infamous for manipulating situations to his own advantage. No wonder the Lord changed his name. These are the *Patriarchs* we're talking about, not some pagans! *This was the same Abraham whom the Lord counted faithful!* Like Abraham and his kin, who among us hasn't needed forgiveness? Which of us is immune to fear, doubt, deception or other inherited stumbling blocks, much less has the right to cast the very stones at others we've tripped over ourselves?

What in the world are we doing to each other with our words? Are we standing in the gate throwing rocks, or speaking soothing, healing, empowering words of blessing? I, for one, am asking the Lord to shine His light on any stones in my heart, any patterns of sin, fear, criticism, insecurity, greed, selfishness, judgment, unbelief or whatever, and then to reveal any I have in my hand ready to throw at someone else. I'm asking Him to set me free as I fall to my knees at the Cross in repentance, and to line up my thoughts

and speech with His mighty Word, taking them completely captive to Christ.

Thinking about the Holy Spirit lifting stones out of my heart reminds me of what I've seen many times in my yard. When we remove a rock, little bugs, spiders and worms start scurrying for cover, and a hole is left where it used to be. *It was covering things we may not have even realized were there*. It's not condemnation but the Lord's *mercy* that reveals the hidden things so we can be utterly set free. Remove your hard places through repentance, but *don't stop there*. Let the Lord refill the spaces they once occupied with HIMSELF. Let Him cleanse the spot with the washing of the Word and the power of prayer, and ask the Lord Jesus to work out Isaiah 42:16 in your heart: *"I will lead the blind by ways they have not known, along unfamiliar paths I will guide them, I will turn the darkness into light before them and make the rough places smooth."*

Consider one of the temptations Christ faced in the wilderness. In Matthew 4:3, it says, *"the tempter came to Him, and he said, 'If You are the Son of God, command that these stones become bread.'"* My question is, have we ever been tempted to turn the stones in our hearts to bread? Have we taken some hard, stumbling thing and fed on it, instead of getting rid of it? Have we ever nourished ourselves on sin, especially if it's a generational thing? Ever clung to anger until it turned to bitterness, because your mother or father was angry? How about moodiness, fear, alcoholism or infidelity—whatever it is that runs in your family? Do you make excuses for it rather than purge it with Truth?

The Lord wants our hearts to feed on TRUTH, not stones, because the words of our mouths spring from them. We need to let Him reveal and remove all the hard stuff, so it won't be gravel we're spewing! *If you allow those things to remain, before long they'll build a WALL between you and God. Do whatever you must to make His Word the light and lamp of your path that smoothes out the rough places and tears barriers down.* Read and memorize it "daily in the gates," and immerse yourself in godly messages, tapes, DVD's, music and every form of media. Use note cards and journals. Tape Scripture passages to your closets, the back of cabinets, mirrors, the dash of your car, in drawers—*anywhere you frequently look.* Be smart enough to know you're not very smart and how *desperately* you need to ingest the Word of God, the Word of Life, food for your soul.

As you do that, I believe a mighty work of transformation will start taking place in your heart. Your mind will begin to be renewed and new things will emerge from your mouth. Criticism will suddenly turn sour on your tongue, and you'll want to spit it out. Complaining won't be able to find a spot amid all the praise you're giving the Lord. Wisdom will find a home in you, and the Holy Spirit will speak it to others through you even when you don't realize it. *As your mouth becomes a source of grace,* you'll be an instrument of righteousness that builds up and edifies the body of Christ, instead of someone whose words tear it down.

And then the last part of Isaiah 62:10 can begin to happen in your life, *"...lift a banner for the people."* The heart that's allowed Spirit and Truth to clear the path is one that can stand in the gate and offer what the elders and the others spoke to Boaz, declarations and prayers of blessing and encouragement. You'll speak words of life and edification that say, "This is the way of the King! Walk in it with me!"—words that become a standard of praise, joy and strength.

The words of blessing spoken over Boaz and Ruth became prophetic, as we'll see. They did become prosperous and famous, and their offspring were absolutely blessed and established. In fact, King David came from their family line as well as the Messiah Himself, Jesus Christ. Oh, my friends, do we realize the power that words of blessing and prayers can have, and what the King of Kings, the Chief Cornerstone, can build through them? I believe the answer is: more than we can possibly imagine! May the Holy Spirit continually fill our mouths with Truth and grace.

Questions & Applications

1. **Ask the Lord to reveal any "stones" in your heart as you seek Him in the Word and prayer. As He does, clear the path through repentance, and rejoice in the grace He gives.**
2. **Ask also for the grace to forgive any who have been less than graceful in their words to or about you.**
3. **Keep your eyes open for opportunities to speak words of life and blessing, especially to "foreigners"!**

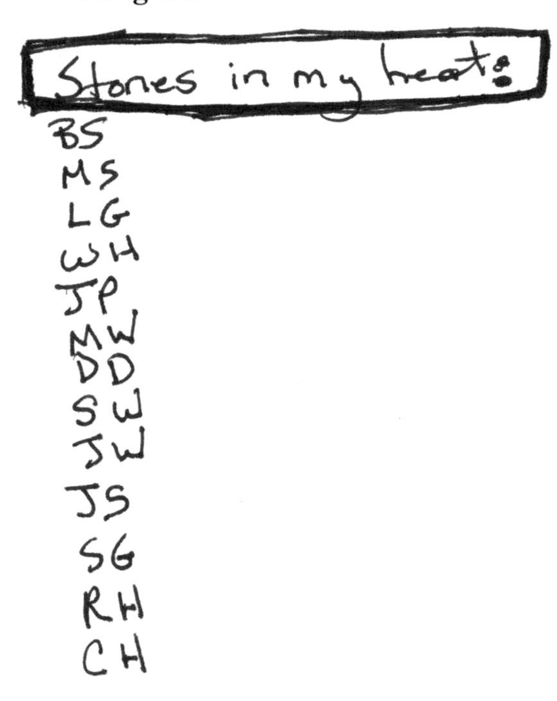

40

Ruth Became...

So Boaz took Ruth and she became his wife... **Ruth 4:13a.**

What a moment! Boaz took Ruth, the one for whom he'd made provision and worked out the legal matters and dreamt of, and, in the sweet little town of Bethlehem, made her his bride. The matter was done, complete and established. The fullness of mercy and passion was poured out. A pagan woman and a man of honor were fulfilling the miraculous plan of the Most High. The business part was finished. No more sandals had to be exchanged. The wedding had arrived, and it was time to rejoice, be glad and give glory where glory was due.

I don't believe words can capture the depth of emotion surrounding that wedding day. I imagine that seeing Ruth, the bride, approaching her redeemer, dressed in splendor and honor, instead of the rags of Moab, would have been breathtaking. And the beauty of the bride and groom standing face-to-face exchanging spoken, as well as unspoken, vows of love and passion must have been overwhelming. (*I can hardly wait for the day with my Bridegroom, King Jesus, when "I will see Him for myself. Yes, I will see Him with my own eyes. I am overwhelmed with the thought," Job 19:27.)*

What a privilege for all who witnessed it. More was happening before them than they could've begun to dream. *I wonder what beginnings we're witnessing today that will astound us tomorrow.* I believe we should all operate with that kind of joyful expectation, knowing our faithful Redeemer is setting in motion a plan formed before we ever drew a breath. The privilege of watching it unfold should thrill our souls.

Ruth probably said many things to precious Boaz on their wedding day, but I imagine that her most powerful expressions were tears of joy and gratitude. She was entering a holy covenant, being renamed and established, set in a position of favor and honor and catapulted from gleaning leftovers in the fields to co-owning them. She was living-out the favor of Almighty God. *Favor given the Bride should never be a source of pride, but of absolute gratitude and humility. Faith was the only thing that brought Ruth to the bridal altar, and it will be our only qualification, too. We have nothing to offer the King, nothing to cause Him to choose us, except for that.*

"Ruth…became." Focus on those two words. After all Ruth was born into, all she'd walked through and all the fears and tears, she now *became*. The sad, desperate Moabite *became* Bethlehem's woman of honor. The foreigner *became* the recipient of scandalous favor. The one whose life had been ripped apart *became* amazingly complete. Beauty was rising up from ashes, and sorrow that had filled deep wells of her heart now *became* inexpressible joy, full of glory. The old *became* new. The crooked *became* straight, and the rough *became* smooth as calloused feet stepped onto destiny's path. Blessing was taking the bride's hand and leading her to his intimate chamber, and her life and legacy would never be the same.

There may have been musicians and singers present at the ceremony, but I believe the sweetest song was silently being sung in Ruth's heart. Fear could flee now. Lack could go somewhere else. Anxiety had no room. Bitterness was unthinkable. Pure love was the only thing given a platform on that sweet, holy day.

You are Ruth, the beloved of the King's heart. Mercy was born in Bethlehem for you, and faith has brought you to the altar with your Redeemer. The business transaction for your redemption was finished at the Cross, and the resurrection of Christ means that you'll be, too. It doesn't matter what your earthly position is, or how worthy you feel. You're the King's passion and delight. You're beautiful beyond compare to His pure eyes, and His heart is full of love for you. The King is taken with you and smitten by you. You are cherished, chosen and changed. You're the recipient of heaven's storehouse, and its favor is yours. You're not who you were, because the King has chosen you.

Insert your name into the phrase, "Ruth became." ____________ became...Now fill in the rest of the sentence. The words that come to mind for me are, "Cynthia became... nothing she deserved, nothing she earned and nothing but a product of mercy." *Rejoice, and again I say, rejoice*. You're no longer who you were, but who the King of Kings says you are. You're the Bride!

Sometimes, while my *head* knows I'm the bride of Christ because the Word says it and the Spirit confirms it, my *heart* screams out, "I'm not worthy! Look at these stones in my heart! Look what I've said and done. Look at all my mistakes! Who am I to become one who carries the name of the Lord Jesus? Who am I to be joined with the King of Glory? The Bride is to be pure and without spot or wrinkle. That doesn't seem to describe me by any stretch of the imagination." Instead of praying, "Lord, send me out to make disciples," my prayer becomes, "Lord, I don't feel worthy to carry Your precious, holy Word!" To this whine, the Lord has replied (rather quickly and firmly, by the way), "GET THIS STRAIGHT. *YOU'RE NOT.* Your righteousness is through Christ alone." *Thank God.*

Yet the Enemy loves to reinforce those feelings of unworthiness. He loves to jab us with reminders of our mistakes and failures. Even as you dwell in Bethlehem, he wants to keep your thoughts and emotions stuck in Moab, the place you were wounded and weary. As I cried out to the Lord for victory in that battle, I sensed Him whisper, "The Enemy is a *created being*. He doesn't come up with his own schemes, he copies Mine. If you study the battles in My Word, you'll see how he imitates them in your own life." Here are a few I came up with:

The battle of Jericho: the Enemy marches around us, trying to intimidate and wear us down. Have you ever felt besieged by circumstances until you're *weary*? Then, at your weakest moment, Satan shouts, trying to make so much noise you crumble in fear. BUT WE'RE THE ONES WHO NEED TO BE GIVING THE SHOUT, BECAUSE "THE BATTLE BELONGS TO THE LORD," (Zechariah 4:6).

David and Goliath: the Enemy wants to appear larger than life and utterly undefeatable. He wants to keep us blinded by fear and unbelief, unaware that the least of us could take one small stone from the River of Life, even the size of a mustard seed, and knock him down. He's banking on the majority of us choosing to hide in the camp, trembling in our boots.

The Cross and the Resurrection: God's ultimate triumph, that which made a public spectacle of the Enemy and his wicked kingdom is another thing he imitates, bringing false saviors and comforters—"redeemers" that appear to provide solutions for your life. He longs to publicly humiliate the Lord Jesus and anyone who follows Him, as the risen Christ humiliated him. *Look at our culture, isn't that spirit all around us? Cross jewelry not allowed in places, the name of*

Jesus forbidden at public events, Christians mocked or sued for practicing their faith...

What's wearing you down? What in your eyes appears larger than life? What's humiliating you? What's keeping you silent? What's making you feel like a Moabite instead of the beautiful Bride you are? Go to Christ. Run to the Word of Truth, and let the Holy Spirit brand it into your heart and mind. Live daily in the humble posture of crying out to the King. *The battle is HIS, and it will be won. Count on it—and count on who you are in Him.*

A few years ago, while watching someone else minister, I felt a burning call to speak the Word. I literally cried right there in front of everyone, as I protested, "Lord, I'm not worthy." I don't think I'll ever forget His precious reply in my spirit, "NEITHER ARE THEY." Praise God. We've all sinned and fallen short, yet through faith we all qualify. Let Romans 5:8 sink in: *"But God demonstrates His own love toward us, in that while we were still sinners, Christ died for us."* He didn't wait for us to get our act together or fall in love with Him before He sealed the deal on our behalf.

Boaz took Ruth as his bride, even though as a foreigner she could easily have been considered unworthy. He dressed her in beauty and jewels, even though her hands were calloused from the fields and her feet were darkened and rough from her long, hard journey. He looked past all the obvious evidences of where she'd been and declared before all witnesses, "This one is *mine*. I'm going to love her and love her WELL." Though our hearts have been adulterous, our feet have wandered far and our hands are scarred by what they've held onto and tried to work out on their own, the Lord Jesus embraces us in His perfect, holy arms, and says, "This one is *Mine." How great is the Lord's mercy and all He's poured out on us! I pray we all have sense enough to RECEIVE IT!*

Ezekiel 16:6 presents a picture of Israel found in an open field, *"struggling in their own blood,"* (NKJ). The original King James calls it *"polluted in thine own blood."* The NIV puts it, *"kicking about in your blood."* None sounds good! I see the phrase representing where we all were when Christ rescued us and brought us to His altar. We were struggling in our own foreign bloodline, our own carnal nature, our own fleshly desires and our own battle plans. We were polluted with the bloodiness of pride, fear, lust, greed, selfishness and an adulterous nature. We were battered and beaten by the false saviors to whom we were turning. We were, like this scene describes, crawling on hard, open ground, bloody, exposed, starving and vulnerable to attack, in endless turmoil and unhealed woundedness, absolutely without hope.

The second part of the verse is the part that sets my heart on fire. Here, the Lord speaks to the bloody struggler, calling out, *"LIVE! Yes, I said to you in your own blood, 'LIVE!'"* Verse 7 gets even more exciting as the Lord says, *"I made you thrive like a plant in the field; and you grew, matured, and became very beautiful."* There's that word again, "became." You were out there in your own field, your own Moab, struggling in your own mess and in a whole lot of trouble, WHEN THE WORD OF THE LORD TRANSFORMED YOU, breathed life into you and established you in thriving beauty in the house of Almighty God.

Verses 8-14 present a beautiful description from the heart of God of just what He does for us, His beloved Bride. Put yourself in that scene, struggling in the field, and hear with fresh ears what the Lord has done. Let it cause you to worship deeply as you rejoice in your salvation. The Lord says He, *"spread the corner of My garment over you and covered your nakedness."* (Just what Boaz did, in a sense, to Ruth back on the threshing floor. I see "nakedness" as describing what we were before He covered us—raw, bare, wounded, poor and without righteousness.) He goes on, *"I swore an oath to you and entered into a covenant with you, and you became Mine."* Once again, you *became...*

God then says, *"I washed you in water; yes, I thoroughly washed off your blood, and I anointed you with oil."* He *is* Living Water and has washed us with *Himself, with His own blood* and His Word. He's poured out the sacred oil of His Spirit, and we've been cleansed and anointed indeed. Next, He describes how He dresses us, *"I clothed you in embroidered cloth and gave you sandals of badger skin; I clothed you with fine linen and covered you with silk."* He clothes us with the royal garments of the holy priesthood of which He's made us members. We're not covered in rags, but in the finest materials—that HE'S EMBROIDERED HIS NAME ON WITH HIS OWN HANDS! Can you imagine His mighty, powerful, holy hands stitching a garment for *you?* The same finger that etched the Ten Commandments in stone PERSONALLY EMBROIDERS YOUR WEDDING GOWN. I'd love to see what that needlework looks like. But spiritually, I know that written all over you are the words, "I WAS. I AM. I AM TO COME. MY NAME IS ON HER PAST, HER PRESENT AND HER FUTURE. THE NAME OF JESUS CHRIST IS ALL THAT IS TO BE SEEN HERE. ALL HER OLD NAMES ARE ERASED, SHE IS NEW."

My, that robe looks good on you—a perfect fit! He then adds jewelry, as if being covered in embroidered silk isn't enough! *"I put bracelets on your arms and a necklace around your neck, and I put a ring on your nose, earrings on your ears and a beautiful crown on your head."* He leaves nothing uncovered or unadorned; no part of us remains untouched by His hand of mercy and heart of glory. He goes on to say, *"You ate pastry of fine flour, honey, and oil. You were exceedingly beautiful, and succeeded to royalty."* Which one of us doesn't want to be beautiful? Isn't most advertising to women directly aimed at that desire? Cry out with the psalmist, *"The Lord will give grace and glory; no good thing will He withhold from those whose walk uprightly. O Lord of hosts, blessed is the man who trusts in You!"* Say with Isaiah 61:10, *"I will greatly rejoice in the Lord, my soul shall be joyful in my God."*

It's critical that we know that we know that we know that our Redeemer lives, that we're His, that we've become what His Word declares and that His Name is our shield, covering us completely. The Enemy will most definitely try to stain your garment, steal your shoes, rip off your jewelry and remind you of that field in which you used to live, polluted in your own blood. Never let his condemnation take root, but allow the Lord use it to stir even more gratitude in your heart as you realize all the Lord's given you in His grace.

I don't know if thoughts of Moab crossed Ruth's mind as Boaz stood before her at the altar, but if they did, I'm sure they only served to stir up more passion and appreciation for her kinsman-redeemer, and only made the day all the more sweet. I don't look at the past with stinging heart-wounds anymore either, but use it to celebrate and enjoy my Bridegroom today. I know from whence I've come, and remember the taste of my own blood and what it feels like to kick around in it. *How precious is being joined to and dressed by the Redeemer. It's a sweet, sweet thing.*

As I wrote this, I went to take care of a few things in the house. While retrieving something in a storage room, I came across a little, old, tattered notebook with pages sticking out everywhere. I opened it to find prayers and heart-cries dating all the way back to 1982. Many entries were from my college days. As I read what was on my heart then, things I'd totally forgotten, I fell on my face in a puddle of tears, until the Lord whispered in my heart, "You didn't think I'd leave you there, did you? Can't you see how I've carried you? Child, I LOVE YOU. My eye was on you, and you were the apple of it, even before yours was on Me. I had your wardrobe and jewels ready long before you realized you were bare. My wing was spread over you when you weren't yet able to see it." What can you say to that, except to collapse in gratitude? The King never wastes our pain or memories of Moab, *but uses them to glorify His Name, as we who've been forgiven much, LOVE MUCH.*

If Ruth hadn't known famine, tasted despair and heartache and suffered poverty, shame and sorrow, her royal wedding garment wouldn't have been nearly so lovely and precious. The nuptials would certainly have been bright, but not nearly as glorious as they appeared against the backdrop of her dark past. I imagine dear Ruth *loved much* on that sacred day. So do I.

Questions & Applications

1. **Is anything making you feel like a Moabite today, instead of the beautiful Bride you are? Ask the Lord for eyes to see yourself as He sees you.**
2. **Did you complete the sentence, (your name) became __________________? If not, do so now.**
3. **Echo Revelation 19:6-8 as a prayer of great joy and anticipation: *"Then I heard what sounded like a great multitude, like the roar of rushing waters and like loud peals of thunder, shouting, 'Hallelujah! For our Lord God Almighty reigns. Let us rejoice and be glad and give Him glory! For the wedding of the Lamb has come, and His Bride has made herself ready. Fine linen, bright and clean, was given her to wear.'"* We will step into that scene sooner than we can imagine, my friends. Hallelujah! Let's start the praise now!**

41

New Birth

So Boaz took Ruth and she became his wife; and when he went in to her, the Lord gave her conception, and she bore a son, **Ruth 4:13b.**

The groom took his sweet bride, showered her with his love and *something was conceived and birthed.* SOMETHING WILL ALWAYS BE CONCEIVED AND BIRTHED WHEN YOU STEP INTO THE INTIMATE HOLY OF HOLIES WITH THE KING OF KINGS. When you, the holy, precious bride of the Risen Christ, enter into sweet union with Him, something will be planted in the "womb" of your spirit. When you unite your heart to Christ's and allow the Holy Spirit to overshadow you, something will inevitably be produced—something sacred. When the Holy Spirit fills us, He creates something new, a new nature, in our hearts that's very different from the old person we've been. If you're in Christ and abiding in His Word, you can expect things that glorify Him to be brought forth. *The Lord's sweet presence brings forth true worship. Passion spills out. Ministry is conceived. Spirit produced fruit grows in abundance. Blessing is brought forth. Gifts, anointing and precious fellowship with the King result.* I don't want to live anywhere else.

Have you seen it happening in your life? You've given your heart to the Lord Jesus, and fruit from that relationship has blossomed and come to maturity. You've known the call to give, to intercede and to love. You've felt heaven's fire burn in your heart, have heard the Lord's wooing voice and have seen Him birth His anointing in you. You can't abide in His mighty, overwhelming presence and receive His Word and not have something stir within you. Holy seed falls on good ground there, and that seed, the Word of God, never returns void. *Let's celebrate, Bride. The King of Glory has come to us and chosen to conceive fruit in our lives that our finite minds and weak flesh simply can't!*

The Holy Spirit wants to birth much in us, including 1 Corinthians 13-kind-of-love, Galatians 5- kind-of-fruit and an Isaiah 61-kind-of-mission plan: anointed to preach good news to the poor, bind the brokenhearted, proclaim freedom, release prisoners from bondage, proclaim the year of the Lord's favor, comfort all who mourn, provide for those in want and bestow a crown of beauty, the oil of gladness and a garment of praise. That's the passage Jesus quoted in Luke 4, proclaiming Himself as its fulfillment. *And that's what He brings forth as we abide in Him.* How amazing that the mighty King of Glory *desires* to abide in us, and allows us to participate with Him in seeing His kingdom come and His will done on earth as it is in heaven. *May we never get over it.*

The early chapters of Genesis in God's precious Word provide an account of God's original creation, including mankind. From the Bible's very first verse we find the Holy Spirit hovering over the waters as the Lord spoke life and form into all He desired to create. God spoke and it was. Just as in Gen. 1:26, where Adam was "conceived" at the word of Jehovah, *what begins in our hearts as His Spirit hovers over its murkiness also comes from His Word. And the Word of the living God always brings forth CHRIST.*

Lamentations 2:19 instructs, *"...pour out your heart like water in the presence of the Lord. Lift up your hands to Him for the lives of your children."* That verse makes me picture my heart the same way Genesis 1:1 depicts the earth before the Lord gave it form: *"darkness was over the surface of the deep, and the Spirit of God was hovering over the waters."* To me, those deep waters represent pain, fear, injury, insecurity, pride—whatever consumes our hearts and darkens them. I know the Enemy of our souls wants to drown us in those dark seas and take us out. At times I've felt like he has a wicked grip on my head and thoughts and is dunking me under, saying, "You may have come this far with the Lord, but you won't survive this round. You need to resign from anything that resembles ministry." It's like a trump card he holds against my heart, and I start falling. I know I should fight back right away, but often I feel completely overwhelmed, finding myself so distracted and oppressed I can barely pray, let alone study.

At times like that virtually all I can do is envision the Holy Spirit hovering over the gloomy, formless waters of my heart, inviting me to pour them into His hands. When I do, He speaks, and brings order out of chaos, gives structure to what was shapeless, establishes what was wandering, brings life to what was dying, binds up what was broken, strengthens what was sick and turns that water into new wine, all the while wrapping my heart in a new wineskin called love. It's a God-given transformed heart where Christ dwells and new things are birthed.

Much like the creation of the world, Christ's first miracle involved water. In John 2 the scene is a wedding, and the distress is a lack of wine. Jesus commands six stone jars to be filled with common water. *What does water become in the hands of the King?* New wine, the best wine, wine fit for a marriage feast, wine offered freely and without charge. *"Come, all you who are thirsty, come to the waters; and you who have no money, come, buy and eat! Come, buy wine and milk without money and without cost,"* (Isaiah 55:1). Whatever the situation or stress you're experiencing, Jesus is ready and willing to reveal His glory through it and bring something out of it that's better than where you started.

As I've cried out to the Lord, asking Him to keep me filled and thrilled with His Word, His Living Water, I've also had this thought: *birth is associated with water breaking.* May the Lord Jesus break whatever holds back the absolute gushing downpour of holy rain in our hearts and bring forth a flood of holy water and new wine. *"All our springs are in You,"* (Psalm 87:7). *"For He will come like a pent-up flood that the breath of the Lord drives along,"* (Isaiah 59:19). Come, Lord Jesus, and perform your Word to us.

If pain, which you've asked the King of Kings to remove, remains in your life, then trust that you're in *labor*—that in His wisdom and perfect timing, there's some water-breaking coming. Believe that God is creating something mighty that will show off the Lord Jesus, something that will look like Him and bring Him praise, even through the generations. I've given birth twice and know for sure that labor is intense, consuming and, without drugs, quite painful! Yet, somehow I never imagined that what the Lord wants to bring forth from me might be painful, too. I always thought the Lord's work in my heart would be easy, but have found spiritual labor to be more like heart surgery—if not childbirth. I no longer believe the verse that says, *"His yoke is easy and His burden is light,"* means that His work never involves hardship. Some lessons hurt, some growth requires pain and some heart-stones that need to be turned to flesh might just grate on us a little on their way out.

Think about the physical birth process: there's conception, a joining together; there's a waiting period, a hidden time when the child is knit together in the mother's womb; then there's obvious evidence on the outside that something's growing on the inside. There's the fullness of time, the due date, followed by labor pains, a pushing forward. At last, the delivery comes, when new life is brought out of that dark, restricted place, and you get to hold and cherish the blessing that was so long in coming.

I've found the same process at work in the Spirit. The Lord has a good plan and purpose for us —for a future and a hope—but it doesn't come to fullness and delivery the same day it's conceived in our hearts. The Lord gives us planting seasons, waiting periods and stretches of time to mature and develop us. Aren't we urged over and over in the Word to wait on the Lord, trust His timing and rest in Him with a quiet confidence that He's knitting our hearts together to look like His? I love the words Eve spoke when she delivered the first baby on earth. Genesis 4:1 records her saying, *"With the help of God I have brought forth a man."* I think she must have been *amazed, overwhelmed and astounded* by what had just happened, as the never-before-seen ushered out of her little womb. New life came into existence. When our little hearts feel overwhelmed, dark and confined, I pray the Lord will continually bring forth *Christ* out of them—that we, like Eve, will always be filled with awe and wonder at the things the Lord might choose to do in and through us.

One morning as I sought the Lord in prayer, I was absolutely overwhelmed by a sense of His vast holiness, the far-reaching, universe-bursting enormity of Him that we can't even begin to grasp. The fact that the holy, pure, timeless, eternal, mighty, powerful, Almighty God, who stretched out the heavens and established the earth with His mere Word, who created all that is and ever will be, who breathed life into man and then gave His own last breath for man's sin, who commands the heavenlies and whose glory fills creation—the One whose very Name causes the nations to tremble and the heavens to bow—would choose to do something through *me* is astounding, awesome and utterly amazing! The thought that He wants to be brought forth from our hearts is *absolutely glorious. "Who is like the Lord our God, who dwells on high, who humbles Himself to behold the things that are in the heavens and in the earth?"* (Psalm 113:5-6).

It's all about Him. It's not about what we conceive and plan, or for what we labor and try to bring forth in our own strength. It's about dying to everything our flesh tries to birth, falling before the Holy One and walking with Him in Spirit and Truth. As we do, He has the freedom in our hearts to produce the desires of His. Can you think of a time you had a bright idea of your own and tried to make it happen? How about a time when you came humbly before the King of Kings and He opened doors? *There's a HUGE difference, isn't there? There's always life and growth in what Christ produces, as opposed to what we try to accomplish ourselves.*

Whatever your labor in the Lord may look or feel like, it's well worth it. As it says in 1 Corinthians 15:58, *"... know that your labor in the Lord is not in vain."* May our efforts in the King always evidence His heart of love. May we cry out, not only for ourselves, but for those around us, echoing the loving care of Paul in Galatians 4:19, *"My dear children, for whom I am again in the pain of childbirth until Christ is formed in you..."*

Scripture tells us we have an Enemy out to steal, kill and destroy everything the Lord wants to bring forth through our lives. Don't think he'll sit back and watch whatever it is without a fight. *Be on guard. Be alert. He wants to devour. Put on the armor. Hide yourself in Christ and stay there.*

Revelation 12:4 tells us, *"The dragon stood in front of the woman who was about to give birth, so that he might devour her child the moment it was born."* Be assured that your Enemy will waste no time in trying to destroy all the

Lord wants to do through your life. Despite this, you're *not* to live in fear but in quiet confidence that, *"greater is He that is in me than he that is in the world,"* and that you'll overcome, as Revelation 12:11 says, *"by the blood of the Lamb and by the word of our testimony."*

Be careful about what gets conceived in your heart, testing everything against the Word of God. Psalm 7:14 says, *"He who is pregnant with evil and conceives trouble gives birth to disillusionment."* The Enemy not only wants to destroy God's plan for you, he wants to create something in you, too: bitterness, unhealed wounds, anger, insecurity, depression, pride, criticism, unfaithfulness, compromise, lukewarmness, selfishness, greed—*anything that'll give him ground to stand on and allow him to root something unholy in your heart. By their very nature, these "babies" can produce nothing but disillusionment, disappointment, sorrow and death.*

We need to take Galatians 5:1 very seriously: *"It is for freedom that Christ has set us free. Stand firm, then, and do not let yourselves be burdened again by a yoke of slavery."* Our Foe wants to enslave us to emotions, lusts, slippery seductions, pride, despair and addictions. He wants to entrap us and then accuse us for being in the trap. He wants us to think we've strayed so far from what the Lord has for us that giving up looks like the best option, or to deceive us into believing God has given up on us—that we've messed-up one too many times, or been too terribly unfaithful as a bride of the Lord Jesus for Him to use us. We need to remember what the Word says in Romans 11:29, *"for God's gifts and His call are irrevocable."* Whatever He's planted in you, He'll faithfully bring to pass. We can't fail so badly that repentance won't immediately bring us back. We can't out-sin His love. We can't shock Him.

May we truly STAND FIRM on the name of Jesus and continually labor in prayer, even when the Lord wakes us at 3 a.m. to do it. May we battle on our knees, Sword in hand, against every foul thing the Enemy wants to bring against us. My young son made a comment the other day completely out of the blue. He said, "Mom, Satan wants to defeat us. BUT HOW CAN HE? WE HAVE JESUS!" *May we have the faith of a little child.* In the prayer He taught His disciples, Jesus told us to call the Most High God, "our Father." Abba. Faithful Daddy. HE IS OUR FATHER. He gave us physical birth with a plan for a spiritual one—to be born again. He's faithful, and we can trust Him to finish everything His mind conceived for our lives before we ever drew a breath. He speaks over us what He spoke in His Word, "Fear not. I am with you. I will do it," and as it says in 1 Thessalonians 5:24, *"The One who calls you is faithful, and He will bring it to pass."*

Questions & Applications

1. **Recall a time when you tried to "birth" something in your flesh, and contrast what happened with something the Lord has done through you.**
2. **The Lord Jesus has an assignment, a plan, a purpose, a thing of glory that He wants to bring forth through your life. Stay in prayer and the Word, and trust Him to bring His good plans to pass. Don't give up when the "labor" gets hard! Keep pressing on, *"running with perseverance the race marked out for us,"* (Hebrews 12:1).**

42

Suffering's End

Then the women said to Naomi, "Blessed be the Lord, who has not left you this day without a close relative; and may his name be famous in Israel!" And may he be to you a restorer of life and a nourisher of your old age; for your daughter-in-law, who loves you, who is better to you than seven sons, has borne him." Then Naomi took the child and laid him on her bosom, and became a nurse to him, **Ruth 4:14-16.**

What Ruth birthed brought praise to the name of the Lord and public testimony to the faithfulness of the King of Kings. Notice that it wasn't *Ruth* the women were speaking to, but Naomi, the bitter one. The one who lost so much back in Moab, she'd asked to be called "Mara." The one who blamed, not blessed, the Lord. The one who said of the Most High God, *"He has made my life very bitter. I went away full, but the Lord has brought me back empty."* It's convicting to recall the many times in my own life that I've blamed instead of blessed my Savior. Occasions when I've considered my circumstances with a heavy heart, instead of anticipating the glory the Lord was planning to bring to His holy Name through them. It's easy to praise God in times of blessing, but it can be tough to look past our flesh and praise Him in trials.

What comes out of our mouths when things aren't going as we think they should? What are we saying about God in those times? Often it's not our words as much as our attitudes that speak volumes. *But how precious is the Lord Jesus, whose mercy far exceeds our need!* He can handle whatever rushes through our hearts. He can take our questions. He knows what we were expecting and how to walk us through His own plan, which is always and forever better. *He is good. He's got His fame in mind. He has the glory of God in the forefront of His thinking. And He knows how to bring it about.* I believe when the Lord does reveal His will for our lives, there won't be one day of pain we'd trade for the blessing of it. We'll bow before His throne and say, "It was worth it all," and every fiber of our being will reflect Romans 8:18, *"The sufferings we have now are nothing compared to the great glory that will be shown to us."*

I pray that we'll patiently wait on the Lord during trials, all the while expecting Him to show off for us and bring praise to His Name. May we, as much as our flesh hates it, *"consider it joy when we face various trials."* I don't want to watch Him unveil His glory and have to live with a deep regret that I didn't trust Him as He was working it out. I don't want pout lines engraved on my face. I don't want doubt, temper tantrums or depression to characterize how I react to what I don't understand. I don't want the King to have to say of me, "Oh, you of little faith!"

It required great difficulty to get Naomi and Ruth out of Moab and into the little, prophetic town of Bethlehem to position them where the Lord wanted them. *Yet, through it all, He was moving them into a place where He could pour into their hands and hearts, and literally into their laps, more than they ever dreamed*—to a place of restoration, new life and great honor so full of His presence and blessing they never desired Moab again. It's been the same with me, and maybe you, too. Whatever our Moab was, we may well have stayed put there were it not for the great upheaval the Lord allowed. We might never have put one toe on the road to Bethlehem if we hadn't been driven by desperation.

Philippians 1:6 states, *"Being confident of this very thing, that He who began a good work in you will complete it until the day of Jesus Christ."* That "good work" may not always look good to our feeble eyes. It may be hugely upsetting, something that totally changes the direction of our lives, something hard, unexpected or very far from the plans we had for ourselves. Moab's upheaval wasn't "good" in Naomi's limited understanding. But I'm certain that as she sat in Bethlehem watching her sweet Ruth loved by the honored Boaz, and held their child on her aging lap, she saw the journey that brought them there with new eyes and a new heart—a heart emptied of bitterness and filled with love and thanksgiving.

We need to fall on our faces before the Most High and thank Him for every upset in our lives, every discomfort that drove us out of Moab and every plan of ours that fell to the ground, so His perfect will could be set in motion. What an unspeakable blessing it was for Naomi to see the end of God's plan, to hold in her arms the fruit of her suffering and hear the women of Bethlehem as they spoke blessings around her. I don't know if she'd ever allowed her heart to dream of that kind of fulfillment, *but there it was in her lap.* This woman who accused the Lord of bringing her back empty now sat with a full heart and full arms. Surely worship and praise rose up from her soul and blended with those of the ladies of Bethlehem. As 1 Corinthians 2:9 puts it, *"...no mind has conceived the things the Lord has planned for those who love Him..."*

I pray that I'll hold in my hands the blessings of the Lord in this life; that I'll see the fruit of the long, hard journey and all He was arranging and positioning me for, until the worship of my heart becomes too deep and rich for words. I hope to say along with David in Psalm 27:13, *"I will see the goodness of the Lord in the land of the living."* But if not, if the glory He's planning isn't fully seen before I leave this tent of flesh and stand before His majesty, then I pray He'll give me the grace to wait, anticipate it with joy and trust Him with whatever brings Him the most fame and praise—and for my worship to be just as rich and deep, nonetheless. *It's not about me. It's about making Him known and His Name famous.*

What the women said of the child snuggled against Naomi's bosom is so precious to me: *"May he be to you a restorer of life and a nourisher of your old age."* Whatever the Lord is up to in your life and heart, He's all about restoration and lasting, satisfying nourishment. In whatever form it takes, His ultimate goal is to bring abundant life to you and glory to His Name; to replace your dead, stone-cold heart with a new, tender one that loves well. It's to save you from your own purposes and plant you in His; to lift you out of Moab's pit and settle you in Bethlehem's bounty.

The Restorer of Life was born for us in Bethlehem, too. The Nourisher of our souls arrived in its humble stable—the King of Israel birthed in that little place. The Holy One sent to restore Jacob and be a light to the Gentiles came from that lowly town. Almighty God, for whom the earth is a mere footstool, poured Himself into flesh and set His feet on humble soil so you could live. He died to enable you to enter the presence of the Most High cleansed and freed of Moab's dirt, to touch Him, taste His goodness and hear His words—to enable you to hold blessing itself against your bosom, as He holds you against His.

It doesn't matter how long you wandered through Moab, how much the locusts have devoured or how deep the pit is from which you need redemption. *He is able.* The

Redeemer's arm is not short. His plate is not too full to turn His attention to your plight. He's never incapable of unraveling the tangles in your heart and knitting it back together with gold. There's nothing He can't do. If some voice whispers that you've strayed too far or been too long-gone for Him to move on your behalf, you can be sure that voice is a lie. *Your Redeemer lives*, and He says, *"See, I have engraved you on the palms of My hands; your walls are ever before Me,"* (Isaiah 49:16). Your name is etched in Jesus' nail-scarred hands. Despite upheavals, you can be sure He hasn't forgotten you and is up to something *good.*

Pondering this, I sense the Lord ask, "How many years do you need redeemed, child? Just how much did those locusts eat?" My reply: "Every year, Lord! The locusts have eaten much. Leave no day untouched by Your great redemption. I want no sliver of my life left outside Your healing touch." The cross of Christ proclaims, "I will redeem you and every year the locusts have eaten, and place the blessing of *Myself* in your lap," echoing Isaiah 44:22, *"I have swept away your offenses like a cloud, your sins like the morning mist. Return to Me, for I have redeemed you."* Let the redeemed of the Lord say so. *Moab is no longer our home, and we need never return there. Emptiness is no longer the condition of our hearts or arms. We've been made complete and filled to overflowing in Christ Jesus, and the fullness of His blessing is ours forever and ever.*

I love the description of Naomi holding Ruth's child and *becoming a nurse to him.* That symbolizes fullness to me. You can't nurse from an empty bottle or a dry bosom. Physically, she couldn't have nursed with her own milk, but I've heard it taught that she did. Of course, the Lord of the impossible could have enabled her if He so desired. Whatever way the Lord provided, she became a nursemaid to her grandchild. I remember nursing my infant daughter with tears streaming down my face, overwhelmed with thankfulness and awe at the child in my lap. I daresay Naomi was full of the same intense emotions.

When you hold the blessing of God with your very own hands (answered prayer and evidence of redemption and restoration) or wrap your arms around His Word and see it come to pass, life is going to spring up from within you. I like to think of it as "liquid life," life that takes the form of Living Water, milk for babes and new wine for the mature. Drink that's full of nourishment and so abundant it has to spill over to others, causing them to grow, too. I pray the King of Kings will bring that type of overflowing fullness of His grace into our laps, that He'll "give us this day our daily bread" (*and milk*), that we'll rejoice in seeing His will come to pass in our lives and those around us and that we'll forever live in that place.

Psalm 65:4 says, *"Blessed is the man whom You choose, and cause to approach You, that he may dwell in Your courts. We shall be satisfied with the goodness of Your house, of Your holy temple."* We're blessed indeed for, through the power of the Resurrection, the King of Glory invites us to approach Him and live in His courts. He promises to satisfy us with His goodness, fill what's empty, bring blessing out of upheavals, restore what's lost, free what's captive, heal what's broken and redeem what sin has stolen away. His home is now ours. His Name is our name. And His Child, the Lord Jesus, is given to us. We hold in the "lap" of our hearts the greatest blessing imaginable, the Lamb slain for our souls, beside Whom all else pales and falls as rubbish. We, above all others, are blessed and have reason to worship.

Can't you imagine Naomi holding that child, rocking him to sleep and singing quiet lullabies? Can't you see her (ignoring every child-rearing book's advice) holding him for hours, loving him too much to even lay him down for a nap and just watching him sleep in her arms? Can't you picture her jumping at his every whimper, scooping him up in his waking hours and dancing with him to a new song, the song of Bethlehem's chorus? Can't you hear her telling him lengthy stories for as long as he'd listen, and saying again and again how blessed he was to be born in the land of the Lord God to such faithful parents? Can't you envision Naomi encouraging the boy to dream big, trust God and believe all of His promises, whispering blessings in his tiny ears, urging him to love the Lord with all his heart, soul, mind and strength and to expect great, miraculous things, reminding him how his very birth was a sign of the Most High's faithfulness and warning him to stay in the courts of the King and avoid Moab at all costs?

I want to cherish what the Lord puts in my lap like that. I don't ever want to get used to His blessings, lose the awe and wonder of His provision and care or ignore His work in my heart and callously take it for granted. I want gratitude to spring from my soul every minute of my life. I want memories of Moab and the upheavals that drew me out of there to continually remind me of Bethlehem's sweetness. I want to nourish all the King gives me with deep pleasure, caring for His provision with passion and excellence. I want to set my face like flint on His with my mind renewed so deeply it's unshakable. I want to constantly play the tape of God's Word in my head, focusing on pure Truth and thinking on things above. I want to rejoice as He says to rejoice and to see more than I ever asked for or imagined occur in my life. *He*, the Most High God, King of Glory and Holy One of Israel, who's taken us foreigners in the field into His care and graced us with unspeakable blessings, *deserves no less.*

Questions & Applications

1. **Is there anything from your past that still needs to be redeemed?**

2. **Reflect on the greatest blessing you could ever hold—the redemption of all that you were and the blessing of all that Christ is. Enter the throne room of the Most High God through the privilege of prayer, and thank Him with fresh passion for the gift of His own Son placed freely in your lap. *"For there is born to you this day in the city of David a Savior, who is Christ the Lord"* Luke 2:11(NKJV).**

43

Generational Blessings

Also the neighbor women gave him a name, saying, "There is a son born to Naomi." And they called his name Obed. He is the father of Jesse, the father of David. Now this is the genealogy of Perez: Perez was the father of Hezron, Hezron the father of Ram, Ram the father of Amminadab, Amminadab the father of Nahshon, Nahshon the father of Salmon, Salmon the father of Boaz, Boaz the father of Obed, Obed the father of Jesse, Jesse the father of David, **Ruth 4: 17-22.**

Never before have I considered lists of families and genealogies interesting. But with the conclusion of the precious book of *Ruth*, they've become richly powerful to me—things meant to stir praise in our hearts. Instead of wondering why in the world they're included in God's Word, I now look at them as the Most High pointing and saying, "Look at this! I'M ABOUT THE GENERATIONS! I'm eternal, and I let you trace my Hand through specific lives. There are treasures to be found even in lists." *Let us see them then, Lord Jesus.*

Here, the lineage of Ruth's son is traced back to Perez (a son of Judah, whose sons were described in Nehemiah 11:6 as "valiant men") and forward to David, the king of Israel, a man after God's own heart. This line gives us a sweet glimpse of the Lord's mercy and blessing, and of His plans even for those who've wandered the farthest. Skipping ahead to the first book of the New Testament, we find that Matthew *starts with a genealogy!*—an account of the Lord working through a family tree. To me, it's a beautiful record of the King's faithfulness to move and work His plan not only in us but also in the hearts of our children, stretching through our descendents until He breaks open the skies. According to Jeremiah 29:11, God's purpose is *"to prosper you and not to harm you, to give you a future and a hope."* He wants the glory of His presence to bless those who seek after Him, *and their children, too.*

The family list given in Matthew 1 is virtually identical to the one given in *Ruth.* Why? It seems to me that when the Lord repeats Himself, He means for us to *get it.* (I find Him repeating Himself to me often!) It's worth noting, however, that the lineage in *Ruth* doesn't include the names of mothers, while in Matthew we find three: Tamar, Rahab and Ruth. Those three little, slipped-in names speak volumes of the Lord's mercy. These were not Sunday School ladies. They weren't the heads of the women's ministry, or ladies you'd expect to find honored in the family tree of Christ.

In Genesis 38, the Bible informs us that widowed Tamar posed as a prostitute and slept with Judah, her father-in-law. The child from that union was Perez, the man to whom the women of Bethlehem referred in their blessing to Boaz by saying, "May your house be like the house of Perez." Joshua 2 tells of Rahab, a prostitute in Jericho who offers shelter to two Jewish spies. (It was the broken one, not the self-righteous one that opened her door.) Spared when Jericho fell, she joined the Israelites and eventually gave birth to Boaz.

I wonder if Rahab's history gave Boaz more compassion for Ruth; if knowing his own lineage helped him appreciate hers, just as remembering our own sinful past helps us show grace to others. This also recalls Hosea 2:19, in which the Lord God says of the unfaithful, adulterous one, who's lived as Rahab did in Jericho, *"I will betroth you to Me forever; yes, I will betroth you to Me in righteousness and justice, in lovingkindness and mercy; I will betroth you to Me in faithfulness, and you shall know the Lord."*

And surely, by now, we understand Ruth's background: foreigner from a pagan land, born into a line that wasn't supposed to mingle with God's chosen people, immersed since childhood in idolatry, kinship to Boaz the result of an unlawful marriage to one of Naomi's sons. What hope this holds for us and our lineages! We, whose hearts know all about deceitfulness and manipulation, whose feet have wandered in unfaithfulness and whose lives have been immersed in much idolatry and self-seeking, are included in the pure line of the children of the King of Kings—those who receive the inheritance of the Most High God through faith in Christ. With no heavenly credentials of our own, we're called *"a royal priesthood, a holy nation, His own special people,"* (1 Peter 2:9). Sinners from birth, we now have the right to be called the children of God (John 1:12) and the privilege of revealing Christ through our redeemed lives.

Let that sink in with fresh wonder. Remember where you were and to all you've been called. Consider God's mercy once again and expect it to overflow you into the lives of others, especially your family line. Fall before the throne of grace with renewed appreciation for your salvation and fresh passion for the high position the King's sacrifice has given you. He is good. His mercy endures forever and through all generations. He *"raises the poor out of the dust, and lifts the needy out of the ash heap, that He may seat them with princes, with the princes of their people,"* (Psalm 113:7-8).

May this knowledge continually bring us to our knees. May any self-righteous, legalistic blinders fall from our eyes as we fall in humble worship before the Lord of Hosts and His grace. That's where I want to anchor my heart, and from where I want all the expressions of my life to spring.

A particular Scripture in the Old Testament concerning our effect on coming generations has always sent a chill down my spine. It's found among the Ten Commandments in Exodus 20:5-6, where the Lord states, *"You shall not bow down to them or worship them* [idols]*; for I, the Lord your God, am a jealous God, punishing the children for the sin of the fathers to the third and fourth generation of those who hate Me, but showing love to a thousand generations of those who love Me and keep My commandments."* If we choose to walk down the road of idolatry or live in what I've labeled as Moab, we're naturally going to lead those in our care down the same path. The sin and pain of that choice will trickle down to our descendents, establishing strongholds that can even grip entire generations. *When we open the doors of our hearts and homes to sin, we're not the only ones affected.*

It's not too difficult to find examples of family lines with repeating patterns of sin (most of us don't have to look beyond our own!): anger, abuse, rejection, pride, unforgiveness, addictions, obsessions, compulsions, laziness, deceit, gossip, nagging, materialism (idolatry), lust, self-centeredness...you name it. The point is, if we have some unconfessed sin rooted in our hearts, it will scatter its seeds, grow in places we never intended and damage those we love most. As the saying goes, "The apple doesn't fall far from the tree." *That puts the fear of God in me and sends me to my knees for the cleansing power of the blood of Christ. It catapults my heart from a casual approach to the Holy God to a desperately earnest one, the pouring-out-your-heart-like-a-river-kind that sees the potential for destruction and cries out for the King's mercy and salvation. It's a dread which understands that on my own I'll open all kinds of dangerous doors, and that the only Hand able to close them is His.*

BUT (thank God for that blessed "but") when we choose the path of the Lord Jesus, when we plant our feet on Bethlehem's solid ground and ask the King of Glory to move with power and passion in our hearts and family line, we can expect an overflow that far, far exceeds any grip the Enemy may have had. Those who love Jesus can expect to experience the kind of love and mercy that's strong enough to reach to a *thousand generations*. When you ask the Lord to fill your heart, soul, mind and strength with love and wisdom, then you're laying out a path of *glory* for your children's precious feet. I want those who come after me to walk with the King until He takes us all home. I want my line full of pure worship.

Rejoice, sweet generations to come! We LOVE the Lord our God, the King of Kings, the Risen Christ, and you'll be blessed by the hearts He gives us. Our devotion to Him will not only be for our good, but for yours as well.

I believe every one of us desires blessing for our lives, for our children's lives and for the generations to follow. *So let's examine our hearts and take care of business with the King*. We need to take a hard look within and ask the Holy Spirit to reveal any strongholds we've allowed the Enemy to build there through unconfessed sin, then repent of it and let the Lord Jesus establish us and our line in true freedom. It's the liberty to live life in abundant love and from a heart of pure, polished gold, to walk with the Holy Spirit and receive power and revelation and to bear blessing's rich fruit. I know from personal experience that it can seem easier at times to resist facing our issues and continue in bondage. *But freedom is worth the cost of dealing with whatever the Lord shows us.*

The King wants us free. When He brings something to our attention, it's not for condemnation but an invitation for cleansing. He wants to bring us to the place where we can breathe-in deep peace and rest; where our sleep becomes sweet and our outlook becomes fresh and joyful. Go there with Him! It's for more than your own sake! *There are little souls, whether your own physical children or not, who are counting on your influence to be pure!* So, let the King purify you.

As the Holy Spirit convicts me about things, I simply agree with Him that they're sin and full of destruction and repent of them. I ask Him to take back ground I've given up in my life and to close the doors sin opened to me and my descendents. I then often feel led to intercede for marital sins, family sins, corporate sins and national sins. (Some great examples of corporate intercession include: Moses in Exodus 32, Job in Job 1 and Daniel in Daniel 9. There are many others.) I ask the Lord to cover every area with the powerful, mighty, cleansing blood of Jesus, to help me resist every temptation to return to my individual patterns, to retrain my thinking and to deliver me from the deadly power of self-deceit.

When a problem arises, I find it all too easy to resort to old reactions and habits, to the way past woundedness reacted. *Wounded hearts can't love well.* There's interference from behind, something grabbing them from "back there." A wound is tender and sensitive; you can't touch it without a reaction. To avoid this, I ask the Lord to go back into my life and remove and destroy with His own blood the root of every hurt, wound and wrong reaction. I pray for deliverance from every curse passed down to me from my predecessors and from every one I've participated in and perpetuated. In short, TO HEAL MY BEHIND! Sin has a price. It releases curses and death that only Jesus can absolve. He alone is able and worthy. And, praise God, He's willing! Freedom is *always* His will! We who've been held captive have great reason to celebrate!

Sometimes I awaken in the middle of the night with heaviness of heart because of some issue I need to deal with before the Lord. Yet, as I begin to pray, I feel absolutely NO condemnation, just a sweet invitation to lay those things at the Cross and be set free from their power. More than anything, it's as if the Lord is extending a gracious offer to repent, urging me to come to His throne out of His great love and mercy. I want to share with you part of one of those prayers that the Lord so clearly answered in my heart. I'm always amazed that He dares speak to us at all. *When King of Glory speaks, it becomes awesome, amazing, holy ground.* For what it's worth, here's my little prayer dialogue:

> "I hate how easily I've been tripped-up, Lord! The Enemy plays his cards, and there I go. Teach me to stand firm! Strengthen me and focus me on Your Face! Face me forward, pressing into You."

> *"Renew your thinking, then. Retrain those old patterns of thought, they're weeds in your garden. If you leave old tracks of thinking in place, even though you're Mine, you can easily slide down them at the first disruption. I reveal them to you so you can be freed through the power of Christ. It's work. It takes effort. It takes time. It takes focus. It requires wrestling against what has held you and then embracing My Truth."*

Let's be free! Let's allow the Lord to cleanse us and establish our place in this generation! Let's be bold about affecting those who come after us! Let's be confident of the call of God on our hearts and lives, and *let's live it out!* Let's get on with it! There's business to be done that only freed souls can accomplish. Let's operate in the fullness and power of the Holy Spirit, and watch with wonder the beginning of the thousand generations touched and blessed by our faithfulness! LET'S BE ABOUT GROOMING THOSE WHO COME AFTER US FOR THE PRIESTHOOD! That thought alone changes my whole perspective regarding my responsibility. *There are Davids, Ruths, Pauls, Samuels, Esthers and more that we're helping to shape for the courts of the King, but we must have free hearts to do it well.*

I pray that we'll STAND in Christ's freedom and never relax on our watch, that Truth will envelop us until deception finds no foothold and that we'll keep on doing what we're all called to do—LOVE WELL—to love the King, to love life and to love everyone who comes across our path. Not too long ago, I told the Lord, "I love you so much, Lord! What do I need to do to hear, 'Well done, good and faithful one!'?" His reply in my heart was, "Love well." Help us to do that, Holy Spirit!

In God's Word, the bride of Christ is spoken of as wearing "fine linen, white and clean," (Revelation 19:8), and how she's to be "without spot or wrinkle." IF YOU'VE EVER WORN LINEN, YOU KNOW SITTING DOWN WILL WRINKLE IT TO PIECES! You can't take a seat without looking like you never ironed it! And on that pure, white fabric, any dirt will surely stick. As part of the Bride, we're not to sit down on our watch! Generations are depending on it! Think of your descendents as being joined to you by a "spiritual umbilical cord." They're intensely connected to you for a season, and what your spirit feeds on will pass on to them. LET US THEN FEAST ON THE KING, THE BREAD OF LIFE!

The cry of my heart is to see so much more than what surrounds me today and to worship with eternity's passion. May we look back through the glimpses of generations in God's Word, especially Jesus', and let them stimulate faith and hope in us. Then, let's turn our gaze forward in the same Word to eagerly anticipate the joy of our King's presence at the promised Wedding Feast of the Lamb, as He unveils His plan for all eternity. May we never underestimate God's call on our lives to our own generation, much less the ones to come, but by the power of the Holy Spirit may we fully complete it.

For me, this study of *Ruth* has been a journey into the freedom and blessing of the King's courts. That's what I desire for my children—and for you, too. As I've asked the Lord to give me His Word to pray for my household, those now living and generations yet to come, He's led me to these passages, which I want to leave you with (add your own as He leads):

> Psalm 23: That the Lord will be their Shepherd, faithfully providing for and leading them by quiet streams of peace. That He'll restore their souls, lead them in paths of righteousness and guide them with His Holy Spirit. That they won't fear, but that He Himself will comfort them and prepare a table before them from which they'll eat richly and drink deeply. And that they'll dwell in His house, in His tabernacle and in the sanctuary of His heart forever and ever.

> Matthew 6—The Lord's Prayer: That God will parent them, so they'll know Him as their Abba-Father and love and live through His Name. That His goodness, mercy and power will be their focus, and that His kingdom will be built in and through them, according to His perfect will. That He'll provide holy, spiritual Bread and make every physical provision for them, steer their hearts far away from temptation and keep them from stumbling. That they'll walk in the freedom of forgiveness, hide themselves in Christ, be delivered from all evil and have no weapon formed against them prosper. And that they'll ever worship

the King of Kings, to whom belongs the Kingdom, the power and the glory for all eternity.

Ephesians 3:14-21: That they'll bow their knees before the King and seek His Spirit for strength in the inner man. That Christ will dwell in their hearts through faith, and they'll be rooted and grounded in the vast grace of God, know the love of Christ that passes understanding and be filled with all the fullness of God. That they'll give Him glory and boast in Him alone, and that He'll do exceedingly and abundantly above everything I've asked for all my descendents.

Zechariah 13:9: That they'll call on the name of the Lord, discern His voice and identify themselves as His.

Zechariah 14:16: That they'll forever worship the King of Kings and feast in His shelter and presence, celebrating Him with great, deep, full joy.

REJOICE! YOU HAVE NO IDEA WHAT YOUR PRAYERS MAY SET IN MOTION. The generations you pray for will rise up and call you blessed. *PRAISE THE KING!!!* Amen and amen.

Questions & Applications

1. **Have you honestly identified, confessed and forsaken any generational sins you may have inherited from your predecessors?**
2. **Are there any sins in your life right now that left unconfessed could affect your children, grandchildren and future descendents? The Redeemer**

desires your freedom, and the freedom repentance brings is sweet, indeed.

3. **One of my favorite songs, especially in reference to this little peek into Ruth, is "My Redeemer Lives" by Nicole C. Mullen. On two particularly difficult days, when my husband and I got in the car that song was belting out on the radio. Needless to say, I bought the CD. My new favorite is "Feels Like Redemption" by Michael English. Whatever your favorite song of redemption, get it out and play it LOUD. If you don't have one, make one up. Lift up those precious hands and offer pure praise to the One who's called you from darkness to light, from the depths to the heights, from Moab to Bethlehem—and straight into the King's heart. You'll be in good company, joining angels and elders who continually do so before the throne of glory and grace. I pray your song will become a lifestyle of thanksgiving and a hymn you live, and that thousands after you will also rejoice.**

44

Conclusion

I pray that your heart, and not just your mind, has followed sweet Ruth to redemption's joy, and that Christ Jesus—the Savior, Messiah, King of Kings and Lord of Lords, the Redeemer of all that was, is and is to come, the Holy Anointed One, the Way, the Truth, and the Life, the Almighty God—is more beautiful than ever to you now. I hope you are rejoicing a little deeper today in that priceless gift called salvation, and that a flame of passion has been fanned in your heart for the One who's so passionate for you. *If so, go forth in His power.*

For, just as we've benefited from Ruth's, there are many, many souls who need to hear of *your* journey to the King of Kings. Desperate in their own "Moabs," they need encouragement to turn their lovely feet toward Bethlehem, the House of Bread—to the Redeemer, Jesus Christ, the Son of the Living God. If you are His, you have a wonderful story to tell. *Ask the Holy Spirit to put the words in your mouth, and go tell it.*

If you have come to this page and know in your heart that you are not yet Christ's, then settle the matter right now. Through his death and resurrection, Jesus has made abundant mercy and grace available to you: for every sin and offense you have ever committed, for all you've been and every place your feet have wandered. The King of Kings, the God of the ages, desires you with a supernatural love and pursues you with the passion of heaven. You haven't gone too far or been away too long, and He hasn't forgotten you.

Lay down all you've clung to apart from Jesus. Tell Him you know you're a sinner and that you desire to turn from those things to Him. Empty your heart before Him. Get real, not religious. Tell Jesus you know that He is the Messiah, the Savior, and that you accept Him as just that, and ask Him to fill to overflowing that precious-in-His-sight heart you just emptied with His Spirit and to consume your life with the joy of salvation. He will do it!

Then, get ready for the adventure of a lifetime, which will stretch into eternity. Dive into the Bible, the precious Word of God, the inerrant lamp for your feet. Join a body of believers, a church, that will love on you, disciple you and be to you as iron sharpening iron. And daily, continually get on your knees and meet with the King. *You'll never be the same. And neither will heaven—because it will become your home!*

May you and your posterity be forever blessed as you abide in the House of Bread with King Jesus. My prayers are with you.

Breinigsville, PA USA
29 July 2010
242658BV00001BA/19/P